Upper Limit Music

Upper Limit Music

The Writing of Louis Zukofsky

Edited by
Mark Scroggins

The University of Alabama Press
Tuscaloosa and London

∞

The paper on which this book is printed meets the minimum requirements of
American National Standard for Information Science–Permanence of Paper for
Printed Library Materials, ANSI Z39.48-1984.

Library of Congress Cataloging-in-Publication Data

Upper limit music : the writing of Louis Zukofsky / edited by Mark Scroggins.
        p.   cm.
Includes index.
ISBN 0-8173-0826-1 (pbk. : alk. paper)
1. Zukofsky, Louis, 1904–1978—Criticism and interpretation.
2. Postmodernism (Literature)—United States.   I. Scroggins, Mark.
PS3549.U47Z93   1997
811'.52—dc20   96-17168

British Library Cataloguing-in-Publication Data available

1 2 3 4 5 6 7 8 9 10 / 06 05 04 03 02 01 00 99 98 97

Contents

II. Toward the Postmodern: Zukofsky's Life of Writing

Acknowledgments

WHILE ASSEMBLING THIS COLLECTION has certainly been a labor of love, it has been nonetheless a labor. Its more onerous aspects, however, have been largely mitigated by the assumption of the pleasurable obligations that I can here recount and acknowledge. The bulk of the essays collected in *Upper Limit Music: The Writing of Louis Zukofsky* were presented in June 1993 at "The First Postmodernists: American Poets of the 1930s Generation," a conference at the University of Maine, Orono. Burton Hatlen, the director of the National Poetry Foundation at the University of Maine, ably organized and managed that conference. Two years later, participants are, it seems, unanimous in recalling it as a model of scholarly interchange and conversation. Burt has been instrumental in forwarding the assembly of this volume and deserves especial praise for his encouragement of younger scholars (like several in this volume), in large part through his editing of the journal *Sagetrieb*. I owe a great debt to Peter Quartermain, who first proposed that I take on this project. His profound erudition, mordant wit, and scrupulous scholarship have long been a model for me, and like Burt, he has been generous with encouragement, advice, and logistical support. Two dear friends, Eric Murphy Selinger and John Taggart, each with his own brand of bemused skepticism, were a source of extremely useful suggestions. Their input has especially worked to shape my introduction. A constant electronic interchange with Marnie Parsons and the poet E. A. Miller has done much to make a seemingly interminable project proceed with dispatch. Guy Davenport, in his correspondence and conversation, remains, well, as Hugh Kenner once put it, *polumetis.*

Perhaps of most importance, Paul Zukofsky generously took time from his own pursuits to look over these essays and make numerous extremely helpful comments; as I suggested to him, perhaps he ought to share editorial credit—though I'm sure he'd as soon fiddle on a Willie Nelson record as have his name on a volume of literary criticism ("Who's Willie Nelson?" he replies—"just kidding!"). His interest and involvement have been invaluable. I consider myself honored as well to have been able to work with the excellent people at the University of Alabama Press. Finally, I must acknowledge the contributors to this volume: their work speaks for itself, and I can only confess myself pleased to have been able to publish it under my name. I suppose that this collection as a whole is quite appropriately offered to the memory of Louis Zukofsky, but I would like to dedicate my part in it to my parents and to Martha Belt.

I would like to thank the following publishers for permission to reprint materials from their publications:

"Z" by bp Nichol is reprinted from *ABC: The Aleph Beth Book,* copyright © 1969, by permission of Oberon Press.

From *Pound/Zukofsky: The Selected Letters of Ezra Pound and Louis Zukofsky* edited by Barry Ahearn, copyright © 1987 by The Ezra Pound Literary Property Trust. Reprinted by permission of New Directions Publishing Corporation.

From *The Cantos* by Ezra Pound, copyright © 1934, 1938 by Ezra Pound. Reprinted by permission of New Directions Publishing Corporation.

From *On Beyond Zebra!* by Dr. Seuss TM and copyright © 1955 and renewed 1983 by Dr. Seuss Enterprises, L.P. Reprinted by permission of Random House, Inc.

Quotations from *On Beyond Zebra!* by Dr. Seuss by consent of Dr. Seuss Enterprises, L.P. © 1955 by Theodor S. Geisel and Audrey S. Geisel, renewed 1983 by Theodor S. Geisel.

From *Collected Poems* by Wallace Stevens, copyright © 1954 by Wallace Stevens. Reprinted by permission of Alfred A. Knopf, Inc.

From *Opus Posthumous* by Wallace Stevens, edit., Samuel French Morse, copyright © 1957 by Elsie Stevens and Holly Stevens. Reprinted by permission of Alfred A. Knopf, Inc.

From *"A"* by Louis Zukofsky, copyright © 1978 Celia Zukofsky and Louis Zukofsky. Reprinted by permission of Johns Hopkins University Press.

From *Collected Fiction* by Louis Zukofsky, copyright © 1989 by Paul Zukofsky. Reprinted by permission of Dalkey Archive Press.

From *Complete Short Poetry* by Louis Zukofsky, copyright © 1991 by Paul Zukofsky. Reprinted by permission of the Johns Hopkins University Press.

Unpublished Zukofsky materials from the Louis Zukofsky collection of the Harry Ransom Humanities Research Center of the University of Texas at Austin, copyright © Paul Zukofsky, are quoted by permission of Paul Zukofsky. These materials may not be quoted by third parties without the express permission of the copyright holder.

Considerably earlier versions of chapters eleven and twelve were published in *Sagetrieb* and *West Coast Line*. Thanks to the editors of those journals, Burton Hatlen and Roy Miki, for permission to reprint them.

A Note on Texts

Citations from the major works of Louis Zukofsky refer to the most recent available texts:

"*A*" (Baltimore: Johns Hopkins University Press, 1993)
Bottom: On Shakespeare (Berkeley: University of California Press, 1987)
Collected Fiction (Elmwood Park, IL: Dalkey Archive Press, 1990)
Complete Short Poetry (Baltimore: Johns Hopkins University Press, 1991)
Prepositions: The Collected Critical Essays of Louis Zukofsky, expanded edition (Berkeley: University of California Press, 1981)
Autobiography [With Celia Zukofsky] (New York: Grossman, 1970)

Other texts will be included in the individual lists of works cited.

There has been no systematic effort to edit Zukofsky's texts, though some of the above editions claim to have incorporated corrections Zukofsky made in his own copies of his works. While the Johns Hopkins *Complete Short Poetry* is an invaluable volume, it does not include the Latin text of Louis and Celia Zukofsky's *Catullus* and perpetuates the single typographical error of the first edition of *80 Flowers,* problems that to my mind cast doubt on the reliability of the text as a whole. The 1993 Johns Hopkins "*A*" is textually quite corrupt, but it is the best we have; to my knowledge, none of the essays in this volume makes reference to erroneous portions of that text.

For the convenience of those who might be using earlier editions of "*A*", references to "*A*" will include both the movement number and the page number in the Johns Hopkins edition (e.g., "A"-12, 142). The text and pagination of the Johns Hopkins "*A*" are identical to those of the 1978 University of California Press "*A*" (a list of some of the errata in this first collected edition of "*A*", as noted by Celia Zukofsky, can be found in *Paideuma* 8:3 (Winter 1979) 585; there are no doubt many more).

Upper Limit Music

Introduction

How might one set about evaluating and introducing the writings of one of this century's most important poets, a poet whose work has all too often been mistakenly dismissed as the verse of a "poet's poet," difficult, obscure—or, worse, ornamental or trivial? In 1973, five years before the poet's death, Guy Davenport named Louis Zukofsky America's "greatest living poet"; but that encomium, coming at the end of an essay asserting that the difficulties of Zukofsky's verse are "in the reader's mind, not in the poem" (106), seems more to be ammunition for an attack on the American publishing industry than a seriously argued evaluation—that is to say, a premise, rather than a conclusion. Hugh Kenner, in a 1978 *New York Times* article, excerpts from which appear in the blurbs of two editions of Zukofsky's long poem "*A*", pronounces that poem "[t]he most hermetic poem in English, which they will still be elucidating in the 22nd century." Such a statement (like the *Choice* blurb, which promises that "*A*" "could provide another lifetime's worth of elucidation and exegesis") might set racing the pulses of young academics with a particularly scholastic bent, but it does nothing to demonstrate the *necessity* of Zukofsky's poetry, nothing to show how one's experience of twentieth-century American poetry is irrevocably impoverished without a knowledge of his work. How, then, if one is convinced of Zukofsky's importance, should one go about securing his place in the canon? Or—to make no bones about it—how might one prove this hitherto neglected figure a truly *great* modern poet?

Is it not enough to point to the unprecedented range and virtuosity of Louis Zukofsky's writings, from the nimble and classical prose of

Little and "It Was" to the inexplicably moving yet enigmatic drama of "Arise, arise"; from the politically earnest and formally dazzling " 'Mantis' " and "A"-7 to the stretches of musical rumination, capturing precisely the rhythm of walking, observation, and napping of "A"-13; from the incisive, prescient criticism Zukofsky wrote during the 1930s, including the first (and still among the best) assessment of Pound's *Cantos,* to the breathtaking sprawl of *Bottom: On Shakespeare,* a work that reads all of Western literature and philosophy under the aegis of Zukofsky's poetic tutelary deity? And is it not enough to attend to the voices of prominent poets who cite Zukofsky as among their most profound and enduring influences: Charles Tomlinson, Robert Creeley, Thomas Merton, Ian Hamilton Finlay, Robert Duncan, Ronald Johnson, of an older generation; Michael Palmer, John Taggart, Charles Bernstein, Ron Silliman, Michael Heller, and Hugh Seidman (among many others), of a younger?[1] And there is the testimony of his contemporaries: for Kenneth Rexroth, "Louis Zukofsky [was] one of the most important poets of my generation" (Zukofsky, *Complete Short Poetry* blurb). For the great Northumbrian poet Basil Bunting, Zukofsky was one of the two living poets (the other being Pound) who had, "in his sterner, stonier way," taught him something about the making of verses. And in the letters of Lorine Niedecker, along with Bunting one of Zukofsky's two closest literary correspondents, Zukofsky seemed almost to represent poetry itself. The voices of critics are there to be heard, as well. Davenport and Kenner, of course, but also Kenneth Cox, Andrew Crozier, the late Eric Mottram, Marjorie Perloff, and Peter Quartermain—all have asserted, and often worked painstakingly to demonstrate, Zukofsky's importance.

But in the end genuflection and hearsay praise must give way to argument and analysis, however partisan it might prove. Nineteen years after Louis Zukofsky's death, his presence on the American poetic landscape shows no signs of diminishing; I, for one, am convinced that when the dust settles he will prove one of the central figures of whatever histories we write of the literature of the twentieth century. The reason is not his prominence during his life; indeed, Zukofsky suffered acutely from what he felt was an unfair isolation and a lack of readership. Nor is it because of his literary friendships or his immediate influence; E. E. Cummings, for instance, had a far wider circle of acquaintances than did Zukofsky and saw his poetry and poetics disseminated far more broadly than Zukofsky's, but his works have weathered the passage of the century far less sturdily than the younger poet's. And it is not merely because of his influence on later generations of poets, though that influence has proved considerable: the entire movement of Language Poetry, for example, can be said to look to Zukofsky as one of its most important precursors. In the last analysis, any claim for Zukofsky's centrality—his *greatness*—must focus on his work itself and on his example as producing, inventing, transforming *poet*. I would prefer simply to point to that work, to say, "read the *Complete Short Poetry,* read '*A*', explore the poetry on its own terms"— but the acts of evaluation and introduction have their own necessity, even as they have their protocols. And beyond that, it is undeniable that Zukofsky's work is on some levels less than inviting: it is prickly, obdurate, resistant both to our commonsense expectations of precisely how a poem means and to our conventional notions of what pleasures a poem should afford. But it is inarguable that Zukofsky's work is at all points concerned with the aural dimension of poetry: the poems themselves constantly advertise their own musical nature, and Zukofsky's writings in poetics repeat over and again the equation of poetry and song. My own point of entrance to the body of work of this twentieth-century master, then, as the title of the present collection of essays indicates, lies in the relationship Zukofsky sketches between his own poetry and the "wordless art of music" (*Prepositions* 19).

In a memorable moment of "A"-12, the most sprawling and conversational movement of his *Cantos*-length long poem "*A*", Zukofsky describes his own poetics:

I'll tell you.
About my *poetics*—

    music
$\int$
    speech

An integral
Lower limit speech
Upper limit music

No?

    ["A"-12, 138]

It is a characteristically gnomic gesture from a poet who would confess later in life that he felt more in common with engineers and scientists than he did with most poets: the former's habits of concrete observation, careful measurement, and precise calculation, after all, accorded better with his notion of the poetic labor than did the latter's all too often unfocused sentiment and personal outpourings. The limits of a mathematical integral of course are asymptotic points that can be approached but never reached. Zukofsky's poetry, then, an integral whose limits are speech and music, moves between the ream of the koiné—of common, information-bearing communication—and the purely musical, where words are deployed wholly without regard for their meanings but interact (and give pleasure) through sound alone. The musical is necessarily but one of the realms in which poetry must operate, for language is inevitably referential, communicative; Zukofsky begins his teaching anthology *A Test of Poetry* by stressing the sensory and intellective aspects of the poem—"The test of poetry is the range of pleasure it affords as sight, sound, and intellection. This is its purpose as art" (vii)—but later in the same work he emphasizes the informative side of poetry: "Good poetry is the barest—most essentially complete—form of presenting a subject. . . . Good poetry is definite information on the subject dealt with, on the movement of the lines of verse, and on the emotion of verbal construction." But while there is no paucity of vivid image, concrete detail, delicate emotion, and painstaking thought in Zukofsky's poems, nonetheless one returns again and again to the *music* of this extraordinary body of work.

The music of Zukofsky's poetry is rarely of the mellifluous sort; if Swinburne or Tennyson achieved an aural texture akin to that of Brahms or Schumann, Zukofsky's "music" has far more in common with the unadorned and angular sonic structures of Webern. The elaborately wrought assonances and consonances and the complex meters of a Swinburne seem heavy-handed beside the wiry, taut play of sound in a poem of Zukofsky's such as 1959's "Wire":

Wire cage flues
    on
the roofs:

Paper ash—whole
    sheets
in gusts—

Flawed by winds
      fly
like doves

[*Complete Short Poetry* 208]

Note the careful weighing of sound here, how Zukofsky constructs
a pattern out of a bare minimum of aural repetitions: ca**ge** | **P**a**p**er;
flue**s** | **r**oo**fs**; a**sh** | **sh**eet**s**; g**us**t**s** | **d**ove**s**; and the flurries of sound of
Wi**re** | **fl**y | **l**i**k**e; **fl**ue**s** | **Fl**awed | **fl**y; **Fl**awe**d** | **w**in**ds** | **d**ove**s**. No
sound, save the *s,* which serves as the closest the poem has to an end-
rhyme, is repeated more than three times, yet there are enough repetitions to establish this brief poem as a remarkably coherent aural
whole, an almost weightless structure of lightly patterned sound
forms.

In *A Test of Poetry,* Zukofsky comments that Swinburne's work
yields "the feeling of a very grandiose shadow built upon very little"
(96), but the reason is not merely that Swinburne has somehow *over-
used* sonic effects, while Zukofsky himself has deployed them spar-
ingly. Indeed, for Zukofsky sound is perhaps the single indispensable
element of an effective poem: "The sound of the words is sometimes
95% of poetic presentation. One can often appreciate the connotations
of the sound of words merely by listening, even if the language is
foreign." Swinburne's defect is not mere intensity of sound: "What is
foreign to poetry," rather, "is the word which means little or nothing—either as sound, image, or relation of ideas" (*Test of Poetry* 58).
Compression—what Pound had expressed, following Zukofsky's
friend Basil Bunting, in the equation *Dichten = Condensare*—is the
hallmark of Zukofsky's poetry, an absolutely astringent discipline that
will allow no excess verbiage, that will permit the poet only the most
condensed and charged structures of language. This discipline is evident throughout Zukofsky's work, even in poems that might otherwise seem whimsical or slight: that is, even when Zukofsky is at his
most high-spirited, one has always the sense that there is no word out
of place, that the words have been handled with a painstaking "sincerity" (Zukofsky's own term) and arranged into a formally satisfying
and coherent "objectification," a tangible and inevitable shape.

There are a number of musics in Zukofsky's poetry, several ways
in which it approaches what Walter Pater proposed as an ideal "condition of music." There are the sounds of the words themselves, cre-

ating aural effects that approximate the effects of literal music on our ears. And there is the notion of the poem as a "song," a composition that by rights ought to be set to music. Quoting Dante, Zukofsky asserts that the art of poetry is "nothing else but the completed action of writing words to be set to music" (*Prepositions* 9). This is not to say that the poet is literally a lyricist, Ira to George Gershwin (or even Auden to Stravinsky). Rather, poetry written as words to be set to music, in critic Kenneth Cox's words, "is concerned for the pitch of vowel and duration of syllable which fit verse to be sung . . . [Zukofsky's poetry] distinguishes song from declamation and declamation from recitative. . . . He seeks not so much expressive word or rhythm as what he calls 'melody,' phrasing, such shaping of syllables as carries conviction without fuss and such changes of tone and pace as, with repetition and crossing of themes, augmentation, imitation and all the other devices of musicians, construct a composition of English words" (82–83). And it is worth keeping in mind, as well, that Zukofsky welcomed the setting of his poems to music.

Beyond these fairly traditional uses of the term "music," there is an analogical use, in which the structures and forms of music become models for the structures of Zukofsky's verse. Most famous, and most significant, is his use of the baroque fugue as a formal model for sections of his great long poem, "*A*". The contributors' notes to Zukofsky's first major publication, the " 'Objectivists' 1931" issue of *Poetry* magazine, which he edited at the behest of Ezra Pound, describe the first movements of "*A*" as including "two themes: I—desire for the potentially perfect finding its direction inextricably the direction of historic and contemporary particulars; and II—approximate attainment of this perfection in the feeling of the contrapuntal design of the [fugue] transferred to poetry; both themes related to the text of Bach's *St. Matthew Passion*." Where the fugue deploys musical subjects and countersubjects to achieve a pleasing density of musical information, Zukofsky's poetry counterpoints various thematic and imagistic materials. This is a music, not of sounds or of aural movements, but of concepts: it is musical, not inherently—that is, it does not draw upon the same sensory resources as what we call music—but analogously. As Zukofsky puts it in a 1930 letter to Pound, his poetic mentor and sponsor, "*A*" "has to be read as a pattern" (*Pound/Zukofsky* 82), in large part because it is modeled on the forms of baroque music, what Pound was in his music criticism fond of calling "pattern music," in contradistinction to what he saw as the undisciplined "gush" of romantic music, especially as interpreted by exceptionally sensitive late nineteenth-century musicians, fond of a plasticity of tempo that maddened the music critic Pound.

My own emphasis on music in Zukofsky's verse (an emphasis derived of course from the poet's own writings) is meant to make clear, not merely that Zukofsky's is a poetry in which sound values are carefully determined, but more important that Zukofsky's is a poetics of redoubtable and even revolutionary formalism, in which structure and shape are the most important elements of the poem. To some degree "music" in the phrase "upper limit music" is simply a trope, a figure for the condition of absolute form to which Pater referred in his famous passage on the "condition of music." Call it *form,* call it *structure, shape,* even *engineering*—whatever terminology one chooses to describe it, at the heart of Zukofsky's works lies an impulse to arrange words in a meaningful, tangible order or, conversely, to force words into an order, invented or found, and observe the meanings that arise from or coalesce out of them. This is a somewhat different sort of formalism from that of a Frost or an Antony Hecht and worlds apart from that of the soi-disant New Formalists, whose militant sponsorship of traditional forms can be read as a rejection of the poet's responsibility *for* form. Zukofsky's is a principled formalism that on the whole rejects inherited forms, an absolute conviction that any shape the human mind can come upon is of itself valuable and meaningful and that words, as the product and producer of human intellect and imagination, can never be limited in their power of suggestion or their meaningful potential. Zukofsky resembles Auden or, say, James Merrill (though God knows he would have relished neither comparison), insofar as they share an appetite for new forms, new shapes in which to cast the poem and insofar as they share an infectious gaiety and enthusiasm for the forms upon which they have happened. But where Auden and Merrill pursue their formal experiments within the general framework of English accentual-syllabic meter and rhyme (with many variations and exoticisms), Zukofsky prefers to deracinate his poetics more fundamentally from the soil of traditional forms: his word-count prosodies, his arithmetically derived distributions of consonant sounds, and his phonetic transliterations from foreign verse, are all original and strikingly successful attempts, in George Steiner's words, "to instance possible procedures for American poetry now and tomorrow" (352).

Zukofsky was among the first American poets to be born in the twentieth century. His immediate poetic forebears, the generation of writers we now classify as "high" modernists, were born in the closing decades of the nineteenth century, and even their most formally progressive, forward-looking works—Pound's *Cantos,* Williams's *Paterson,* Eliot's *Waste Land*—retain a sense of having with difficulty broken out of Victorian forms and mindsets. The shadow of Browning always lurks behind Pound, emerging for instance in the *Pisan Cantos* when Pound celebrates Churchill's election defeat: "Oh to be in England now that Winston's out"; at one memorable point in *Paterson,* Williams begins quoting his own early Keatsian poem *The Wanderer,* betraying an ambivalent nostalgia for its lush diction; and the androgynous Tiresias of Eliot's waste land, "old man with wrinkled dugs," ostensibly an archetypally modern figure, bears a distinct resemblance to the speaker of Tennyson's dramatic monologue "Tiresias," published in 1885, the year of Pound's birth. But Zukofsky, like Auden, was at home in our century, never having known another. While it is not inappropriate to consider him a contemporary of the high modernists (especially given his friendships with Pound, Williams, and Moore), Zukofsky, especially in his later works, is every bit as "new" or experimental as such poets of our own fin de siècle as Clark Coolidge, Susan Howe, or Michael Palmer.

In his later years, Zukofsky would claim closest relation, not to the poets of the preceding generation to whose work his own seems most similar —Pound, Williams, Eliot, Moore—but to Wallace Stevens, the most formally conservative poet of the modernist revolution and one who would parody Williams's formal experiments as "reject[ing] the idea that meaning has the slightest value and describ[ing] a poem as a structure of little blocks" (*Letters* 803). Stevens is an unlikely precursor for the author of "A"-23 and *80 Flowers,* but Zukofsky would claim in 1971 that his own works were "closer to [Stevens's] than to that of any of my contemporaries in the last half century of life we shared together" (*Prepositions* 27). To juxtapose Zukofsky and Stevens is instructive, in that it highlights both the continuities between Zukofsky and an earlier tradition of poetry in English and the radical breaks that twentieth-century writers would effect between themselves and earlier modes of poetic expression. The cultural milieu in which Zukofsky came of age, for instance, was not that of Stephen Foster, Bliss Carman, and Sarah Bernhardt, as it was for Stevens, but that of Krazy Kat, E. E. Cummings, Charlie Chaplin, and the frenetic cultural ferment of the American twenties. And the problem of the death of God, which would in one form or another haunt Stevens most of his life, Zukofsky claimed to have put behind him at about the age of sixteen. But the problem of knowledge, of the foundations of our epistemological certainty—what Stevens formulates as the relationship of "reality" and the "imagination"—and the vexed, insoluble relationship between poetry and the world of power and politics ("things as they are") loom every bit as large in Zukofsky's career as they do in his older contemporary's.

The difference lies perhaps in emphasis and in terminology. Where Stevens's terms are thinly reworked versions of the concepts deployed by Wordsworth, Coleridge, and the other romantics, Zukofsky sets aside the question of the status of the phenomenal world: the poet must "live with the things as they exist" or as they are perceived; it is immaterial whether they have an existence apart from our perceptions. The real problems of knowledge, as Zukofsky explores them in his poetry, lie in the social, interpersonal bases of our shared worldview, in the extent to which our communications one with another are made in the medium of a language that we have inherited and that itself shapes us. The truly radical agenda of Zukofsky's work lies not in an exploration of any conventional epistemology, the relationship between *subject* and *object,* or (as in Stevens) "imagination" and "reality," but in an exploration of the very medium in which we know and communicate knowledge: Stevens's epic theme mourns the death of the Gods; for Zukofsky, a poet can spend his life exploring the words "the" and "a," "both of which are weighted with as much epos and historical destiny as one man can perhaps resolve. Those who do not believe this are too sure that the little words mean nothing among so many other words" (*Prepositions* 10).

In addition to being perhaps our first thoroughly modern poet, Zukofsky is not coincidentally perhaps the most "American" of American poets: the son of Yiddish-speaking immigrants, himself exposed to no formal English until he began public school on New York's Lower East Side, Zukofsky's uneasy assimilation into, and ultimate mastery of, an ostensibly hostile Western tradition is emblematic of the sense of both conquest and alterity at the heart of whatever we might regard as the twentieth-century American mind. Perhaps the alien nature of the American tongue itself, as that tongue presented itself to a small, thin boy awash in the patois of Irish and Italian American New York streets, gave rise in Zukofsky to a sense of the ultimately provisional nature of language itself ("the foreignness," as Walter Benjamin puts it, not of *a* language, but "of languages" [75])— and beyond that of nationality. At any rate, Zukofsky grew up with a sense of the American vernacular as firm as that of his older friend Williams and a similar conviction that poetry could not be written in an inherited tongue or in inherited forms. In Zukofsky, the Poundian imperative to "make it new" has a specifically American resonance and speaks to a cultural agenda that harnesses the European past to an American future, without succumbing to a specious or stifling "internationalism" like Pound's own. When Pound, visiting America in 1939 after a twenty-eight-year exile, touted Father Coughlin to him, Zukofsky could only reply, "Whatever you don't know, Ezra, you ought to know *voices*" (*Prepositions* 165). Zukofsky himself was always listening to American voices, which kept him grounded in an American reality.

In the past decade, two aspects of Zukofsky's work seem to have attracted critical interest and generated critical partisanship (as opposed, that is, to the interest and partisanship of other poets). First, there is the redoubtable daedalian artistry of Zukofsky's work, his compositional habits of inventing outlandishly difficult and unconventional forms, of submerging impossibly arcane schemata beneath the surface of a syntactically disjunct text, of packing his severely compressed lines with unidentified citations, quotations, translations, and transliterations from the full range of a capacious and eclectic reading. This aspect of Zukofsky's corpus has given rise to something akin to the Joyce or Pound critical industries (though on a far smaller scale): readers who, by the evidence of their own explorations of the Zukofskyan text, value Zukofsky's work primarily *for* its very hermeticism. The work of such readers is invaluable and even necessary, but hermeticism alone cannot justify a high valuation of Zukofsky's work: Spenser and Joyce, for instance, are undeniably hermetic, but there are many aspects of their works to admire aside from their concealed significations. Spenser, his multiple allegories aside, is one of English literature's master storytellers. *Finnegans Wake,* though it may pack in an enormous and heterogeneous cargo of reference, is on its surface a non-stop carnival of joyous linguistic play. It is unwise to justify a writer's importance solely on the basis of the exegetical labors to which he has given rise.

Another reading of Zukofsky stresses the very surface difficulty of his poetry, which is seen as somehow empowering for the reader, who is forced thereby to become an active participant in the constitution of the work's meaning. This seems to me a far more fruitful position, despite the facts that, on the one hand, the model of the reading process it posits for conventional poetry is a patently impoverished one, and, on the other, the coincidence of syntactic/semantic ambiguity and readerly participation is by no means assured: there are perfectly intelligent and goodwilled readers who will not hesitate to simply set aside a difficult text in favor of something more immediately rewarding, less demanding of their time. But I am convinced that there is value in the uncertainties and obscurities of Zukofsky's poetry, that there is a certain liberated exhilaration in being cast upon one's own resources in navigating the tightly compressed word-walls of "A"-22 and -23 or *80 Flowers,* the crabbed, foreign-sounding transliterations of *Catullus,* or even the strung-out syntactic ambiguities of a brief lyric like "A B C," the tenth poem of the sequence "I's (pronounced *eyes)*":

> He has wit—
> but who has more—
>
> who looks
> some way more
>
> withal
>
> than
> one eye
>
> weeps, his voice
> [*Complete Short Poetry* 216]

In the space of eight lines, this little poem involves us in inextricable ambiguities. "He has wit" is surely declarative, but should the remaining phrases of the poem, devoid of punctuation save for two dashes and a comma, be read as statements or questions: "he has wit—who has more wit than he?" or "he has wit—but there is another who has more wit"? Is the second "who" to be identified with the first? What is implied by "some way more / withal / than / one eye": does it imply keeping both eyes open, not letting either of one's eyes be blurred by tears? And is "his voice" somehow to be equated with looking "some way more," or with "one eye / weep[ing]"? The archaic adverb "withal" (Shakespearean?) is a miniature community of ambiguities: which of its dictionary definitions ought we to read here, "besides," "thereby," "thereupon," or "still"? (And of course a pun on "with all" irresistibly suggests itself.) And what relationship does the title, "A B C," bear to the poem as a whole? In the tiny compass of these eight lines, the reader has become enmeshed in a web of meaningful possibilities, none of which claims hegemony over the others. Initially bewildering, the experience soon reveals itself as liberating: if the text makes no attempt to impress upon its reader anything resembling a unitary meaning, then generating multiple meanings through one's reading is precisely the point. Zukofsky's poetry does not license readerly free play (it is not a Rorschach blot), for it claims of its reader an attention commensurate with the intelligence it embodies, but it does stimulate, and reward, an astonishing amount of participatory involvement on that reader's part, a participation that eventually opens into a sense of liberation.

But should this liberation, above all private and often only momentary, be transposed to the realm of the political? Can one argue the importance of Zukofsky's work on the basis of the ideological implications of its very obscurity? Several readers, in part following the lead of the poetics writings of the post-Zukofsky Language Poets, have done precisely that. I remain determinedly agnostic as to whether one should accord Zukofsky's poetry a political value on the basis of its disruptions of conventional discourse, keeping in mind Charles Altieri's lapidary essay title "Without Consequences Is No Politics."[2] At the very least, however, one must concede that Zukofsky's is a poetry that both challenges and energizes its readers, pressing them to be on their toes at all times, to take an almost unprecedented role in piecing together the syntaxes and meanings possible within each passage. Zukofsky writes English as if it were a foreign language (to paraphrase Hugh Kenner on the American modernists), and he puts his readers in the position of novice language learner striving, say, to work through Apollonius of Rhodes's *Argonautica* with nothing but a Greek lexicon and a deal of spare time. Such an experience is admittedly repugnant to some readers, especially those who desire the "disappearance of the world" Ron Silliman observes in the forms of popular fiction: "the consumer of a mass-market novel such as *Jaws* stares at a 'blank' page (the page also of the speed-reader) while a story appears to unform miraculously of its own free will before his or her eyes" (13). But then, little worthwhile comes without effort. In Lear's words, "nothing will come of nothing"; or in Emerson's, "He that would bring home the wealth of the Indies, must carry out the wealth of the Indies" (59).

One ultimately returns to Zukofsky's own measure: "The test of poetry is the range of pleasure it affords as sight, sound, and intellection." The intellective rigor of his poetry is plain enough, the condensed and distilled equations of, in his own words, a "finer mathematician" (Interview 274); and for those who prefer the poetry they read to exercise their intelligence—and exercise is itself a certain pleasure—Zukofsky's work is of almost inexhaustible interest and delight. But it is their pleasures of sight and sound—of the poem as tangible, audible shaped object—that will ensure the survival of Zukofsky's works. No poet of the twentieth century has had a better ear than Zukofsky's nor a surer sense of poetic form. And certainly no poet has combined such matchless talents with the tireless ambition, bold experimentation, and sheer dogged determination necessary to produce a range of masterworks as varied as the corpus that includes *Bottom: On Shakespeare,* the novel *Little, 80 Flowers,* and the whole completed structure of *"A"*. The poetry of the twentieth century has been shaped in large part by the generation of poets born in the last decades of the nineteenth; much of the most fascinating and challenging poetry of our own fin de siècle and, beyond it, the poetry of the twenty-first century, may in large part be dominated by the influence and example of Louis Zukofsky.

Upper Limit Music is the first grouping of essays on Zukofsky since 1979, when Carroll F. Terrell published his *Louis Zukofsky: Man and Poet.* While that collection remains a piece of necessary equipment for Zukofsky scholars, both for its critical essays and its indispensable bibliography, the circumstances of its preparation—it was compiled in the months immediately following Zukofsky's death in May 1978 and drew largely upon a special 1978 issue of the Pound journal *Paide-uma*—made the *Man and Poet* volume something of a (not unpleasing) mixed bag of biography, criticism, bibliography, and general Fest-schrift. *Upper Limit Music* focuses more narrowly upon the critical but with a concomitant realization that in the case of a poet such as Zuk-ofsky, whose works are not yet canonized and whose life has not yet been written, it is not inappropriate to incorporate the biographical within the critical. Zukofsky's works, as well, are tightly bound up with extraliterary events, both of his historical era and of his own life; to separate the writing and the man who writes would be, I think, a mistake.

The shape of this collection and its concerns are in large part an outgrowth of its original occasion. Most of these essays, that is, began as papers presented at the University of Maine at Orono in June 1993, on the occasion of a conference entitled "The First Postmodernists: American Poets of the 1930s Generation." While all of these essays are concerned with providing new readings of Zukofsky's works, they have in large part fallen into two broad categories: those that address Zukofsky as a poet of the thirties, involved like his contemporaries in the political, poetical, and cultural struggles of that turbulent decade, and those that examine his work in terms of its "postmodernism," roughly speaking the manners in which it builds upon, extends, and breaks from the modernist poetics of the generation of writers im-mediately preceding him.

The first generation of critics to take notice of Zukofsky pursued such genealogies with a vengeance; they were for the most part schol-ars who came to his work primarily through a reading of Pound, and their interpretations of his work were informed (not inappropriately, I might add) by their assimilation of Pound's methods and poetics. In such light, Zukofsky seems both epigone and innovator, disciple and founder of his own school—Aristotle to Pound's Plato. (Paul Smith, for instance, in one of the finest readings of "*A*", describes that work as "a sustained and important attempt to write a way out of [Pound's] shadow" [133].) But readings of Zukofsky as Poundian disciple seem long since to have reached their limit, and scholars are finding Zuk-ofsky of increasing interest, not only in his own terms, but in the terms of his various nonliterary and quasi-literary contexts, contexts including but by no means limited to the political and economic situ-ations within which his works were written and situate themselves.

Alec Marsh's essay on Pound and Zukofsky, for instance, focuses not on any unidirectional notion of "influence"—of Pound's influencing Zukofsky, or vice versa—but on the interchange and interplay of ideas (and misunderstandings) between the two poets and the various manners in which each of them responds to a given literary/political/economic problem, the relationship of poetic production to a labor theory of value. In so doing, Marsh broaches the problem of the relationship of the political and the aesthetic as it appears in Zukofsky's writings; this problem was one of the major literary debates of the American 1930s, and its ramifications constitute one of the principal themes of the essays here collected.

Like Marsh's, several of the essays in this volume address the context in which Zukofsky's work was produced and try to remedy the shortcomings of the various formalist, decontextualizing readings of his work that have been advanced in the past. Norman Finkelstein explores a fascinating moment in literary history by placing Zukofsky in contrast to the *In Zikh* group, a contemporaneous school of New York Yiddish modernists, and examines the implications of Zukofsky's conscious decision to become a Jewish-American poet writing in English and to ally himself with the poetic modernism of Pound rather than that being advanced by his fellow Jews. Steve Shoemaker opens this volume by looking at Zukofsky's crisis of assimilation, not only in relation to his friendship with the increasingly anti-Semitic Pound, but also as it is played out in his reading of the protomodernist culture hero Henry James; in this view, Zukofsky's "Objectivist" modernism—at once a gesture in literary politics, the formation of a "movement" of Objectivist poets, *and* a set of formal and stylistic innovations—is as much a strategy by which to survive Pound's implicit (and explicit) vilifications as it is a set of developments of Pound's own aesthetics.

Other essays more directly address Zukofsky's situation within the political and economic contexts of the thirties. It is impossible to deny that Zukofsky was a Marxist during an era when perhaps a majority of American artists and intellectuals confessed an allegiance to the Left; my own essay looks at his relationship with the formal power structure of American literary Marxism, particularly as embodied in the periodical *New Masses,* and argues that the Party's rather narrow definition of what sort of writing would serve the proletarian cause was a source of continual conflict for Zukofsky, whose own resolutely modernist aesthetic was formed out of his reading of Apollinaire, Pound, Stein, and other writers whose works served to foreground the materiality of the text itself, to draw attention to the medium of language itself.

During the Depression, of course, many of America's most prominent writers and artists could find work only through government programs. Zukofsky was no exception; he worked for the Works Progress Administration (WPA) in New York City, concentrating mostly on a project known as the *Index of American Design*. While the manuscripts he wrote for the *Index* are as yet unpublished, they are of considerable interest and cast a fascinating light on Zukofsky's other writings. Barry Ahearn examines the *Index* material within the context of Zukofsky's WPA career as a whole, and his leftist affinities, and looks at the relationship of Zukofsky's readings of particular cultural artifacts to the economic and political matrixes out of which those readings are produced: unsurprisingly, Zukofsky emerges as a canny, if unconventional, Marxist cultural critic. Ira B. Nadel, concentrating primarily on different *Index* articles from Ahearn, emphasizes Zukofsky as *American* cultural critic and shows how the *Index* material situates him in the tradition of such earlier writers as Henry Adams and William Carlos Williams. Both critics clearly demonstrate how the cultural skills Zukofsky honed in working on the *Index*—a close attention to the craftsmanship involved in producing an artifact and to the cultural and economic matrices out of which that artifact proceeded—served him in writing his "poem of a life," "*A*".

Although he is inextricably situated within the political economic contexts of the thirties, Zukofsky must be read as a *writer* within those contexts; a close examination of his early works, for instance, reveals as much about the astonishing degree of ambition and invention possessed by this young poet as it does about his material or philosophical circumstances. Ming-Qian Ma locates Zukofsky's first major work, "Poem beginning 'The,' " within a context of modernist quotational practice and shows further how " 'The' " breaks with the practice of such quoting poets as Pound and Eliot and inaugurates a poetics of what Ma felicitously names "postmodernist citationality." Peter Quartermain magisterially examines the neglected prose work *Thanks to the Dictionary*. This piece, out of print for many years, is one of Zukofsky's most astonishingly experimental early works and looks forward, in its surrender of authorial control, to the aleatorical poetics of such contemporary postmodernist masters as Jackson Mac Low and the late John Cage. Susan Vanderborg reads a Kabbalistic fracturing of language in Zukofsky's lyrics of the thirties, particularly in the political sestina " 'Mantis,' " and meditates upon the relationship between the raw sounds of words and the effects of those words in the world of economic exploitation and political oppression. Just as Marsh and Shoemaker critically examine Zukofsky's relationship with Ezra Pound, P. Michael Campbell looks at Zukofsky's surprising avowal of kinship with Wallace Stevens, whom various critics have perhaps unfairly stigmatized as a reactionary force within modernist poetry and have placed at the head of a twentieth-century tradition diametrically opposed to Pound, Eliot, and Williams's "revolution of the word." The commonalities between the works of Zukofsky and Stevens, Campbell's essay implies, cast into doubt such facile balkanizing of the field of modern American poetic production.

"A"-12, the central long section of Zukofsky's "epic," can in several ways be read as the fulcrum upon which the poem, and Zukofsky's whole poetics, turn. Burton Hatlen reads this section in terms of Zukofsky's own notion of "fugal" form and argues tentatively that we can read a transition from modernism to postmodernism in the "incomplete" form of the movement as a whole. Of course, wherever one determines the precise locus of shift to be, whether in "A"-12, in the manner in which quotations are deployed in " 'The,' " or in the chance composition of *Thanks to the Dictionary,* it is abundantly clear that Zukofsky's writing maps out in some detail the trajectory of writing practices toward what we now regard as the postmodern: this is evident not least in the extent to which such contemporary poets as Charles Bernstein, Ron Silliman, Ronald Johnson, and John Taggart have made use of and paid homage to Zukofsky's innovations.

Such acknowledgments of Zukofsky's pathfinding achievements tend to focus on his later writings, work in which various postmodern or poststructuralist problematics—the death or dispersal of the author, the indeterminacy of textual meaning—can be read as coming to the fore. Marnie Parsons examines the final section of Zukofsky's *"A"*, "A"-24, a text that is an arrangement, to Handel's harpsichord music, of various of Zukofsky's earlier texts, both prose and poetry; one significant fact about "A"-24, which appears under Zukofsky's name and as a section of *his* epic, is that it was composed not by the poet but by his wife, Celia. "A"-24, then, positions itself as a text whose author we cannot with assurance name. In its multiple voicings, it makes not sense, but "nonsense," a not at all pejorative description of how these four simultaneously sounded texts (five, including Handel) interact to produce a plenitude of meaning.

Finally, Kent Johnson presents a notational reading of Zukofsky's last completed work, the volume of short poems *80 Flowers.* Johnson finds in the *Flowers* persuasive parallels with classical Chinese poets and sees in their fractal compression the promise of a whole new poetics, perhaps one similar to that which Williams foresaw when he wrote, reviewing Zukofsky, "With a fleck of the bright future a whole world can again be imagined and the music picks up again. I hear a new music of verse stretching out into the future" (165).

Williams, of course, writing in 1947, had no way of foreseeing the dazzling limits to which his younger friend would press his poetics. Williams wrote of necessity in prospect, but the present essays as a whole aim to begin a retrospective assessment of this major writer's achievements. A mere thirteen papers cannot begin to encompass the breadth of Zukofsky's art, nor can they do any more than hint at the continuing impact of his work upon the practice of poetry in the English-speaking world. Nonetheless, let their conversation begin— the conversation of poets, critics, and scholars, all admirers of Zukofsky's achievement—keeping always in mind that Zukofsky's poetry speaks for itself and demands of us as readers an attention and openness commensurate with the pleasures and knowledges it yields:

> why deny what you've not
> tried: read, not into, it:
> desire until all be bright.
> ["A"-22, 528]

Notes

1. Creeley has no fewer than five pieces on Zukofsky in his collected essays and has contributed a foreword to the *Complete Short Poetry;* Heller is author of *Conviction's Net of Branches,* the only extant full-length study of the Objectivists, Zukofsky's short lived "school"; Taggart's recently published *Songs of Degrees* includes three indispensable essays on Zukofsky's poetry.

2. This essay is part of an exchange in Robert Von Hallberg's collection *Politics and Poetic Value;* see also Jerome J. McGann, "Contemporary Poetry, Alternate Routes" and "Response to Charles Altieri," and Jed Rasula, "The Politics of, the Politics in." Useful overviews of the issues at stake in the intertwining of poetics

and politics are Charles Bernstein's edited volume, *The Politics of Poetic Form* and Hank Lazer's omnibus review essay, "The Politics of Form and Poetry's Other Subjects." The Language Poets' own writings are voluminous, and a fair sampling can be found in Andrews and Bernstein, *The L=A=N=G=U=A=G=E Book;* a useful account of their political claims is Hartley, *Textual Politics and the Language Poets.* Marjorie Perloff, perhaps the first "mainstream" critic to take note of Language Writing, is resolutely unwilling to commit herself as to whether that work's political claims have validity. See "The Word as Such: L=A=N=G=U=A=G=E Poetry in the Eighties." Quartermain and Stanley, in otherwise quite useful studies, edge toward Language Poetry orthodoxy in reading the ideological valence of Zukofsky's work.

Works Cited

Altieri, Charles. "Without Consequences Is No Politics: A Response to Jerome McGann." *Politics and Poetic Value.* Ed. Robert Von Hallberg. Chicago: U of Chicago P, 1987.

Andrews, Bruce, and Charles Bernstein, eds. *The L=A=N=G=U=A=G=E Book.* Carbondale: Southern Illinois UP, 1984.

Benjamin, Walter. *Illuminations.* Ed. Hannah Arendt. Trans. Harry Zohn. New York: Schocken, 1969.

Bernstein, Charles, ed. *The Politics of Poetic Form: Poetry and Public Policy.* New York: Roof, 1990.

Bunting, Basil. Preface. *Collected Poems.* Mt. Kisco, NY: Moyer Bell, 1985.

Cox, Kenneth. "The Poetry of Louis Zukofsky: '*A*'." Agenda 9.4–10.1 (Autumn 1971–Winter 1972): 80–89.

Creeley, Robert. *Collected Essays.* Berkeley: U of California P, 1989.

Davenport, Guy. *The Geography of the Imagination: Forty Essays.* San Francisco: North Point, 1981.

Emerson, Ralph Waldo. *Essays and Lectures.* Ed. Joel Porte. New York: Library of America, 1983.

Hartley, George P. *Textual Politics and the Language Poets.* Bloomington: Indiana UP, 1989.

Heller, Michael. *Conviction's Net of Branches: Essays on the Objectivist Poets and Poetry.* Carbondale: Southern Illinois UP, 1985.

Lazer, Hank. "The Politics of Form and Poetry's Other Subjects: Reading Contemporary American Poetry." *American Literary History* 2.3 (Fall 1990): 503–527.

McGann, Jerome J. "Contemporary Poetry, Alternate Routes." *Politics and Poetic Value.* Ed. Robert Von Hallberg. Chicago: U of Chicago P, 1987. 263–276.

———. "Response to Charles Altieri." *Politics and Poetic Value.* Ed. Robert Von Hallberg. Chicago: U of Chicago P, 1987. 309–314.

Perloff, Marjorie. "The Word as Such: L=A=N=G=U=A=G=E Poetry in the

Eighties." *The Dance of the Intellect: Studies in the Poetry of the Pound Tradition.* Cambridge: Cambridge UP, 1985. 215–238.

Quartermain, Peter. *Disjunctive Poetics: From Gertrude Stein and Louis Zukofsky to Susan Howe.* Cambridge: Cambridge UP, 1992.

Rasula, Jed. "The Politics of, the Politics in." *Politics and Poetic Value.* Ed. Robert Von Hallberg. Chicago: U of Chicago P, 1987. 315–322.

Silliman, Ron. "Disappearance of the Word, Appearance of the World." *The New Sentence.* New York: Roof, 1987.

Smith, Paul. *Pound Revised.* London: Croom Helm, 1983.

Stanley, Sandra Kumamoto. *Louis Zukofsky and the Transformation of a Modern American Poetics.* Berkeley: U of California P, 1993.

Steiner, George. *After Babel: Aspects of Language and Translation.* Oxford: Oxford UP, 1975.

Stevens, Wallace. *The Letters of Wallace Stevens.* Ed. Holly Stevens. New York: Knopf, 1966.

Taggart, John. *Songs of Degrees: Essays on Contemporary Poetry and Poetics.* Tuscaloosa: U of Alabama P, 1994.

Terrell, Carroll F., ed. *Louis Zukofsky: Man and Poet.* Orono, ME: National Poetry Foundation, 1979.

Von Hallberg, Robert, ed. *Politics and Poetic Value.* Chicago: U of Chicago P, 1987.

Williams, William Carlos. *Something to Say: William Carlos Williams on Younger Poets.* Ed. James E. B. Breslin. New York: New Directions, 1985.

Zukofsky, Louis. Contributor's note. Spec. issue of *Poetry* 37.5 (February 1931): 294. (Special issue: " 'Objectivists' 1931").

———. [Interview ("Sincerity and Objectification").] With L. S. Dembo. *Louis Zukofsky: Man and Poet.* Ed. Carroll F. Terrell. Orono, ME: National Poetry Foundation, 1979. 265–281.

———. *A Test of Poetry.* 1948. New York: C. Z. Publications, 1980.

Zukofsky, Louis, and Ezra Pound. *Pound/Zukofsky: Selected Letters of Ezra Pound and Louis Zukofsky.* Ed. Barry Ahearn. New York: New Directions, 1987.

I.

Cultural Poetics, Political Culture
Zukofsky in the 1930s

1

Between Contact and Exile
Louis Zukofsky's Poetry of Survival

STEVE SHOEMAKER

THE FIGURE OF HENRY JAMES looms at the periphery of Objectivist beginnings, presiding over the transfer of impetus and imprimatur from the first-generation modernism of Ezra Pound and William Carlos Williams to what Williams called "another wave of it" (*Selected Letters* 95). In 1927, the year the Objectivist wave first began to swell, Williams published his first full-length novel, *A Voyage to Pagany,* described by Pound as an attempt to grapple with "the Jamesian problem of U.S.A. v. Europe, the international relation, etc." (*Literary Essays* 397). This same year Pound began to edit a little magazine whose title, *The Exile,* evoked a state of existence that James had done more to explore than anyone else, at least according to Pound's own estimate. In fact, Pound had at this time been estranged from the land of his birth for nearly twenty years, a period roughly equal in duration to the term of James's absence from America before the return visit of 1904–1905 that produced *The American Scene.* The itinerary of that visit, as Louis Zukofsky pointed out more than once in his writings, took the novelist who famously "never went down-town" to the Jewish ghetto of New York's Lower East Side and probably close by the crowded apartment that housed the infant Zukofsky and family.

It seems oddly fitting, then, that in 1927 Pound should publish Zukofsky's important early work, "Poem beginning 'The' " in *The Exile.* Through the transatlantic negotiations of *The Exile,* and more particularly through his contact with Zukofsky, Pound effected a literary return that went part of the way toward matching James's 1904 homecoming. As for Zukofsky, the "contingency" of James's visit to the Lower East Side seemed to him "a forecast of the first-generation

American infusion into twentieth-century literature" (*Autobiography* 13). The publication of "Poem beginning 'The' " in *The Exile* represents Zukofsky's first major contribution to that literary infusion. At the same time, however, his residence in America, the result of his immigrant family's journey in a direction opposite to that of Pound's exile, cemented an affinity with Williams, whose approach to the Jamesian "international relation" emphasized the cultivation of specifically American roots. Like Pound, Williams expressed his artistic stance on the question of national and international literatures through his editorship of a little magazine, *Contact,* which insisted on "the essential contact between words and the locality which breeds them, in this case America" (1). And like Pound's *The Exile,* Williams's *Contact* included the work of the young Louis Zukofsky in its pages.[1]

For Zukofsky, however, the possible meanings of both "contact" and "exile" are complicated by a set of cultural problems not addressed by most critical readings of the "supranational movement called International Modernism" (Kenner 33). A more detailed consideration of Zukofsky's reaction to James's visit to the Lower East Side in 1904, recorded in Zukofsky's *Autobiography* (1970), provides an entrance into the difficulty, but Zukofsky has ensured that the approach will be oblique. The *Autobiography* is an unusual document whose teasing title belies its content, at least if the book is approached with other, more familiar autobiographies in mind. A slim volume of sixty-three pages, according to a numbering scheme that takes separate account of two title pages, colophon, epigraphs, and dedication, the book presents eighteen of Zukofsky's shorter poems in twenty-two musical "settings," the latter all composed by his wife Celia according to "forms" (madrigal, plain chant, etc.) suggested by the poet. Interspersed among these settings, one finds six brief prose statements, one as short as two lines, none longer than a paragraph. The book's epigraphs, in similarly concise manner, defend such apparent reticence in a purported "autobiography":

> I too have been charged with obscurity, tho it's a case of listeners wanting to know too much about me, more than the words say.
> —*Little*

> As a poet I have always felt that the work says all there needs to be said of one's life.
> [*Autobiography* 5]

Readers, or rather "listeners," who seek to understand the man are directed to the work, to the novella *Little,* for example, or to *"A"*, Zukofsky's 826-page "poem of a life," composed over a period of nearly fifty years. But since *Little,* when it is not primarily "a kind of linguistic heaven of infinite play" (Sorrentino vii), concerns itself mostly with Zukofsky's son Paul, a violin prodigy, and since *"A"* has been called "the most hermetic poem in English, which they will still be elucidating in the 22nd century" (Kenner, *"A"* jacket), we might be forgiven for hovering over those six prose statements in the *Autobiography,* couched in the "plain" language of "fact."

The reference to James occurs in the first such declaration, which reads in its entirety as follows: "But the bare facts are: I was born in Manhattan, January 23, 1904, the year Henry James returned to the American scene to look at the Lower East Side. The contingency appeals to me as a forecast of the first-generation American infusion into twentieth-century literature. At one time or another I have lived in all of the boroughs of New York City—for thirty years in Brooklyn Heights not far from the house on Cranberry Street where Whitman's *Leaves of Grass* was first printed" (13). This careful selection of "bare facts" positions Zukofsky as both an American and a New Yorker. Drawing on the familiar scheme of his immediate surroundings, Zukofsky maps his life, inviting us to consider a nexus of "contingencies" both spatial and literary, to imagine perhaps the proximate coexistence of Whitman-James-Zukofsky. If we attempt to correlate even the few "points" we are given, however, Zukofsky's implied superimposition of the literary and the lived suggests gaps, distances, and displacements that threaten a violent distortion of any resulting "map." We might wonder, for example, about the *literary* distance between James and Whitman in relation to Zukofsky's own work. But even if we suspend such speculation to concentrate on more concrete facts, we get no further than the paragraph's first sentence before encountering another gap of sorts: in locating the Lower East Side as the object of James's investigation and Manhattan as the site of Zukofsky's birth, this sentence's somewhat slippery declaration of fact avoids a more precise designation of Zukofsky's birthplace, the Lower East Side, and partially compensates for the omission by singling out the East Side as the special object of James's attention, though it was only one stop on the novelist's New York itinerary.

Such an arrangement of words by the always finical Zukofsky takes on more significance when in the next sentence we come upon the phrase "first-generation American infusion," an expression that rather delicately handles the phenomenon of mass immigration at the turn of the century and that elides any direct mention of Zukofsky's Jewishness. Louis, the youngest of four children, was the first member of his family to be born in America, more particularly in the Jewish ghetto of the Lower East Side. Like the other three central Objectivists—Charles Reznikoff, George Oppen, and Carl Rakosi—his parents were Jews who immigrated to America around the turn of the century (his father in 1898, his mother in 1903). Louis grew up speaking Yiddish first, English second. The *Autobiography*'s second paragraph of "facts" credits Zukofsky's "first exposure to letters" to the vital Yiddish theaters of his youth, where by the age of nine he had seen "a good deal of Shakespeare, Ibsen, Strindberg and Tolstoy performed—all in Yiddish" (33), but this first, and ostensibly most "bare" paragraph, emphasizes Zukofsky the American over Zukofsky the Jew. This question of emphasis is an important one in his career as a poet. Addressing Zukofsky's dual loyalties, Harold Schimmel has suggested that Zukofsky is simultaneously "the most American of all Jewish poets" and "the most Jewish of all American poets" (235). This double identity is often difficult for Zukofsky to sustain without one element's conflicting with or even eclipsing the other, as the passage under consideration subtly attests.

To pursue the meanings of Zukofsky's facts a bit further, we need only turn to *The American Scene*. The most casual reading of this record of James's impressions of America in 1904 and 1905 reveals his alarm at the massive influx of immigrants at the turn of the century. Indeed, Zukofsky's term "infusion" encodes a reference to *The American Scene* that, I would argue, opens up Zukofsky's textual "gaps" into a veritable pit at the heart of his brief text. Specifically, it evokes two section titles, "The Scale of the Infusion" and "The Effect of the Infusion," from James's chapter, "New York and the Hudson: A Spring Impression" (116–139). Leading up to James's visit to the Lower East Side, these sections are part of a sequence dealing with the effects of mass immigration under such titles as "The Obsession of the Alien," "The Ubiquity of the Alien," and "The Eclipse of Manners." In writing these "impressions," James grappled with a social phenomenon of undeniably vast proportions. There were nearly 28 million immigrants to the continental United States in the period 1820–1910; in 1905 immigrants were arriving at an average rate of 24,000 a day (Quartermain 10). Among the results of this "infusion" was a fantastic density of population in New York City. The tenth ward, which included the Lower East Side apartment of Zukofsky's youth, had a population of over 300,000 per square mile by 1890 (Jacob Riis, cited in Ahearn 2), much of it, like all the Zukofskys other than Louis, foreign born and unschooled in the English language. It is unsurprising, then, that James found the presence of "the alien" a powerful ingredient of "the general queer sauce of New York." Even in Central Park, not far from the "upper reaches of Fifth and Madison avenues," there were sunny summer afternoons that "showed the fruit of the foreign trees as shaken down there with a force that smothered everything else." The "alien," James concluded, "was as truly in possession, under the high 'aristocratic' nose, as if he had had but three steps to come" (117). Indeed, the "alien" turns out to be the common New York element that allows for "singleness of impression" wherever one goes: "Is not the universal sauce essentially *his* sauce, and do we not feel ourselves feeding, half the time, from the ladle, as greasy as he chooses to leave it for us, that he holds out?"

It is not difficult to register the fastidious novelist's distress at this paradoxically universal alien, despite the goodwill that grants the park's "babel of voices" the adjective "cheerful," praises the lively interest of the scene, and desires to pay "proper tribute" to the "great field of recreation" (118). The "dense Yiddish quarter" of the Lower East Side, however, provides a still more strenuous test of Jamesian attention. Here James is staggered by a "scene that hummed with the human presence" (132), a "great swarming, a swarming that had begun to thicken" (131) as he and his guide had crossed to the East Side. The Jewishness of the population contributes markedly to the effect, for "[t]here is no swarming like that of Israel when once Israel has got a start" (131). James finds himself confronted "at every step" with "the signs and sounds, immitigable, unmistakable, of a Jewry that had burst all bounds," with not only density but increase, until "multiplication, multiplication of everything was the dominant note." James's immersion in such "overflow" calls up a watery metaphor, elaborated by a string of strange and unpleasant images: "It was as if we had been thus, in the crowded, hustled roadway . . . at the bottom of some vast sallow aquarium in which innumerable fish, of over-developed proboscis were to bump together, for ever, amid heaped spoils of the sea"

(131). The bizarre image of fish "with over-developed proboscis" recalls, of course, stereotypical Jewish physiognomy; the "sallow" aquarium is presumably muddied by the dark Jewish presence; the surrounding "heaped spoils" evoke another stereotype, of Jewish greed and acquisitiveness—this despite the pervasive poverty of the immediate context. In addition, James writes of "the intensity of the Jewish aspect" and of an "excess of lurid meaning" in the faces he encounters on the Lower East Side.

In *The Jew's Body* (1991), Sander Gilman has written of the ways that representations of the body, bound up with definitions of race, are used to enforce powerful categories of social organization and division. In the case of the Jew, "scientifically" classified as "black" in the nineteenth century, dark skin color was interpreted as a sign of disease, inferiority, and atavism. As this classification of Jewish "blackness" declined in popularity, skin color as the mark of Jewish difference gave way to an emphasis on "the Jewish nose" in both scientific and popular thought, but the signification remained the same. Gilman traces this shift and follows its consequences well into the twentieth century, focusing on the rise of modern rhinoplasty in Germany as a response to the Jewish desire for "invisibility," for an escape from the persecution that accompanied visibly Jewish identity. The point here is simply that James participates in a long tradition of anti-Semitic representations of the Jews and particularly of the Jewish body. The "Jewish nose," the "overdeveloped proboscis" James opposes to the " 'aristocratic' nose" of the Upper West Side, is one prominent sign of not only Jewishness but Jewish atavism. Thus the Jews of the ghetto are "innumerable fish" in "some vast sallow aquarium"; they "swarm" in a way that seems more appropriate to vermin or insects than people, a connection James does eventually make ("a swarming little square in which an ant-like population darted to and fro" [134]). The bristling "complexity of firescapes" everywhere evident on the East Side brings this analogy to fuller expression, suggesting to James "the spaciously organized cage for the nimbler class of animal in some great zoological garden . . . a little world of bars and perches and swings for human squirrels and monkeys" (134). This "infusion" of the "alien," with all the horror and wonderment it is capable of arousing, is the pit Zukofsky skirts in the *Autobiography*. Could he have read James without seeing in his own image an image of the "alien," at worst an atavistic, animalistic Other, a member of the "ugly race" (Gilman, *Jew's Body* 193)?

The actual scene of Zukofsky's reading of James is glimpsed in the twelfth movement of "*A*", a movement devoted to family and to tradition. The sequence in question is concerned more particularly with fathers and sons, with the patriarchal line of descent connecting Zukofsky's grandfather, Maishe Afroim, Zukofsky's father, Pinchos, Zukofsky himself, and, finally, his son Paul. James enters the text at one of the poem's more straightforward moments, as the poet sits at table with his father. Since we learn elsewhere in "*A*" that Pinchos worked as a night watchman in the same shop where he pressed pants from six in the morning until nine or even eleven at night, except for Fridays when he left before sunset to keep the Sabbath, it is not surprising that in this scene he drowses while Zukofsky occupies himself with "my guest Henry," presumably by way of an edition of *The American Scene* bearing a photograph of the author:

> What a face has the great American novelist
> It says: Fie! Nancy, finance.
> I have just met him on Rutgers Street, New York
> Henry James, Jr.,
> Opposite what stood out in my youth
> As a frightening
> Copy of a Norman Church in red brick
> Half a square block, if I recall,
> Faced with a prospect of fire escapes—
> Practically where I was born.
>   ["*A*"-12, 148]

The pages of "*A*" place Zukofsky in the Jamesian scene and allow him to encounter James himself ("I have just met him on Rutgers Street"), but the encounter's frame makes it clear that James is now triply a "guest" in Zukofsky territory—"*A*", the East Side, Zukofsky's own apartment. Zukofsky inverts James's act of reconnaissance; his exclamation "What a face" subjects the novelist to the same sort of searching gaze that found "an excess of lurid meaning" in the Jewish faces of the Lower East Side (including, just perhaps, that of Zukofsky's father?). As Zukofsky whimsically imposes his own meanings, the face in the photo is made to speak, to indulge in the penchant for homophonic transliteration ("Fie! Nancy, finance") that Zukofsky used to generate entire poems and even whole books and to reintroduce, if only fleetingly, economics, a frequent theme in "*A*". As the passage continues, the fire escapes that prompted James's zoo analogy are juxtaposed with the scene of Zukofsky's own birth, refigured as part of the landscape of his childhood. Zukofsky completes his decentering of James's perspective by bringing things full circle, bestowing on James an "intensity of Jewish aspect" as he is imagined walking down the street with "[t]he look of a shaven Chassid" ("A"-12, 149).

Of course, such a transformation, such an "identity" of James and Jew, cannot be sustained for long, even imaginatively ("Were it possible to either him or Chassid" ["A"-12, 149]). In the next transition of "A", the image of James as Chassid leads to an interpolated quotation:

> Said the Chassid:
> If you do not, Lord, yet wish to redeem
> Israel, at least redeem the Gentiles.
>   ["A"-12, 149]

The Chassid's charitable entreaty contrasts with James's less generous attitude toward the Jews and with Zukofsky's own lingering resentment, unexpressed in the more public *Autobiography*, but present in "A"-12.

> I cannot be too grateful for what you did for Rutgers Street
> (Or for Baltimore, "That cheerful little city of the dead")
>   ["A"-12, 149]

Even here Zukofsky is sly; the syntactical ambiguity of "I cannot be too grateful," which might at first be taken as an actual expression of gratitude for James's record of his visit, only gradually resolves into irony as Zukofsky reproduces James's description of Baltimore. The next two lines reinforce the sense of cultural distance, the distance that James, despite the sensitivity Zukofsky admired, was unable to bridge:

> You went down-town once
> At that no beard shaking the head
>   ["A"-12, 149]

James's imagined Chassidic double, a golem momentarily conjured into being by Zukofsky, vanishes as the poem continues its meditation on fathers and sons—inspired, perhaps, by the presence of the devoutly religious (and full-bearded) Pinchos—proceeding to a vision of Jacob's dream in the desert presaging the founding of Israel. The beardless, unredeemed James, we presume, continues to occupy his uneasy place in Zukofsky's eclectic "tradition," which must accommodate Gentile and Jewish elements from all reaches of Zukofsky's experience: Aristotle and Spinoza, Henry James and Pinchos Zukofsky.

As we have seen, this accommodation can be difficult, but James offers only an inkling of the problem's true scope. James's casual anti-Semitism in *The American Scene* is disturbing, even potentially dangerous, but it comes and goes, appears and disappears, in the rapid flux of the novelist's ceaseless metaphor-making. His zoo analogy seems to be intended to apply ultimately to all of New York, though it was directly spurred by his observations of the Lower East Side. He does his best to restrain his visions of "the Hebrew conquest of New York" (132), trying hard to see the ever-present "swarm" as "a quality of appealing surrounding life" (131). He even goes so far as to offer a vision, albeit not for long, of the Lower East Side as "the New Jerusalem on earth," with its "farspreading light and its celestial serenity of multiplication" (133). In opposition to the "dark, foul stifling Ghettos of other remembered cities," the Lower East Side suggests a "city of redemption"; even the "tenement-house" lodging "some five-and-twenty families" seems remarkable for "conditions so little sordid, so highly 'evolved' " (135). Zukofsky, however, would in the mid-1930s have to deal, not with James's attempts at balance, but with an Ezra Pound increasingly passionate in his anti-Semitism.

In his 1918 essay on James, Pound had expressed admiration for the novelist's treatment of "race," but this admiration had been ambivalent. More or less equating nation and race, Pound had praised James for his "great labour, this labour of translation, of making American intelligible, of making it possible for individuals to meet across national borders" (*Literary Essays* 296). The point of James's "whole great assaying and weighing," his "research for the significance of nationality" (296), had been to promote "communication" and "peace" based not on eliminating differences but on "a recognition of differences, of the right of differences to exist, of interest in finding things different" (298). At the same time, however, Pound suggested approvingly that James's novels were founded on another truth, on "the major conflicts which he portrays," conflicts of "race against race, immutable" (298). By the 1930s this latter truth would dominate Pound's outlook, particularly his thinking about Jews. As Pound became more and more obsessed with economic questions and more sympathetic to Mussolini and fascism, he came to see in the Jews a "negative principle," "the dangerous embodiment of otherness and confusion," as Robert Casillo has expressed it. Casillo has charted in great detail the development of Pound's thought on this point, arguing convincingly that the roots of Pound's anti-Semitism go deeper than economics and an association between Jews and "usura," that anti-Semitism itself "is the crucial factor in the development of his fascism," that "[s]imply put, anti-Semitism goes further to explain Pound's fascism than vice versa" (16). As Pound put it to Wyndham Lewis, he objected "as much to semitism in matters of mind as in matters of commerce" (quoted in Casillo 36). His extensive objections to "semitism," which he consistently treats as a biological and racial category, cover a wide territory: including religion, philosophy, economics, nature, sexuality, and language. He blames Jews for monotheism (bringing with it code worship, the decline of "pagan" values, and the concept of sin), "abstraction," usury, a divorce from nature and the decline of agriculture, hatred of sexuality, and unclear thought and expression. The very scope of the attack indicates the degree to which "Jewishness" becomes a conceptual dumping ground for the whole range of evils in Pound's cosmology.

But there is also a physical, bodily dimension to the assault. Where James's stereotypes stop short of traditional anti-Semitic associations of Jews with filth and disease, Pound's do not. Pound reduces the Jews to "the demonic status of germs and bacilli, invisible 'carriers' of plague and disease, a swamp, an enormous 'power of putrefaction' " (Casillo 3). In writings and radio speeches of the thirties and forties, Pound rails against the "Hebrew Disease" and the "Jewish poison," finds Christianity "verminous with Semitic infections," claims that the Jews have "wormed into the system" and "infected the world." James's "ant-like population" seems benign compared to Pound's references to Jews as "rats," "bed-bugs," "vermin," "plague," "syphilis," and "disease incarnate." In response to plague conditions, then, Pound urges the necessity of "purge," "a racial Solution," "world prophylaxis," "clearing fungus," and "maintaining antisepsis" (Casillo passim).

As Casillo has shown, Pound's anti-Semitism, even at its most virulent, cannot be separated from his larger cultural project, a project that for a time included the Objectivists, a group of American poets on whom, and through whom, he clearly hoped to have a transatlantic influence. Pound's hostility to the Jews attained its full vehemence only gradually, but the first foreshadowings of its final intensity corresponded, ironically, with the height of Objectivist publishing activity in the late twenties and early thirties, the years of "Poem beginning 'The' " (1927), *Poetry*'s " 'Objectivists' 1931" issue, and *An "Objectivists" Anthology*. In hindsight, we are able to see that Pound's hostility is complemented and opposed by an Objectivist aesthetic of resistance, endurance, and survival in the texts of the period. The historical pressures of the day are registered in these texts and in the "collective" dynamics of Objectivist publishing. At the center of the Objectivist vortex, from its very inception, were historical forces that threatened to blow it apart even as the Objectivists sought to fashion a future for modernism.

Zukofsky's "Poem beginning 'The,' " the work that contributed importantly to the group's initial formation by bringing Pound and Zukofsky together in the first place (and by bringing Zukofsky to George Oppen's attention), uncannily anticipates at least some of the terms of the group's eventual dissolution. "A"-12's meditation on Jewish tradition was written in 1950 and 1951, when Zukofsky was about forty-six years old, but the dual problem of Jew and writer in America had been one of Zukofsky's earliest themes. In "Poem beginning 'The,' " the precocious culmination of his early poetic development, written when he was twenty-two years old, Zukofsky both pays homage to and sometimes takes issue with a whole range of modernist works, particularly Eliot's *The Waste Land*. Where Eliot numbered every ten lines of his poem and provided footnotes for scholars, Zukofsky parodically numbered *every* line and prefaced the poem with a playful index.[2] Surveying the field of modernist cultural production from the perspective of a Jewish American writer embarking on the same search for a viable "tradition" that would later consume "*A*", Zukofsky confronts the difficulty of his position in a dizzying mix of poetic styles. Following Pound and Eliot in the use of a modernist idiom free to draw on a discursive field ranging from advertising jargon to classical diction, from the Vaudevillian to the pseudopoetic, he self-consciously stages his groping after an acceptable and accepting "culture."

Zukofsky writes, for example, of his experiences as a Jew at Columbia University, which promulgated its own project of culture based on the "Great Books":

162 Is it the sun you're looking for,
163 Drop in at Askforaclassic, Inc.,
164 Get yourself another century,
165 A little frost before sundown.
166 It's the time don'chewknow,
167 And if you're a Jewish boy, then be your
           Plato's Philo.
        [*Complete Short Poetry* 14–15]

Sending up John Erskine, his English professor at Columbia (Ahearn 19–21), Zukofsky also dramatizes a genuine dilemma. "The sun," indexed in one of Zukofsky's semicomic notes to the poem as "Power of the Past, Present, and Future" (*Complete Short Poetry* 8), is the object of Zukofsky's version of the modernist return to "sources"; sometimes associated with the Jewish people in Zukofsky's writing, it represents a powerful source of energy that Zukofsky hopes to tap, a feat he achieves linguistically by punning on the homophones "sun" and "son" (Zukofsky himself). His purpose is to reclaim the sun from its modernist role as the merciless desiccator of the Eliotic wasteland ("26 And why if the waste land has been explored, traveled over, circumscribed, / 27 Are there only wrathless skeletons exhumed new planted in it sacred wood" [10]); along the way he implies that the writers of the Eliot school had a hand in planting at least a few of the skeletons "exhumed" in their own writings. In a letter to Pound, Zukofsky explains that he intended the poem to demonstrate that there was still hope for "fruit of another generation" (*Pound/Zukofsky* 76–77). What it would mean for Zukofsky to speak for his own "generation," however, was not easy to discern.

His experience as a "Jewish boy" at Columbia, for example, seems to demand that Zukofsky become a twentieth-century "Philo"— Philo Judaeus, that is, the first-century Alexandrian Jewish philosopher who attempted to reconcile Judaism with Hellenism and who was considered a traitor to Jewish tradition for his efforts (Tomas 54). Already estranged from orthodox Jewish tradition, Zukofsky is at first tempted by Columbia's "classical" offerings, with their lure of the forbidden ("like . . . roast flitches of red boar" [*Complete Short Poetry* 15]). But he quickly became discontented with Columbia's academic version of "culture" and its designs upon him, which Zukofsky punningly registered as a cultural program that would "make me fit / 176 For the Pater that was Greece / 177 The siesta that was Rome" (*Complete Short Poetry* 15). Rebelling against a program that treated his Jewishness as alien, that considered him unfit, Zukofsky was nevertheless determined that "culture" would provide his escape from the poverty of his upbringing ("243 And why is it the representatives of your, my, race are always hankering for food, mother?" [*Complete Short Poetry* 17]). Zukofsky resigns himself to the necessity of "assimilation"—

251   Assimilation is not hard,
252   And once the Faith's askew
253   I might as well look Shagetz just as much as Jew
        [17]

—but even in so doing, he adopts the aggressive stance of a Shylock ready to put his acquired culture to his own uses:

254   I'll read their Donne as mine,
255   And leopard in their spots
256   I'll do what says their Coleridge,
257   Twist red hot pokers into knots.
258   The villainy they teach me I will execute
259   And it shall go hard with them,
260   For I'll better the instruction,
261   Having learned, so to speak, in their
            colleges.
        [*Complete Short Poetry* 18]

Dense with reference to the English literary tradition—the Bible, Shakespeare, Donne, Coleridge—this passage twists that tradition into knots of Zukofsky's own making. At its deepest stratum of reference lies a question taking us to the heart of both English and Hebrew tradition, and to the core of the problem, race: "Can the Ethiopian change his skin, or the leopard his spots?" (Jeremiah 13:23).

Zukofsky proposes for himself a multiple, shifting cultural identity ("254 I'll read their Donne as mine / 255 And leopard in their spots"), but his allusion ironically acknowledges the difficulty, if not impossibility, of the project, an effect intensified if we overlay the biblical allusion with a line from Donne's "Elegie on the Lady Marckam": "Of what small spots pure white complaines! Alas." Invoking a (racial) standard of "pure white" that has already made an appearance in "Poem beginning 'The' " (again punningly: "291 Even in their dirt, the Angles like Angels are fair" [19]), the line's emphasis on spoiled purity also resonates with the full context of the line from Jeremiah. The high biblical prophetic fury of Jeremiah 13 threatens nothing less than the complete destruction of the Jewish people: "And I will dash them one against another, fathers and sons together, says the Lord. I will not pity or spare or have compassion, that I should not destroy them" (13:12). The chapter's closing lines invoke once again that state of purity, of perfect and untarnished whiteness promising survival if not salvation, that has haunted Zukofsky's poem:

> Woe to you, O Jerusalem
> How long will it be
> before you are made clean?
> [13:27]

How long will it be? The question projects a futurity that "Poem beginning 'The' " takes up as its burden. Seen in this light, the passage under discussion not only dramatizes the conflict of cultural identity faced by the young Zukofsky but stages that conflict on a world historical scale, connecting it to the fate of the Jewish people.

As a response to literary modernism, and an attempt to imagine its future, "Poem beginning 'The' " seems to suggest, subtly and allusively, that the great modernist exiles whom Zukofsky admired—Pound, Joyce, and Eliot—are in the final analysis "self-exiled men," unequipped to understand the true hardships, and terrors, of the Diaspora. In the twenties and thirties, the nascent Objectivist movement embodies one possible modernist future, but the Objectivist presence also skews the field, sometimes unsettling modernist assumptions and raising questions about the meanings of key terms, like "exile." Objectivist writing and publishing practices often reveal, at a very early stage, tensions and conflicts in the ideology of modernism that subsequent critical readings have until recently tended to smooth over. Not only is there no place for Zukofsky's ethnic identity in the ideal of international modernism, but that ideal involves assumptions about the permissible range of "difference" that become, at least in Pound's case, more sinister as the cultural stakes rise. With the advent of the

Great Depression and the rise of fascism in Europe, Pound's sense of crisis, and the accompanying desire for a "new civilization," are increasingly matched by the chaotic and "revolutionary" character of world events. The problem of cultural identity articulated by Zukofsky in "Poem beginning 'The,' " and the concomitant problem of Jewish exile and Jewish survival, become urgently tied to overt political and social conflict on the contemporary scene. "Poem beginning 'The,' " written in 1926, had registered alarm at events in Germany:

68   Somehow, in German, the Jew goat-song
         is unconvincing—
        . . . .
72   Time, time the goat were an offering

and in Italy, home of both Pound and Mussolini, "Il Duce":

75   Black shirts—black shirts—some power
        is so funereal.
        [*Complete Short Poetry* 11]

By the early thirties, the growing atmosphere of world crisis would precipitate a crisis within Objectivist ranks, a clear falling out among the principal writers of that movement.

Mussolini's power, "funereal" for Zukofsky, seemed increasingly attractive to Pound as he turned more and more from the realm of aesthetics to the realm of economics and politics. In Pound's estimate, his prose belonged to the "sphere of action, not to 'art and letters' " (Alpert 430), and in the early thirties he wrote a lot of it, including a book, perhaps *the* book, that TO, Publishers, significantly, did not publish. When the press ceased operations in 1933, it abandoned various projects, including an ambitious long-term plan to publish Pound's complete critical works in six to ten volumes (Sharp 45). Next in line would have been Pound's *ABC of Economics,* written in a ten-day burst of activity in February 1933. A subsequent burst of energy that same month produced another treatment of economic and political themes, *Jefferson and/or Mussolini* (Carpenter 498). In both books, Pound's sympathy with Mussolini was in evidence. At the time, George and Mary Oppen cited their own "economic" reasons for not publishing *ABC of Economics* and shutting down TO, Publishers. But in her autobiography,

Meaning a Life (1978), Mary Oppen wrote also that upon reading the book and discussing it among themselves, she and George found it "absurd" (135) and could not in good conscience agree to publish it.

It is *Jefferson and/or Mussolini,* though, that provides the clearest terms for understanding the conflicts beginning to tear the group apart. Here many of Pound's most cherished ideas about art will be transferred into the realm of historical and political action. Most of *Jefferson and/or Mussolini*'s "radiant gists" will be familiar to readers of *The Cantos*—as when Pound suggests that an explanation of Jeffersonian democracy would be made easier with "a little grammar or a little mediaeval scholarship" (22) at one's disposal. Throughout, the book's hurried attempts at political and historical analysis are interlarded with references to Fenollosa, Frobenius, and Confucius. Sometimes the intended connections seem arbitrary and forced, as we might expect in a book that insists on the "fundamental likenesses" between Thomas Jefferson and Benito Mussolini, similarities that are only evident, Pound acknowledges, when one does away with superficially dissimilar "top dressing" (11). In other cases, Pound's arguments may be easily extrapolated from the opinions expressed in his literary criticism. In what is probably the most important political application of his aesthetic ideas, Pound translates his "great artist" approach to the literary tradition into a "great man" theory of history. He insisted repeatedly, for example, that Jefferson "governed with a limited suffrage, and by means of a conversation with his intelligent friends" (14), an image of governance not far from Pound's own conception of the operations of literary modernism. A quickly sketched dialogue justifies the reigning principle of Pound's approach to politics, a principle closely linked to his "great man" thesis: "I can 'cure' the whole trouble by a criticism of style. Oh, can I? Yes. I have been saying so for some time" (17).

The style of the great man, the great man of style. Here is Pound's nutshell analysis of Mussolini's greatness: "THE SECRET OF THE DUCE is possibly the capacity to pick out the element of immediate and major importance in any tangle; or, in the case of a man, to go straight to the center, for the fellow's major interest. 'Why do you want to put your ideas in order?' " (66). This is Pound's fondest dream of himself as an artist translated into the realm of historical action; Mussolini is his twin, playing out the role Pound increasingly desires for himself. In seeing Mussolini as "artifex" (34), Pound opens the way to see himself as a great leader. But there is a variation on this theme that is of particular interest in an Objectivist context, shedding light on Pound's role as overseer of the next wave of modernism. Elsewhere in the book, Pound refers to Mussolini as not an artist but an editor. In his guise as editor, Mussolini receives credit for a general increase in clarity of expression, for the way in which "Italians [were] getting up and saying what they meant with clarity and even with brevity," as opposed to the "gas, evasion and incompetence" on display at the British House of Commons (74). Mussolini's presence at the top of the Italian hierarchy inspires such clarity all down the line: "And even here is the hand or eye or ear of the Duce, the Debunker par excellence, for the deputies and ministers know that there is an EDITORIAL eye and ear—precisely—an editor, who will see through their bunkum and for whom they will go to the scrap-basket just as quickly as an incompetent reporter's copy will go to the basket in a live editorial office" (74). Pound's analogy crosses the boundary between art and life. Under the watchful eye, the guiding hand, and the listening ear of Mussolini, "the Debunker," it is *people* who are in danger of going to "the scrap-basket" if they fail to meet his high editorial standards.

Effective editorial control, as Pound has long maintained, must be based on a rigorous principle of exclusion. Applied to life and politics, this principle is a direct corollary of his belief in the necessity of assembling an intelligent elite. For his part, Pound tells us he has lived "among the more refined spirits of my epoch" (28). Of his political goals, he writes: "The most I could DO would be to persuade a few of the more intelligent people in all three countries [America, Russia, Italy—sites of three 'revolutions'] to try to find out . . . where and what are the others, and what are the relations possible" (41). The question, "Who is worth meeting?" (68) guides Pound's approach to life and action. But as I have suggested, careful principles of selection must be matched by mechanisms of active exclusion. At times, Pound is quite explicit about this political necessity: "Certain kinds of enemy would be shipped to the *confino*" (70). Often, it is implied by his rhetoric: "fascism meant at the start DIRECT action, cut the cackle, if a man is a mere s.o.b. don't argue" (70). "NO individual worth saving" is likely to be bothered by the "reasonable and limited obedience practiced to given ends and for limited periods" demanded by the fascist state (100). Even the sort of disease metaphor anticipating his later call for "prophylaxis," "purge," and "antisepsis" makes its appearance within a page of Pound's analysis of Mussolini's "editorial" capacities: "A decent concept of a twentieth century world is like a decent concept of a town or family, you don't want your neighbour down with cholera; you don't want your family full of sickly members all yowling for help" (75).

As Pound's editorial protégé, a member of his literary "family," Zukofsky was a disciple of Poundian principles of order but one with a cultural agenda of his own. From the first, that agenda would have to compete at some points with Pound's, but as Pound's "editing" practices began to converge with the fascist program of "antisepsis," the competition would escalate. The two men, of two different generations and two different ethnic backgrounds, who referred to each other as "Sonny" and "Papa" in their correspondence, were caught in a conflict that was at once private and public, intimate and historical. As Pound's thirst for order assumed political dimensions, his manner became not only authoritative but authoritarian. If in 1918, in his essay on James, he had written of the need for "a recognition of differences," in the thirties Pound increasingly set himself up as an arbiter of difference. *Jefferson and/or Mussolini* gives us, I think, a context for understanding a statement in a 1935 letter of Pound's that seemed to confuse Zukofsky at the time. By this time, the two men were still writing to one another, and still discussing publishing prospects, but their exchanges were often charged with tension. In March, 1935 Pound wrote: "I think it would be BAD EDITING to print you in England." The next sentence issues a warning: "Be careful or you'll fall back into racial characteristics, and cease to be L/Z at all" (*Pound/Zukofsky* 163). In his new Mussolini-style "editorial" role, Pound instructed Zukofsky that to acknowledge his ethnic identity as a Jew would be to surrender his identity, his difference, to be absorbed into a mass of "racial characteristics." When Pound had written about James almost thirty years before, "race" had been an important component of "difference"—and it still was, after a fashion. But the Jews as a people had begun to fall off the scale of acceptable difference as they had begun to be targeted for the fascist "purge." In an earlier letter to Zukofsky, Pound had already made the threat quite explicit, again urging Zukofsky to assert his (non-Jewish) difference, "[i]f you don't want to be confused with yr/ ancestral race and pogromd" (158). When it came to the Jews, the need for a recognition of difference had been superseded in Pound's thought by the need for what he called in his 1935 *Guide to Kulchur* (dedicated, ironically, to Zukofsky and Basil Bunting), a "totalitarian" synthesis (45).

In the letter to Zukofsky quoted above, Pound paused to capture his new editorial style in an image: "E.P. with two pronged fork of terror and cajolery" (158). As Zukofsky dodged the sharp points of that fork, his ability to negotiate between his Jewishness and the larger culture, to "leopard in their spots," was more than ever on the line.[3] The prospect of a culture (or *Kulchur*) requiring a totalitarian synthesis made it increasingly clear that the "bartering" of "wisdom and learning," proposed as his salvation in "Poem beginning 'The,' " was an enterprise fraught with dangers in its own right. Culture could easily provoke hostility rather than allay it. When James left the streets of the Lower East Side and entered the "civilized" cafés, his alarm was exacerbated "increasingly as their [i.e., the cafés'] place on the scale was higher" (139). These "torture-rooms of the living idiom" (139), where the English language was put to Jewish uses, were relatively *more* disturbing as the cafés rose on the social scale; a more elevated position meant more serious encroachment on the cultural order. "Assimilation," as Zukofsky's verse has already suggested, is both an accommodation to, and a transformation of, dominant cultural modes. The fascist program of "antisepsis" that Pound would eventually support was formulated in response to just such cultural crises as that signaled by James's worries about the "Accent of the Future" (139). Responding in turn to such hostility, Zukofsky and the other Objectivists forged an aesthetic, and an ethos, of survival.[4] This response, which drew on an awareness of Jewish history and a core of Jewish identity, was present from the movement's inception and became more important with the rise of fascism in the thirties.

In 1926, Zukofsky drew on his Jewish heritage to close "Poem beginning 'The,' " and its search for a viable tradition, with a poem translated from the work of the modern Yiddish poet Yehoash. His translation substitutes the pronoun "we" for the pronoun "I" in order to create an image of collective survival:[5]

321   We shall open our arms wide,
322   Call out of pure might—
323   Sun, you great Sun, our Comrade,
324   From eternity to eternity we remain true to you
325   A myriad years we have been,

326 Myriad upon myriad shall be.

327 How wide our arms are,
328 How strong,
329 A myriad years we have been,
330 Myriad upon myriad shall be.
      [*Complete Short Poetry* 20]

Just as his earlier allusion to the book of Jeremiah opened the poem up to the sweep of historical time, and to the burden of Jewish fate implied by that sweep, Zukofsky's conclusion calls upon the capacity of resistance and endurance displayed by the Jews in the face of recurring threats to their existence as a people. The unfolding story of literary modernism, with its heavy investment in the future of modernism's "self-exiled men," is supplanted by a larger story of exile, contact, and survival.

Notes

1. The first run of *Contact* appeared from December 1920 to June 1923; the second run, which included poems by Zukofsky, appeared for three issues in 1932.

2. Ahearn has pointed out these correspondences between the two poems in his introduction to *Zukofsky's "A"*.

3. Zukofsky's early letters to Pound display what Sander Gilman has described as "Jewish self-hatred." In a letter of 19 December 1929, for example, he refers to himself as an "antisemite" (*Pound/Zukofsky* 28). But by the mid-1930s, Zukofsky has become more resistant to Pound's assaults. On 15 March 1935, a little less than a year after Pound had brandished his "two pronged fork of terror and cajolery," Zukofsky writes, "Maybe it's time Sonny bawled out papa" and proceeds to mount a spirited counterattack (*Pound/Zukofsky* 164). This chronology of increasing resistance is complicated, however, both by the conciliatory tone to which Zukofsky returns in many later letters and by his public defense of Pound in later years. But when Zukofsky writes of Pound in 1948 that he "never felt the least trace of anti-Semitism *in his presence*" (*Prepositions* 165, emphasis added), he chooses his words carefully, implicitly exempting from consideration the charged letters the two men exchanged in the thirties. See chapter 3 for a nuanced discussion of the correspondence and what it reveals about Zukofsky's sense of his own Jewishness.

4. In his essay, "The Mind's Own Place," George Oppen writes of American immigrants' developing—and it seems likely that he has Jewish immigrants particularly in mind—"a morality of crisis, an ethos of survival" (136).

5. Harold Schimmel notes the substitution of "we" for "I" (244); John Tomas

observes that the change "makes the poem into a triumphant affirmation of his [i.e., Zukofsky's] tradition, and Zukofsky into the representative of a people" (62). I emphasize the importance given to survival itself as a positive value.

Works Cited

Ahearn, Barry. Zukofsky's "A": An Introduction. Berkeley: U of California P, 1983.

Alpert, Barry S. "Ezra Pound, John Price, and The Exile." Paideuma 2.3 (Winter 1973): 427–448.

Carpenter, Humphrey. A Serious Character: The Life of Ezra Pound. Boston: Houghton Mifflin, 1988.

Casillo, Robert. The Genealogy of Demons: Anti-Semitism, Fascism, and the Myths of Ezra Pound. Evanston, IL: Northwestern UP, 1988.

Gilman, Sander. Jewish Self-hatred: Anti-Semitism and the Hidden Language of the Jews. Baltimore: Johns Hopkins UP, 1986.

———. The Jew's Body. New York: Routledge, 1991.

James, Henry. The American Scene. New York: Charles Scribner's Sons, 1946.

Kenner, Hugh. Mazes: Essays. San Francisco: North Point, 1989.

Oppen, George. "The Mind's Own Place." Montemora 1 (1975): 132–137.

Oppen, Mary. Meaning a Life: An Autobiography. Santa Barbara: Black Sparrow, 1978.

Pound, Ezra. ABC of Economics. London: Faber & Faber, 1933.

———. Guide to Kulchur. New York: New Directions, 1970.

———. Jefferson and/or Mussolini. London: Stanley Nott, 1935.

———. Literary Essays of Ezra Pound. Ed. T. S. Eliot. New York: New Directions, 1967.

Quartermain, Peter. Disjunctive Poetics: From Gertrude Stein and Louis Zukofsky to Susan Howe. Cambridge: Cambridge UP, 1992.

Schimmel, Harold. "Zuk. Yehoash David Rex." Louis Zukofsky: Man and Poet. Ed. Carroll F. Terrell. Orono, ME: National Poetry Foundation, 1979. 235–245.

Sharp, Tom. "Objectivists," 1927–1934: A Critical History. Diss. Stanford University, 1982.

Sorrentino, Gilbert. Foreword. Collected Fiction. By Louis Zukofsky. Elmwood Park, IL: Dalkey Archive P, 1990. vii–ix.

Tomas, John. "Portrait of the Artist as a Young Jew: Zukofsky's 'Poem beginning "The" ' in Context." Sagetrieb 9.1–2 (1990): 43–64.

Williams, William Carlos. Contact 1 (December 1920).

———. Selected Letters. Ed. John C. Thirlwall. New York: McDowell, Obolensky, 1957.

Zukofsky, Louis. Pound/Zukofsky: Selected Letters of Ezra Pound and Louis Zukofsky. Ed. Barry Ahearn. New York: New Directions, 1987.

2

The Revolutionary Word
Louis Zukofsky, *New Masses,* and
Political Radicalism in the 1930s

MARK SCROGGINS

[*New*] MASSES is just one more wailing place and the whole left now-a-days is a mob of wailers. I do very much believe in leftism in every direction, even in wailing. These people go about it in such a way that nobody listens to them except themselves; and that is a[t] least one reason why they get nowhere. They have the most magnificent cause in the world.
—Wallace Stevens, 9 October 1935 (*Letters* 287)

America when I was seven momma took me to Communist Cell
meetings they sold us garbanzos a handful per ticket a ticket
costs a nickel and the speeches were free everybody was an-
gelic and sentimental about the workers it was all so sincere
you have no idea what a good thing the party was.
—Allen Ginsberg, "America" (*Collected Poems* 147)

THE LINE DIVIDING RESPONSIBLE HISTORIOGRAPHY from diverting anecdote is always a fine one, as Pound's doctrine of the "luminous detail" amply illustrates. "Luminous details," as Pound explains in *I
Gather the Limbs of Osiris,* are "Certain facts [that] give one a sudden
insight into circumjacent conditions, into their causes, their effects,
into sequence, and law. . . . A dozen facts of this nature give us intelligence of a period—a kind of intelligence not to be gathered from
a great array of facts of the other sorts." While luminous details are
"hard to find," they are happily "swift and easy of transmission" (*Selected Prose* 22–23). But when is a detail "luminous," and when is it
merely amusing? And how often does the apocryphal attain the status
of the historical, merely through its conceptual *rightness?*[1] Anecdotes,

of course, have an ambiguous status within the discipline of literary history, and their evidentiary value is certainly far less than that of the document. Nonetheless the anecdote, particularly the anecdote that fulfills expectations one has perhaps already entertained, can have powerful imaginative resonance. I would begin, then, by disclaiming for a moment the demands of responsible literary history and recounting a couple of diverting (if familiar) anecdotes concerning the poet Louis Zukofsky's political years. The first, Hugh Kenner's, has been repeated several times before, so I can paraphrase: sometime in the 1920s, Columbia expellee Whittaker Chambers, card-carrying member of the U.S. Communist party (CPUSA), brought his friend Zukofsky to a meeting of his West Side party cell and sponsored him for membership. Ma Bloor herself, presiding over the meeting, decided that the young poet was a "bourgeois intellectual" and vetoed his induction ("Poem as Lens" 165). (As Celia Zukofsky would later recall, "they suggested that he join someplace on the east side" [quoted in Terrell 50].) According to Kenner, this chilly reception set Zukofsky on a tangent away from the Communist Party: "debarred from membership, [he] soon cooled in fervor though he retained a lifelong respect for Marx's intelligence" ("Poem as Lens" 165). Guy Davenport's account of Zukofsky's political disengagement, less Buster Keaton and more John Keats, derives from direct conversation with the poet: it is as succinct as Kenner's, and though it lacks the element of uneasy social comedy present in the tableau of the well-dressed, obviously intellectual young poet confronted by the redoubtable mother of the revolution, has its own suspiciously neat literary symmetry: Zukofsky, "the friend of Whittaker Chambers at Columbia in its Reddest heyday . . . read Gibbon with an eye to seeing what Marx would have done about it all and thus bade farewell to Marx and all his host" (194).

I for one am not prepared to write the history of Louis Zukofsky's political years—much less to encapsulate and domesticate that history in a wry anecdote—and I do not think it yet possible to reach any unassailable conclusions concerning Zukofsky's relationship to American literary radicalism in the 1930s. It will take extensive and painstaking examination of the relevant documentary evidence before we can ever be certain about the precise extent of Zukofsky's active involvement in leftist politics during the "committed" decade of the 1930s. More interesting at present, now that both the American and Soviet Communist parties have passed into history (at least under their old names), is determining the relationship between Zukofsky's Marxism—an indisputable biographical fact—and the poetry and statements of poetics he wrote during the period in which Marxist ideology was a central element of his mental landscape. Are Zukofsky's political and poetic radicalisms integrated, of a piece? Or is he, like so many of his contemporaries, unable to resolve the seeming contradictions between a progressive political stance and a poetic modernism that the left coded, in Alan Wald's words, as "expressions of a reactionary ideology that reproduce[s] the fragmentation experienced in bourgeois society" (*Revolutionary Imagination* 3)? As I hope to outline in this essay, Zukofsky's relationship with the radical literary periodical *New Masses,* and with that magazine's editorship, is emblematic of his ultimate inability either to persuade a socialist-realism-minded Communist Party literary orthodoxy to accept his leftist poetic modernism or to force his own poetic productions into the realistic, hortatory mode that the Party, over the latter part of the thirties, would increasingly favor. While this inability (or unwillingness) on Zukofsky's part to reach an accommodation with the established literary Left must at the time have seemed a signal failure, from the perspective of sixty years' history it appears an index of much of what contemporary readers value in Zukofsky's work: its political anomalousness, that is, is synecdochic of the larger obduracy of Zukofsky's poetry as a whole. His refusal to fit his work into accepted party standards is of a piece with that work's refusal to fit comfortably any conventional measure of poetic ordinariness.

The relationship between Zukofsky's politics and poetics, of course, has been both explored and denied in the twenty years or so in which the academy has been seriously reading the poet. Kenner and Davenport, for instance, critics ranging from centrist to reactionary in their own political views, and decidedly conservative in cultural outlook, narrate the political "curve" of Zukofsky's work—which moves from a heavy emphasis on the class war in the twenties and thirties to an equally stressed investment in the domestic realm of familial affection from the forties onward—as a process of education, of a young man realizing his youthful follies as he comes to maturity. (The favored emblem for such a reading might be the two halves of "A"-9: the first, composed between 1938 and 1940, casts phrases from Marx's *Capital* into the formal scheme of Cavalcanti's "Donna mi prega"; the second, composed a decade later, sets to the same meter, even the same rhyming words, language from Baruch Spinoza's *Ethics*.) Zukofsky's early leftism, far from being an integral element of his thought and poetic, is in this account merely an indiscretion of youth, the sort of folly that even John Reed would have outgrown, had he lived, and to which only the hardest-boiled of party hacks—men like Mike Gold or Joseph Freeman—would cling till death.

I think that this narrative of Zukofsky's political career is to some degree an oversimplification, one that stems, at least in Kenner's case, not so much from a rejection of a political poetry *per se* as from Kenner's own rejection of Marxism, both as a viable political philosophy and as an intellectual framework capable of accommodating the radical experiments of modernism. For more "progressive" critics there are many attractions in taking seriously Zukofsky's political allegiances of the thirties, not least of which is his usefulness as a counterexample, a politically committed experimental poet who, through his leftist orientation, stands in contrast to the reactionary giants of the first generation of modernism, the "fascist beasts" (Basil Bunting's term) Yeats, Pound, and Eliot. Zukofsky, that is, serves some critics as a progressive antidote to the canonical figures of high modernism, living proof that modernist poetics are not *necessarily* invested in fascism or reaction. As Burton Hatlen puts it, the first part of "*A*" "represents a sustained effort to write, within a poetic mode that derives from Pound, a democratic and socialist response to the elitist and fascist political epic that Pound himself was writing during the 1930s"— that is, *The Cantos*. Hatlen argues that Zukofsky overcomes the disjunction between poetry and politics by situating the poet's labor within an "explicitly Marxist conception of labor as the distinctively human act by which we collectively transform the world and make it our own" (206). Edward Schelb and Michael Davidson have each explored the ways in which Zukofsky's formal experiments can be situated within a Marxist ideology, and work as it were to deconstruct traditional conceptions of meaning and social value. And in an argument reminiscent of the poetico-political statements of various of the "Language" Poets, Peter Quartermain's *Disjunctive Poetics* rejects the political "content" of Zukofsky's poems—for a reading of "*A*"-9, for instance, "it is irrelevant whether Zukofsky here is a Marxist or a Buddhist" (87)—but finds a liberatory potential precisely in the poetry's difficulty or obscurity.[2]

These critics have admirably explored how Zukofsky's poetry, especially the first third of "*A*", can be read as an attempt to formulate a specifically Marxist modernism, a poetics in which the interplay of form and content works in a truly dialectical manner; in so doing, they amply demonstrate that political criticism of Zukofsky has long since passed the point of merely examining the poetry at the points where it explicitly addresses political subjects and has itself moved to a more truly dialectical, formalist interpretive mode. But this criticism moves too much within an exclusively *literary* space; except for a few pages by Eric Homberger (163–186) and Linda Simon, there has been little attempt to read Zukofsky's literary Marxism (or Leninism) within the immediate literary-historical context of the American thirties, a context in which, as several critics' work is increasingly demonstrating,[3] various leftist literary movements loom every bit as large as the modernist avant-gardes: a context in which writers whom we now regard only as literary figures or stylistic innovators—Edward Dahlberg, Kenneth Rexroth, Stanley Burnshaw—were for a time passionately committed and verbal spokesmen for the revolutionary Left. Too often Zukofsky's work is read in the black-and-white categories of modernist poetics and Marxist-Leninist theory, as if those poetics and that theory could be considered outside their historical moments. When we hear that Zukofsky is a "poet of the Left," we too often overlook Wallace Stevens's bitter words in a 1935 letter to Ronald Lane Latimer, responding to Stanley Burnshaw's review (in *New Masses*) of *Ideas of Order,* a review that chastised Stevens for his unwillingness to take a firm political stand (see Longenbach 143); Stevens writes, "I hope I am headed left, but there are lefts and lefts, and certainly I am not headed for the ghastly left of MASSES" (*Letters* 286). We forget exactly how variegated the "lefts" of the American 1930s could be; three weeks later Stevens would identify his own odd left: "I am pro-Mussolini, personally" (289).

Zukofsky of course was no fan of Mussolini—his citation of the dictator in "Poem beginning 'The' " smacks of both revulsion and satire: "74 'Il Duce: I feel God deeply.' / 75 Black shirts—black shirts—some power is so funereal" (*Complete Short Poetry* 11)—though he was always something of an elitist in aesthetic matters. That elitism coexists uneasily with a Marxism that seems perfectly natural for a first-generation child of Russian Jewish immigrants, a 1920s-era Columbia graduate, and herein lies the importance of Zukofsky's example, an importance beyond that of a mere counterweight to Eliot's

MARK SCROGGINS

and Pound's conservatism. Zukofsky's career as a fellow traveler, and the degree to which his very serious leftist commitments influenced the theories of poetics he propounded in the early thirties, represent an early and important instance of an American poet trying to come to grips with the tension between the political and literary spheres, realms that the American pragmatist tradition—in so many ways Zukofsky's own—has tended to separate.

The relationship of poetry and politics has been an important issue at least since Plato's *Republic,* and it has become almost oppressively so for the politically committed poet and student of poetry in a culture where it seems increasingly that, as Auden writes, "poetry makes nothing happen." In order to contribute perhaps no more than a slight readjustment of perspective to the ongoing discussion of the political in Zukofsky's work, I want to examine, perhaps obliquely, a pair of intertwined subjects: on the one hand, I want to consider Zukofsky's attitude toward and relationship with *New Masses,* the most prominent organ of American Marxist literary production in the 1930s and a magazine that would take a more hard-line pro-Stalinist bent as the decade proceeded. And on the other, I want to unpack the political rhetoric and implications of some of Zukofsky's early published writings, viewing them in the light of the aesthetic increasingly promoted by the influential figures and important literary organs of the Left. What these readings reveal, I think, is that even as Zukofsky's works pioneer new ways of examining the political, the modes of those works make them incompatible with the aesthetic models that the leftist literary establishment of the thirties, especially toward the end of the decade, set forth as orthodoxy. I would not want to speculate on what made Zukofsky leave the Party's sphere of influence other than to register two points: Zukofsky broke off his more or less serious flirtation with Communism at a time when millions were leaving the Party and the Left, when the gap between the rhetoric of American communism and the practices of the Soviet government had grown too wide to be comfortably bridged. And second, Zukofsky's strongest allegiance was first and finally to his poetry (though I would not want to suggest that this was not at times a severely challenged and conflicted allegiance). The refusal of the Left and its literary organs to accept his leftist modernism, combined with the disillusionments of the late 1930s, must have made further fellow traveling a practically unendurable prospect.

There were a number of leftist literary magazines in the 1930s—magazines with such names as *Anvil, Dynamo, Liberator,* and various publications sponsored and run by local John Reed Clubs—but until the founding in 1934 of *Partisan Review,* a journal whose skeptical relationship to the Comintern would eventually lead it to outright Trotskyism, *New Masses* had unquestioned preeminence among them.[4] *New Masses* was founded in 1926 in large part to promote fine writing on the Left and in its early years happily sacrificed Party orthodoxy for literary excellence, publishing pieces by Left-leaning writers of dubious political credentials and even by nonleftists like Ezra Pound whose names lent credibility to the attempt by *New Masses* to establish itself as a serious literary journal. While I may be somewhat unduly simplifying what was actually a complex and shifting editorial policy, I think it fair to say that over the course of the 1930s *New Masses* shifted its focus more and more toward a rather amorphously defined "proletarian" aesthetic based loosely upon the "proletarian literature" then being explored in the Soviet Union. The most strenuous promoter of this aesthetic was *New Masses* editor Mike Gold, born Izhok Granich in 1893 in the Chrystie Street neighborhood of the Lower East Side, a few blocks from where Zukofsky himself would be born in 1904. In an editorial published in *New Masses* in 1926, Gold would describe his ideal proletarian littérateur in memorable, Whitmanian words: "Send us a giant who can shame our writers back to their task of civilizing America. . . . Send a soldier who has studied history. Send a strong poet who loves the masses, and their future. . . . Send us a joker in overalls. Send no saint. Send an artist. Send a scientist. Send a Bolshevik. Send a man" (Gold 139). Gold himself, as Joseph Freeman describes him, set the fashion for this strapping Shakespeare-with-a-lunchbucket: "He affected dirty shirts, a big, black, uncleaned Stetson with the brim of a sombrero; smoked stinking, twisted, Italian three-cent cigars, and spat frequently and vigorously on the floor" (quoted in Aaron 86).[5]

While Mike Gold and his hypothetical proletarian bard might seem a radical contrast to the slim, effete, and above all nattily dressed Zukofsky, the coincidence of his birth proximity to Gold—whom Edward Dahlberg would (with much hindsight) call "the barking Cerberus of pleb fiction" (286)—was not lost on Zukofsky; he mentions it to his literary mentor Ezra Pound in a 1928 letter: "we were brought up together on Chrystie St., tho' I never met him down there and have seen him only once" (*Pound/Zukofsky* 17). Zukofsky claims no close acquaintance with Gold; when Pound questions him about the *New Masses* editor, the installments of whose *Jews Without Money* have aroused his interest, Zukofsky confesses, "I suppose Mike Gold is alright. . . . I don't think I've missed anything not seeing more of him in N.Y.—saw him once anyway. N. Masses a pretty bad best—I'd just as soon have H[ound] & H[orn]" (*Pound/Zukofsky* 62). Zukofsky's attitude toward *New Masses* in the late twenties and early thirties, it appears, was pretty much one of amused contempt. Part of this impression might be attributed to the fact that most of his published comments about *New Masses* occur in correspondence with Pound, from whom one could expect enthusiasm neither for Marxist theory nor for proletarian realism, at least in the crude form in which *New Masses* all too often dished it out. But Zukofsky's discomfort with the direction of *New Masses*' editorial policy goes beyond a desire to distance himself from the magazine in his letters to Pound: what separates Zukofsky, himself a committed Marxist, from the apparatus of the Communist literary establishment, is his simultaneous commitment to a modernist poetics derived from the works of Apollinaire, Pound, Eliot, Williams, Cummings; as he writes to Pound in 1933, "I am not here writing as a member of the U.S. Communist Party—I am sure that as far as they're concerned papa [Pound] & child [Zukofsky] & Unk Bill Walrus [Williams] are in the same galley" (*Pound/Zukofsky* 148).

And as far as Mike Gold would be concerned, Zukofsky is probably right. Gold's 1930 statement of the aesthetics of the new "Proletarian Realism" leaves little space for a poem such as "Poem beginning 'The,'" or even as overtly political a work as the early sections of *"A"*: "Swift action, clear form, the direct line, cinema in words; this seems to be one of the principles of proletarian realism" (Gold 207); "No straining or melodrama or other effects; life itself is the supreme melodrama. Feel this intensely, and everything becomes poetry—the new poetry of materials, of the so-called 'common man,' the Worker moulding his real world" (Gold 208). Most drastically for a writer with as intensely verbal an imagination as Zukofsky's, the poet must use "As few words as possible" and must eschew "verbal acrobatics": "this is only another form for bourgeois idleness. The worker lives too close to reality to care about these literary show-offs, these verbalist heroes" (Gold 207). For Zukofsky, this aesthetic must seem a severely limiting one, not least because of the purely instrumental role it implicitly assigns literature: "Proletarian realism is never pointless. It does not believe in literature for its own sake, but in literature that is useful, has a social function. . . . Every poem, every novel and drama, must have a social theme, or it is merely confectionary" (Gold 207). And Zukofsky knows as well that his own advocacy of the formal innovators and innovations of poetic modernism sets him apart from, allows him a little place among Gold and his collaborators: the *New Masses* editors, he writes in 1931, are a bunch of "New Asses" who "need continual tutoring," and who would "probably fire me out because my name has occasionally been associated with E.P. and W.C.W. and that *lump* Kewmangs" (*Pound/Zukofsky* 96). While the modernist movement has something to teach the Communists—just as Pound's "Bowmen of Shu," for instance, corrects Whittaker Chambers's story "You Have Seen the Heads" (See *Pound/Zukofsky* 96)—Zukofsky doubts that the writers of *New Masses* are likely to accept that tuition. Gold himself appears in *"A"*, neither as literary writer nor literary editor, but as hack propagandist; he is "Carat" in "A"-1: "What's your next editorial about, Carat, / We need propaganda, the thing's / becoming a mass movement" (3).

Zukofsky's first two major publications, the February 1931 issue of *Poetry,* " 'Objectivists' 1931," and the 1932 *An "Objectivists" Anthology,* are editorial arrangements rather than acts of actual authorship, but it would be foolish to underestimate the ideological forces involved in anthology making, then as now the primary weapon in various canon-making and breaking strategies. Zukofsky's two collections are by no definition agitprop, but each of them shows markedly leftist tendencies. The " 'Objectivists' 1931" *Poetry* contains work by a number of clearly left-wing poets—Norman MacLeod, Harry Roskolenkier, Whittaker Chambers, John Wheelwright—and mentions Herman Spector and Sherry Mangan as also-rans in its editor's notes; Zukofsky's explanatory manifesto, "Program: 'Objectivists' 1931," cites Lenin as "a great writer" (272) and mentions among other "particulars" "the Russian Revolution and the rise of metallurgical plants in Siberia" (268). While the left-wing poets of *Poetry's* "Objectivists" issue are for the most part absent from *An "Objectivists" Anthology,* much of the work in that volume is of a political nature: Zukofsky's "A"-1–7, Williams's "A Morning Imagination of Russia" and "The Pure Products of America," among others, and Frances Fletcher's "A Chair," a poem that almost certainly alludes to the 1927 executions of Sacco and Vanzetti, five years later still vivid in the minds of the Left.[6] And while the preface to that volume, " 'Recencies' in Poetry," is for the most part an attack on the current critical establishment, T. S. Eliot in particular, Zukofsky closes with a memorable image of the intersection of the "good poems of yesterday" and the progressive politics of today: "Stalin has been spending some of his time in his one or two rooms not destroying Shakespeare, but has been reading the not really predacious Englishm[a]n on his vacation" (25). Earlier in the essay Zukofsky has advocated a poetry free of "predatory intent" (18), the propagandistic advocacy so strongly prescribed by Gold and other cultural commissars of the Party; in this passage, he demonstrates that even Stalin, the current icon of revolutionary values, is able to enjoy and learn from the works of Shakespeare, a perennial culture hero of Zukofsky's, and is "not really" political, or "predacious."[7]

My own essay's title, of course, is itself a quotation from " 'Recencies' in Poetry": "*Impossible* to communicate anything but particulars—historic and contemporary—things, human beings as things their instrumentalities of capillaries and vein binding up and bound up with events and contingencies. The revolutionary word if it must revolve cannot escape having a reference" (16).[8] This, I think, is one of the few moments in which Zukofsky's writings on poetics assert a definite political dimension to poetic language itself. While Burton Hatlen is right to trace dialectical patterns through the first ten sections of "*A*", and Michael Davidson is correct as well when he asserts that Zukofsky, in " 'Mantis' " and "A"-9, "use[s] formalism not to aestheticize social tensions but to return a degree of use-value to a poetry increasingly instrumentalized by social agendas" (523), at no point does the poet himself explicitly theorize the political implications of his poetic forms and modes. What Zukofsky implies in this passage of " 'Recencies' " is actually fairly straightforward: if one's language is to be "revolutionary," is to have a political impact, it must have a "reference," it must deal with "historic and contemporary" particulars rather than with abstractions. And here he has it both ways, hearkening back both to Pound's Imagist manifesto, which demands the poet "go in fear of abstractions" (*Literary Essays* 5) and to the "scientific" proletarian realism of Gold and company, which demands above all the treatment of actual fact, "the *real conflicts* of men and women . . . Away with all lies about human nature. We are scientists; we know what a man thinks and feels. . . . No straining or melodrama or other effects; life itself is the supreme melodrama" (Gold 208). By his treatment of "historic and contemporary particulars," Zukofsky simultaneously pursues the modernist poetics of his elders Pound and Williams, no matter how bourgeois or reactionary their politics, and fulfills at least the liminal requirements of a proletarian poetics, no matter how far his work might otherwise diverge from what Mike Gold or Joseph Freeman would recognize as proletarian literature.

The major divergences between Zukofsky's modernism and proletarian realism are clear: Zukofsky's poetry, for all of his own emphasis on "clarity," is a difficult poetry, relying on tactics of juxtaposition and montage that, however easily apprehensible they may be in the cinema, pose formidable difficulties for the average reader. When Gold advocates "cinema in words," he means thereby something exceedingly straightforward: "Swift action, clear form, the direct line" (Gold 207); Zukofsky, on the other hand, sees his own work "partak[ing] of the cinematic principle" (*Pound/Zukofsky* 112) to the extent to which its formal structures resemble those of Eisenstein's montage: he writes Pound in 1931, "Advertising & montage, Mr. E.,—Eisenstein has nothing on us" (*Pound/Zukofsky* 121).[9] For such proponents of proletarian literature as the poet Herman Spector, modernist poetry is fundamentally decadent, the product of "sophisticated dilettante[s]" in an "age of the freak in matters esthetic" (quoted in Klein 74). (Zukofsky's own response to misreading and assaults is to chastise his readers for not paying enough attention: in " 'Recencies' " he grouses, "the absence of a habit of reading 4 or 5 times for a meaning—in certain readers is probably regrettable" [9].) In addition, no matter how profoundly Zukofsky's work may treat the class struggle, it almost wholly lacks the hortatory element essential to Gold's vision of proletarian writing. It analyzes, dramatizes, and deconstructs, but it does not inspire to action: the poem is, as Zukofsky puts it in " 'Recencies,' " an "object unrelated to palpable or predatory intent" (18). The poem supplies the information, the knowledge, that may make the mind "more temperate" (in Pound's phrase from *Mauberley*), but it only "records" "state and individual"; it does not supply the necessary "application," the political action that must follow education (19). The very notion of "proletarian literature," it would seem, is for Zukofsky a problematic one: "By all means a literature of the proletariat—which will be

MARK SCROGGINS

only literature after all—if there are writers. They will never get across to the proletariat if they are not" (19).

A lesson that both Cary Nelson and Jerome McGann have been propounding for some time is that as significant as the actual mode of a poet's work is its medium of dissemination, the material venue in which that work is presented to the public.[10] While Zukofsky's political sympathies might lie with the crowd at the *Daily Worker* or *Dynamo,* in the early 1930s he—like his contemporaries John Wheelwright and Sherry Mangan, also modernist poets committed to leftist causes[11]—generally published his poetry not in such leftist journals as *New Masses* but in little magazines associated with the apolitical avant-garde: *Blues, Pagany, Contact,* and so forth. This is, I think, a crucial fact: Zukofsky's Marxism is no doubt as sincere as that of many a fellow traveler published in a John Reed Club journal, and his theoretical stance no doubt more subtly considered than that of many Party members—and those who doubt Zukofsky's grasp of Marxian economic theory might consider the ease and the force with which he debates Pound in the latter stages of their correspondence, a correspondence that quite nearly becomes what Paul Zukofsky (with no little irony) calls it, a "primer in economics" (309)—but even taking these facts into consideration, no matter how evident the Marxist "argument" of Zukofsky's poems might be, their strident formal modernism pretty much forecloses the possibility of their being published in journals like *New Masses,* dominated by the aesthetic of proletarian realism. What results is the slightly odd spectacle of sections of *"A",* a poem that James Laughlin would in 1938 call an "epic of the class struggle" ("Notes"),[12] appearing in such journals as the avant-garde *Pagany* and the grudgingly experimental but thoroughly bourgeois *Poetry* (Chicago).

What fueled much of the political radicalism of the thirties, of course, was the spectacular collapse of the American capitalist economy that began in 1929, the Great Depression. Even as the wrenching human tragedy of the Depression forced thousands of writers and intellectuals to what would once have seemed desperate conclusions— the conclusions, that is, of the Communist Party—and as Roosevelt's New Deal put into operation many of the very reforms the Left had long advocated, thereby validating what the twenties would have seen as extreme programs, the economic disaster also worked to destroy a large proportion of the network of little magazines that had sprung up during the 1920s to publish avant-garde and experimental writing. The Objectivist Press, edited by Zukofsky and underwritten by Oppen, was only one of many publishing ventures that went under in the mid-1930s. Just as the possibilities of publishing his work in the little avant-garde magazines seemed to be disappearing, at the same time—that is, over the course of the mid to late 1930s—it seems that Zukofsky was becoming more personally involved in leftist literary organizations. Zukofsky was a member at least through 1938 of the League of American Writers, the United States affiliate of the International Union of Revolutionary Writers, and Eric Homberger has discovered a mention in a 1937 *Daily Worker* of one "Louis Zukonski" being elected by a division of that body to a committee organizing support for striking steelworkers (171). After the undignified petering out of The Objectivist Press, Zukofsky apparently became closely associated with *New Masses* itself, spending much time at the editorial offices and serving as an unpaid editorial adviser.[13] This, then, is an intriguing conjunction, especially when one considers that there is a substantial period in the late 1930s (approximately late 1935 through 1941) where Zukofsky's only significant periodical publications appear in *New Masses,* that bastion of proletarian writing.

Mike Gold's aesthetic of "proletarian realism" was in full dominance over *New Masses* by the late thirties, when Zukofsky published two sections of "A"-8 in the magazine. The late thirties were a hard time for American Communists, of course: fast slipping away were the heady days of the Popular Front and the Spanish Civil War, during which Communist Party organs for a short while became a forum for all those who would support a common Loyalist cause, no matter how "suspect" their allegiances might have been a few years before. By 1939, the Hitler/Stalin Pact, a joining of hands by the leader of the proletarian revolution and the embodiment of fascism, only served to drive away the remaining vacillators who had not been disillusioned by the Moscow show trials of 1936 and 1938, which had driven loyalists like Gold into what Paul Buhle calls "a hard-nosed sectarianism" (180), an intense hard-line Stalinism. Homberger characterizes what Zukofsky resorted to in the late thirties as "writ[ing] for his desk drawer" (182), withholding his work from public examination; in part this is true, since "A"-8, which was composed between 1935 and

1938, only saw complete publication in 1958. But the sections of "A"-8 that Zukofsky *did* publish seem to me an interesting variation, rather than repudiation, of Homberger's notion. I would submit as example the publication of a poem entitled "March Comrades" in the 3 May 1938 *New Masses* and, by way of contrast, the final appearance of that passage of verse in "A"-8, first published in 1958. These documents make clear, I think, that Zukofsky had fully realized by 1938 that the only common ground between the aesthetic of Gold's *New Masses* and his own concatenation of "historic and contemporary particulars" was one in which the intellectual complexities and aural splendors of the ongoing "*A*" must yield to the merely hortatory.

A brief examination of both the contents and the contexts of these two passages is revealing. "March Comrades," as is evident from its refrain—"This is May Day! May!"—is something of a marching song, a May Day hymn "for a workers' chorus": appropriately, it appears in the May Day issue of *New Masses* for 1938, under a small, only marginally competent, cartoon of a crowd of strikers with pickets:

"March Comrades"
(Words for a workers' chorus, from " 'A' 8")

Workers and farmers unite
You have nothing to lose
   But your chains
   The world is to win
This is May Day! May!
Your armies are veining the earth!

Railways and highways have tied
Blood of farmland and town
   And the chains
   Speed wheat to machine
This is May Day! May!
The poor's armies veining the earth!

Hirers once fed by the harried
Cannot feed them their hire
   Nor can chain
   Hold the hungry in
This is May Day! May!
The poor are veining the earth!

Light lights in air blossoms red
Like nothing on earth
   Now the chains
   Drag graves to lie in
This is May Day! May!
The poor's armies are veining the earth!

March comrades in revolution
From hirer unchained
   Till your gain
   Be the freedom of all
The World's May Day! May!
May of the Freed of All the Earth!

(The poem appears in the middle column of a three-column page, folded within an article on the American Federation of Labor; such a layout, in which poem, prose, and cartoon decoration are juxtaposed in uneasy hierarchy of text and decoration, reminds this reader of nothing so much as the presentation of poetry in that bastion of bourgeois respectability, the *New Yorker.*) There is elsewhere in this issue a brief column urging "Unity on May Day," hailing, among other triumphs for democracy, "the swift progress of Socialism in the Soviet Union and the uprooting of Trotskyist wreckers and spies." The specter of the Moscow trials casts a long shadow over this *New Masses;* a column two pages further on reveals that Trotsky himself has "degenerate[d] into an accomplice of fascism": "Whatever it may mean to Trotsky subjectively, his 'revolution,' objectively, is nothing but counter-revolution and the triumph of fascism" ("His Main Enemy" 10). And finally, on page 19, there is a lengthy "Statement by American Progressives" on the Moscow trials, confidently citing the "clear presumption of the guilt of the defendants": "Drastic attack must be met by drastic defence: it is in this light that we regard the trials." This document is signed by well over a hundred writers, artists, and intellectuals, a group that exemplifies the reach of the American Communist Party's soon-to-be-abandoned Popular Front strategy of welcoming Left-leaning intellectuals of politically heterodox beliefs. Among the signators are Nelson Algren, Malcolm Cowley, Stuart Davis, Mike Gold, Dashiell Hammett, Langston Hughes, and Dorothy Parker. Zukofsky's name is conspicuous by its absence: one can only speculate whether he was asked to sign and refused or was never asked (the powers that be simply assuming that he would refuse). Present among the names, however, is that of Morris U. Schappes, who five years before, in *Poetry* itself, had attacked Zukofsky's *An "Objectivists" Anthology* as the work of "deracinated bourgeois poet[s]," who, piqued by capitalist society's devaluation of poetry itself, have withdrawn into "rootless esotericism"; Zukofsky and company, he advises, ought to model their work upon Louis Aragon's *The Red Front* (343). Zukofsky bristles in reply, quoting Lenin and observing that Schappes "admires only those 'poets' who 'express' their 'service' to the revolutionary proletariat in the worst public-school honored manner of Milton" ("Objectivists Again" 117).

There is unintentional irony in this exchange, not merely because Zukofsky and Schappes will find themselves side by side five years later in an issue of *New Masses,* but because "March Comrades" measures up far more closely to Schappes's political aesthetic, the crowd-rousing, exhortative mode of Louis Aragon—or, for that matter, to Mike Gold's unesoteric, readily grasped proletarian aesthetic—than to the principles of sincerity and objectification Zukofsky himself had put forward seven years before. "March Comrades" is, on the face of it, a concession to the poetry that *New Masses* would have. But it is not wholly a concession: Zukofsky frames his song, noting that it is merely the "words" for a chorus and that it is only a section of "A"-8, a larger whole. Its revision and final publication are even more revealing about the distance between Zukofsky's own aesthetic and the aesthetic of the leftist establishment.[14] Interestingly enough, strictly speaking nothing has been *changed* in the revision—almost the whole of Zukofsky's revising, as one can also see comparing the *An "Objectivists" Anthology* versions of "A"-1 through "A"-7 to their final publications, consists of omission. Omitted here is the entire first stanza, with its heavy-handed restatement of the Communist Manifesto; "This is May Day! May!" becomes the barer but more suggestive "This is May" ("A"-8, 48). The final stanza shows the most drastic changes: "March Comrades" had ended on a crescendo, a more than slightly bombastic iambic tetrameter line, punctuated embarrassingly with capitals: "May of the Freed of All the Earth!" The passage from "A"-8 ends on a quiet, tentative note, not unhopeful but not at all bombastic or hortatory:

March
From hirer unchained

Till your gain
   Be the
World's

                    ["A"-8, 49]

This is no longer a hymn or a chorus but a calm, carefully modulated coda to such a song.

In the context of "A"-8 as a whole, this passage takes on an even more complex aspect, as it reveals itself as a lyrical interlude in a large-scale fugal structure of juxtaposed themes and subjects. "A"-8 is the longest of the first eight sections of "A", as long as the first seven sections combined. It explores to the greatest degree yet the task Zukofsky sets himself in "A"-6, when he asks, "Can / The design / Of the fugue / Be transferred / To poetry?" ("A"-6, 38). Preceding this song are statements (in the musical sense) of the section's eight separate and interwoven themes, themes that include Bach's St. Matthew Passion, the nature of labor, Bach's life and career, and a variety of perspectives on history, including those of Karl Marx, Brooks Adams, and Brooks's brother Henry.[15] The song follows a series of meditations on the nature of thought and fact and how capitalist advertising works to occlude the true relations of existents. Following the song is a three-page passage in which the distribution of "n" and "r" sounds is determined by the equation of a conic section: that passage is itself a concatenation of topics and quotations that range from Communist Party history, to quantum physics, to interwoven fragments of the poems Zukofsky would collect in his teaching anthology A Test of Poetry. All of which says, in short, that the twenty-three lines of poetry to which Zukofsky has reduced the bombast of "March Comrades" are far more resonant and complex in their context in "A"-8 than they are as "Words for a workers' chorus" in a May Day issue of the New Masses. Zukofsky's poetry can indeed serve the cause of the revolution—but to do so it must be both radically decontextualized, taken out of its place in the larger structures of his work, and padded out to grandiloquence and soapbox bluster, obscuring the careful music that Zukofsky, with hindsight and political levelheadedness, will excavate from its lines.

When Zukofsky finished "A"-8 in 1937, it was the most advanced and fully realized section to date of his "poem of a life," the most ambitious poetic figure he had yet written, and among the most achieved products in English of the modernist "revolution of the word." And he had nowhere to publish it, save for the two brief and relatively minor passages that appeared in the *New Masses* in 1937 and 1938—two small and uncharacteristic gargoyles, perhaps, placed on exhibit without regard for their function within the structure of the cathedral as a whole. It is perhaps useless to speculate about what might have happened had the Marxist literary establishment accepted and encouraged Zukofsky's own gropings toward a thoroughly materialist modernism, if *New Masses,* for instance, had been edited by a man like Kenneth Burke rather than by Michael Gold. His achievement in poetry would not have been greatly augmented, I think, but he might have had the opportunity to formalize and theorize what remains among the most interesting, if also among the most problematic, bodies of political poetry of this century.

Notes

I was well along in preparing this essay for publication before my attention was drawn to Jenny Penberthy's essay on Lorine Niedecker, " 'The Revolutionary Word': Lorine Niedecker's Early Writings, 1928–1946" (*West Coast Line* 7 [26.1] [Spring 1992]: 75–98); I think it not inappropriate that our two essays should share a title, given their shared points of reference. Penberthy's work focuses not merely on the political in the works of Niedecker and Zukofsky but also on the often ignored surrealism of Niedecker's early writings. "The Revolutionary Word" is reprinted, in expanded form, in *Niedecker and the Correspondence with Zukofsky* 17–47. Thanks are due as well to Marnie Parsons and to Peter Quartermain, who first brought "March Comrades" to my attention.

1. See, for instance, the meeting between Henry James and Ezra Pound in the opening pages of Hugh Kenner's *The Pound Era,* which more than one critic has taken as historical narrative.

2. For a detailed career-long analysis of the political in Zukofsky's early poetry, see Mottram.

3. See, in particular, Nelson and Kalaidjian.

4. On small leftist magazines, see Nelson 206–233; on *Partisan Review,* see Wald, *New York Intellectuals* 75–97.

5. On Gold, the *New Masses,* and the notion of a proletarian literature, see Klein 70–86, Buhle 171–183, and Kalaidjian 35–58. For a provocative reassessment of Gold's career, see Bloom.

6. An allusion too subtle for Morris U. Schappes, who finds the poem "impoverish[ing]" the "reader's rich experience" ("Historic" 341).

7. I quote here from the version of " 'Recencies' " in *An "Objectivists" Anthology;* while Zukofsky reprinted much of this essay in his collection *Prepositions* (14–18), he has purged it of all of its overtly political and topical material.

8. Jenny Penberthy points out quite rightly that this passage of " 'Recencies' in Poetry," which began as an August 1931 lecture at the Gotham Book Mart, is in large part as well a response to Eugene Jolas's "Revolution of the Word" manifesto, published in the June 1929 issue of his magazine *transition* (Penberthy 19, 25). In that "Proclamation" Jolas asserts, "PURE POETRY IS A LYRICAL ABSOLUTE THAT SEEKS AN A PRIORI REALITY WITHIN OURSELVES ALONE" (quoted in Penberthy 26). Zukofsky counters that the "revolutionary word" "is not infinite. Even infinite is a term" (" 'Recencies' " 16).

9. Zukofsky was intensely interested in the cinema during the 1930s. He reviewed Chaplin's *Modern Times* in 1936 in a fascinating and perspicacious essay, unpublished at the time (*Prepositions* 54–64), and in the early thirties had a hand in a (never to be published) screenplay of Joyce's *Ulysses.*

10. See the many illustrations in Nelson, which illustrate the interplay between design and text in the works he examines, paying special attention to small left-wing magazines and their layouts; see as well McGann, *The Textual Condition* and *Black Riders,* which examine the pedigree of the modernist book.

11. For a historically fascinating account of Wheelwright's and Mangan's careers, see Wald, *Revolutionary Imagination.*

12. Zukofsky, in a letter to Lorine Niedecker dated around 1953, would downplay the political thrust of the early sections of "*A*", warning her especially not to take Laughlin's description too seriously; the political elements in "A"-8 are to be understood as historical materials for a poem, not as messages meant to have a proactive effect in the extrapoetic world. Clearly one must approach Zukofsky's postwar comments carefully: there is much hindsight involved here. See Stanley 107.

13. The only mention I have seen in print of this moment in Zukofsky's career is in Sharp (47), though Barry Ahearn confirmed his association with *New Masses* to me in conversation.

14. According to Marcella Booth's catalog of the Zukofsky manuscripts at the University of Texas (52–53), "A"-8, including the *New Masses* text of "March Comrades," was drafted between August 1935 and January 1937; it was revised, heavily in sections, in October 1957 in preparation for its 1958 publication.

15. On the themes of "A"-8, see Ahearn 75–78.

Works Cited

Aaron, Daniel. *Writers on the Left: Episodes in American Literary Communism*. 1961. New York: Columbia UP, 1992.

Ahearn, Barry. *Zukofsky's "A": An Introduction*. Berkeley: U of California P, 1983.

Bloom, James D. *Left Letters: The Culture Wars of Mike Gold and Joseph Freeman*. New York: Columbia UP, 1992.

Booth, Marcella. *A Catalogue of the Louis Zukofsky Manuscript Collection*. Austin: Humanities Research Center, U of Texas, 1975.

Buhle, Paul. *Marxism in the USA: Remapping the History of the American Left.* London: Verso, 1987.

Dahlberg, Edward. *The Confessions of Edward Dahlberg.* New York: George Braziller, 1971.

Davenport, Guy. *The Geography of the Imagination: Forty Essays.* San Francisco: North Point, 1981.

Davidson, Michael. "Dismantling 'Mantis': Reification and Objectivist Poetics." *American Literary History* 3.3 (Fall 1991): 521–541.

Ginsberg, Allen. *Collected Poems, 1947–1980.* New York: Harper & Row, 1984.

Gold, Michael. *Mike Gold: A Literary Anthology.* Ed. Michael Folsom. New York: International, 1972.

Hatlen, Burton. "Art and/as Labor: Some Dialectical Patterns in *"A"*-1 through *"A"*-10." *Contemporary Literature* 25.2 (Summer 1984): 205–234.

"His Main Enemy! The People." *New Masses* 27.4 (May 3, 1938): 10.

Homberger, Eric. *American Writers and Radical Politics, 1900–39: Equivocal Commitments.* New York: St. Martin's P, 1986.

Kalaidjian, Walter. *American Culture Between the Wars: Revisionary Modernism and Postmodern Critique.* New York: Columbia UP, 1993.

Kenner, Hugh. "Oppen, Zukofsky, and the Poem as Lens." *Literature at the Barricades: The American Writer in the 1930s.* Ed. Ralph F. Bogardus and Fred Hobson. University, AL: U of Alabama P, 1982. 162–171.

———. *The Pound Era.* Berkeley: U of California P, 1971.

Klein, Marcus. *Foreigners: The Making of American Literature, 1900–1940.* Chicago: U of Chicago P, 1981.

Laughlin, James. "Notes on Contributors." *New Directions, 1938.* Norfolk, CT: New Directions, 1938.

Longenbach, James. *Wallace Stevens: The Plain Sense of Things.* New York: Oxford UP, 1991.

McGann, Jerome. *Black Riders: The Visible Language of Modernism.* Princeton, NJ: Princeton UP, 1993.

———. *The Textual Condition.* Princeton, NJ: Princeton UP, 1991.

"The Moscow Trials: A Statement by American Progressives." *New Masses* 27.4 (May 3, 1938): 19.

Mottram, Eric. "1924–1951: Politics and Form in Zukofsky." *MAPS* 5 (1973): 76–103.

Nelson, Cary. *Repression and Recovery: Modern American Poetry and the Politics of Cultural Memory, 1910–1945.* Madison: U of Wisconsin P, 1989.

Penberthy, Jenny. *Niedecker and the Correspondence with Zukofsky, 1931–1970.* Cambridge: Cambridge UP, 1993.

Pound, Ezra. *Literary Essays.* Ed. T. S. Eliot. New York: New Directions, 1968.

———. *Selected Prose, 1909–1965.* Ed. William Cookson. New York: New Directions, 1973.

Quartermain, Peter. *Disjunctive Poetics: From Gertrude Stein and Louis Zukofsky to Susan Howe.* Cambridge: Cambridge UP, 1992.

Schappes, Morris U. "Historic and Contemporary Particulars." Rev. of *An "Objectivists" Anthology. Poetry* 41.6 (March 1933): 340–343.

Schelb, Edward. "The Exaction of Song: Louis Zukofsky and the Ideology of Form." *Contemporary Literature* 31.3 (1990): 335–353.

Sharp, Tom. "The 'Objectivists' Publications." *Sagetrieb* 3.3 (Winter 1984): 41–47.

Simon, Linda. "A Preface to Zukofsky." *Sagetrieb* 2.1 (Spring 1983): 89–96.

Stanley, Sandra Kumamoto. *Louis Zukofsky and the Transformation of a Modern American Poetics.* Berkeley: U of California P, 1994.

Stevens, Wallace. *The Letters of Wallace Stevens.* Ed. Holly Stevens. New York: Knopf, 1966.

Terrell, Carroll F. "Louis Zukofsky: An Eccentric Profile." *Louis Zukofsky: Man and Poet.* Ed. Carroll F. Terrell. Orono, ME: National Poetry Foundation, 1979. 31–74.

"Unity on May Day." *New Masses* 27.4 (May 3, 1938): 8.

Wald, Alan. *The New York Intellectuals: The Rise and Decline of the Anti-Stalinist Left from the 1930s to the 1980s.* Chapel Hill: U of North Carolina P, 1987.

———. *The Revolutionary Imagination: The Poetry and Politics of John Wheelwright and Sherry Mangan.* Chapel Hill: U of North Carolina P, 1983.

Zukofsky, Louis. "March Comrades." *New Masses* 27.4 (May 3, 1938): 14.

———. " 'Recencies' in Poetry." *An "Objectivists" Anthology.* Ed. Louis Zukofsky. Var, France: TO Publishers, 1932. 9–25.

———. ed. *An "Objectivists" Anthology.* Var, France: TO Publishers, 1932.

———. ed. " 'Objectivists' 1931." *Poetry* 37.5 (February 1931). [Special issue of *Poetry*]

Zukofsky, Louis, and Ezra Pound. *Pound/Zukofsky: Selected Letters of Ezra Pound and Louis Zukofsky.* Ed. Barry Ahearn. New York: New Directions, 1987.

Zukofsky, Louis, and Morris U. Schappes. "Objectivists Again." *Poetry* 42.2 (May 1933) 117–118.

Zukofsky, Paul. Afterword. ("The Baron Speaks.") *Collected Fiction.* By Louis Zukofsky. Elmwood Park, IL: Dalkey Archive P, 1990. 301–311.

3

Jewish-American Modernism and the Problem of Identity

With Special Reference to the Work of Louis Zukofsky

NORMAN FINKELSTEIN

When we consider the aesthetics of the Jewish-American modernists, whether they wrote in Yiddish or English, we discover that the psychosocial conflicts that beset them are both voiced and silenced in their poetic theories. Cultural identity and literary affiliation, poetic production and audience reception, tradition and rebellion: these dialectical terms form the unstable ground that these writers endlessly traverse; they constitute the historical matrix out of which their complex, volatile aesthetic is born. And as Terry Eagleton reminds us, "The aesthetic is that which speaks of historical conditions by remaining silent—inheres in them by distance and denial. . . . 'Real' history is cancelled by the text, but in the precise modes of that cancellation lies the text's most significant relation to history." Thus we are concerned "with the specific operations whereby the ideological produces within itself that internal distantiation which is the aesthetic" (177).

If the aesthetic is, at least in part, a matter of ideological distantiation, then that process should be peculiarly visible in the poems, as well as the statements on poetics, made by Jewish-American modernists. When poets write about the goals they set for their poems—the techniques that the poems are to deploy, the subjects that they are to address, the traditions they are to oppose or continue, the aspects of human experience in which they are to ground their utterance—then we should take them at their word. A productive aesthetic stance is never "wrong" or "right," though it may be (and perhaps always is) constituted in part by ideological beliefs—in the sense of Louis Althusser's famous formulation of ideology as "a representation of the imaginary relationship of individuals to their real conditions of existence." The cultural conflicts of Jewish-American poets in the twenties and thirties can be understood partly in terms of their self-representation, which was shaped in turn by their "imaginary" relationships to "real" conditions. In turning to the aesthetics of these figures, we must explore the relationship between their ambivalent psychosocial selves and their stated literary aims. In Eagleton's terms, we must consider the "specific operations" through which the ideological concern over Jewish-American identity "produces within itself" that "distantiation" which is the poetics of Jewish-American modernism.

I

In 1920, a new movement in Yiddish poetry was launched with the publication in New York City of an anthology called *In Zikh* (*In Oneself*). This anthology, prefaced by a crucial manifesto by Jacob Glatshteyn, A. Leyeles, and N. B. Minkov, was soon followed by a magazine, also called *In Zikh,* which was to continue publication until 1940. Self-consciously modernist in their stance, the Inzikhists, or Introspectivists, looked to their Gentile contemporaries in Europe and the United States for literary models but at the same time were deeply rooted in the secular Yiddish literature that had come into being in nineteenth-century Poland and Russia. Thus, like all Jews caught up in the process of assimilation (or perhaps to put it more accurately, the Jewish crisis of modernity), the Introspectivists were acutely aware of living between two worlds. Hence the revealing comedy of the following passage, from a discussion of Gentiles and Yiddish literature, which appeared in *In Zikh* in July 1923:

> Recently, the *In Zikh* had its own experience with Gentile colleagues.
> The American journal, *Poetry,* got hold of an issue of *In Zikh.* And this is what the editors wrote to us:
> "Unfortunately we cannot read your journal. We would like to know in what language it is printed. Is it Chinese?"
> *Poetry* is published in Chicago. Several Yiddish newspapers are printed in Chicago. Yiddish periodicals, collections, books, are published there. There are certainly also Chinese laundries in Chicago, and the lady-editors of *Poetry* have probably seen a ticket from a Chinese laundry in their lifetime. And, after all that—not to mention

that any intelligent person would know the difference between the way Chinese and Yiddish look—to ask whether a Yiddish journal is Chinese does not reflect very positively on the intelligence of the *Poetry* people.

But after all, this is not important.

What is important is: How long will Yiddish literature be unknown among the Gentiles? How long will they think of us—in literature—as Hotentots?

[Harshav and Harshav 797–798]

Here we find the disquieting combination of verbal anxiety and verbal aggression associated with the modern Jewish passage into the dominant culture, focused, in this instance, on the matter of poetic production and reception. Outraged by the neglect and ignorance demonstrated by a Gentile literary group that they ironically regard as "colleagues," the editors of *In Zikh* lash out, using terms that betray their self-conscious marginality. The Gentile, English-speaking literary culture of America in the twenties is justifiably suspected of anti-Semitism. The defensive response by these embattled Jewish modernists, with its derogatory references to Chinese laundries, Hottentots, and lady editors, is marked by the ambivalence of an assimilating minority, as it both asserts its difference and seeks acceptance by the dominant culture. The Introspectivists anxiously remind themselves and their readers that Yiddish-speaking American Jews are full members of white, Western society, neither Chinese nor Hottentot.

These racial categories are not chosen arbitrarily. The Chinese are "Oriental," and it was standard for anti-Semites to regard the Jew as Oriental and therefore as an alien other to Western culture. Furthermore, Yiddish was the language of the *Ostjuden,* the Jews of Eastern Europe. As Jews in Western Europe went through the process of assimilation, the *Ostjuden* came to signify the "bad" Jews, whose alien ways were a source of anxiety for Western Jews hoping to enter the European mainstream. Ironically, this image was gradually reversed: by the late nineteenth century, as the notion of self-hatred developed among assimilated Western Jews, the *Ostjuden* were romantically recast as authentic, "good" Jews. This double bind, "The Invention of the Eastern Jew," as Sander Gilman calls it, signifies "the slipperiness of the Jew's precarious position. . . . Thus the splitting of the identity of the Jew into polar opposites took place in an antithetical manner that mirrored the division of the self into 'good' and 'bad' aspects" (*Jewish*

Self-Hatred 270). This ambivalent splitting becomes the inheritance of the Yiddish writers of *In Zikh*: assimilated, "Western"-identified Jews born in Eastern Europe, transplanted in New York City, and insisting that neither they nor the language of which they are so proud is "Chinese."

And if they are not Chinese, they are certainly not Hottentots. The use of the term "Hottentot" evokes a tradition of racist beliefs (including scientific beliefs) that extended through the nineteenth century and into the twentieth. In his study of the Hottentot stereotype, Gilman observes, "The antithesis of European sexual mores and beauty is the black, and the essential black, the lowest exemplum of mankind on the great chain of being, is the Hottentot" (*Difference and Pathology* 83). Thus it is not merely their status in the literary sphere with which the Introspectivists are concerned; in this case, literary reputation is a metonym for their reception as Jews within American civil society. How do the genteel lady editors of *Poetry,* holding their Chinese laundry tickets and indecipherable copies of *In Zikh,* "see" these partially assimilated Jewish writers? Against such infuriating, threatening figures, the Introspectivists feel compelled to assert their class consciousness and masculinity. But given their European origins, they also intuitively understand that

> The black and the Jew were associated not merely because they were both "outsiders" but because qualities ascribed to one became the means of defining the difference of the other. The categories of "black" and "Jew" thus became interchangeable at one point in history. The line between the two groups vanished, and each became the definition of the other. The ultimate source of this identification was the need to externalize the anxiety generated by change in European (read Christian) middle-class society, a society under extraordinary tension during the course of the nineteenth century. The black no longer satisfactorily bore projections of anxiety. Too distanced, too controlled by the power of colonial empire, the black became part of the European world of myth. The Jew, however, daily present in society and demanding access into a bourgeois life seemingly so stable and well defined in terms of its Christian identity, was perceived as the radical par excellence. And the Jew was thus seen as one with the image of the black present in the fantasy world of European myth.
>
> [*Difference and Pathology* 35]

The Introspectivists internalize these racist myths and bring them to the New World, where the issue of assimilation remains crucial to their lives and work. As they simultaneously seek acceptance and assert their Jewish difference, they are caught in yet another double bind that we can observe in their rhetoric of literary reputation. In other words, the Introspectivists are suffering from an American Jewish version of what John Murray Cuddihy names, in the title of his enduring study of assimilation, *The Ordeal of Civility*. As Cuddihy explains,

> Diaspora in the West forced a bitter choice on the emancipated Jew-ish intelligentsia (ultimately, also, on the Jewish "masses"): either *Yid-dishkeit* lacked something and the West had something to offer, or *Yiddishkeit* had something and the West had nothing (essentially) to offer. In the former case, assimilation or conversion was in order, to acquire that "something"; in the latter case, reduction rather than conversion was indicated—that is, an essentially reductive analysis that would strip the apparently "superior" culture of its apparent superiority (thus elevating the apparently "inferior" and marginal subculture).
> [66]

The Introspectivists were much too far from traditional Jewish life, too heavily invested in modern Western values—but at the same time, too faithful to Yiddish—to consider such a choice seriously. Thus, theirs was the bitterness of ambivalence, a never-ending ordeal. The *In Zikh* discussion concludes in a more reasonable, if not resigned, manner:

> A self-respecting Yiddish literature can react to this phenomenon in two ways.
> First, it can ignore the external world altogether and wait until the weight, the importance and the inner value of our work forces the Gentiles to see us, to consider us and ask pardon for past misrep-resentations.
> Second, it can inform the non-Jewish journals that all they have printed about Yiddish thus far is false, silly misrepresentation and it can undertake the translation of the best, most characteristic Yiddish works, thus forcing them to have respect for Yiddish.
> [Harshav and Harshav 798]

Unfortunately, neither of these possibilities materialized. Yiddish literature, especially poetry, continued to be ignored by Gentile culture in the United States; the "importance and inner value" of the work went unrecognized, and it was not until 1969, with the publication of Irving Howe's and Eliezer Greenberg's *Treasury of Yiddish Poetry,* that a comprehensive body of translations became available. By then, such a book was needed as much by Jews as by Gentiles, for subsequent generations of American Jews did not learn Yiddish. In Europe, the Yiddish-speaking community was destroyed and, with it, the extraordinary potential for a modernist poetry in a genuinely international language. But even before the Holocaust, throughout the twenties and thirties, *In Zikh* continued to lament the isolation of its poets. The responsibility for this condition, however, was gradually shifted to American Jews, who were seen as not only abandoning Yiddish but repudiating it, treating it with contempt. "The pettiest Jewish scribbler in English," writes A. Leyeles in 1937, "the lowest reporter on an English newspaper feels sky-high above Yiddish—whether it's the Yiddish press or the demanding, original Yiddish literature. So many years in America, such a fine literature created here, and we remain strangers to our neighbors as if we had lived in Siam or had written in some Eskimo dialect" (Harshav and Harshav 801).

But although the Introspectivists defended Yiddish against assimilating, English-speaking Jews, they were still ambivalent about their literary forebears, especially in the early years of the movement, before it became clear that Yiddish literature in its entirety was in danger of extinction. Another column in *In Zikh* in 1923 (obviously a year for taking stock) asserts repeatedly that "[w]e have no tradition," that "there is more direct relationship between an Introspectivist and a German Expressionist or English Vorticist than between us and most Yiddish poets of the previous periods." Furthermore, this "direct relation" to "all of Modernism" sets the *In Zikh* group apart from other Yiddish writers, producing "the impression of foreignness in the eyes of those who regard Yiddish poetry merely as a part of Jewish culture, who are looking for thread-weaving, who emphasize, throughout, the word 'Jewish' " (Harshav and Harshav 794). For the Introspectivists, Jewish identity was only one thread in the Yiddish poetry they wished to produce.

II

The Introspectivists were not aware, as they struggled with questions of identity, audience, and artistic affiliation, that about the same time, one erstwhile English Vorticist was considering the vitality of Yiddish and the potential of a Jewish contribution to modernist writing:

9 Dec. 1929   Rapallo
Dear Z.

   The Reznikof [*sic*] prose very good as far as I've got at breakfast. . . . Capital in idea that new wave of literature is jewish (obviously) Bloom casting shadow before, prophetic Jim [Joyce] etc.

   also lack of prose in German due to all idiomatic energy being drawn off into yiddish.

   (not concerned with the "truth" of these suggestions but only with the dynamic.)

                                                                                              yrs
                                                                                              EP

           [*Pound/Zukofsky* 26–27]

It is a singular moment in literary history. Pound's brief speculation concerning Yiddish "energy" is probably prompted by the novelty of a Jewish disciple, a young man whose first language was Yiddish and who had deployed translations from that language to great effect in a work that Pound admired and published, the formidable "Poem beginning 'The.' " Zukofsky, as Harold Schimmel points out, "was a born American." It was not "his fate . . . to attend NYU Law writing free verses in Yiddish (as Glatstein and Minkoff did)" (236). Zukofsky, unlike the European-born Introspectivists, not only admired the Anglo-American modernists, but felt secure enough, confidently American enough, to write his poetry in their—and his own—language. Nevertheless, he too endured the ordeal of civility and perhaps more painfully than any of the Introspectivists, who, despite their anxieties about race, class and gender, suffered mainly from neglect. Direct dealings with Ezra Pound, however much Zukofsky sought and won his approval, had an even more unsettling effect on the younger poet's sense of himself as a Jew.

   In his reply to Pound's letter (December 19, 1929), Zukofsky speaks of his article on Reznikoff (later revised into the crucial Objectivist essay "Sincerity and Objectification") being written for the *Menorah Journal.* Anticipating its rejection (and indeed, it was subsequently turned down), he writes: "If 'they' take it. Do I luf my peepul? The only good Jew I know is my father: a coincidence." He then asks if he can quote Pound's letter as an endorsement in order to convince the *Menorah* editors to take the Reznikoff piece. Later in the same letter Zukofsky calls himself an "antisemite" and exclaims "I hope you don't feel the Jews are roping you in" (*Pound/Zukofsky* 27–28).

The components of this scenario must be delicately unpacked. Zukofsky, who stands at the center of the Objectivist tradition, was then developing some of its most important principles by applying the lessons he had learned from Pound and Williams to the poetry of Charles Reznikoff. "Sincerity and Objectification: *With Special Reference to the Work of Charles Reznikoff*" was intended for the *Menorah Journal;* after the piece was turned down, it became part of Zukofsky's introductory "Program" in the February 1931 Objectivist issue of *Poetry.* (For at least one month, that magazine had an editor who could tell Yiddish from Chinese!) In some respects, the *Menorah Journal* would seem the appropriate venue for Zukofsky's essay. Not only did *Menorah* publish Reznikoff frequently, but according to Alan Wald, it promoted a "particular combination of anti-assimilationism and cosmopolitanism," a spirit of "cultural pluralism" (30) in which Zukofsky's writing would appear to share.

Yet Zukofsky and the *Menorah* editors did not see eye to eye. However much Reznikoff's poems and plays on Jewish subjects represented Zukofsky's Objectivist ideals, they appealed to *Menorah* more as literary embodiments of the Jewish or "Hebraic" humanism at the heart of the *Menorah* project. As Robert Alter reports, "what is most important for *Menorah* writers is to be able to talk about Judaism in the same terms, in the same refined accents, that the secular high priests of the polite English world used to discuss their culture and history" (52). This genteel version of American Jewish intellectual life, which regarded Judaism as a "spiritual aristocracy" (Alter 52), had little in common with either Zukofsky's avant-garde modernism or his working-class roots. No wonder that in a letter to Pound written the following month (January 12, 1930), he bitingly refers to the *Menorah* staff as "the Sanhedrin," anticipating by many years but also ironically reversing what Alter will call *Menorah's* function as "permanent critics of the Jewish Establishment, almost a kind of shadow rabbinate" (54). In the same letter, Zukofsky expresses regret over his desire for acceptance by their " 'thoughtful' heads" and notes that he had already criticized the *Menorah* group in "A"-4 (*Pound / Zukofsky* 32). He is probably referring to these mordantly senescent lines:

> Wherever we put our hats is our home
> Our aged heads are our homes,
> Eyes wink to their own phosphorescence,
> No feast lights of Venice or The Last Supper light
> Our beards' familiars; His
> Stars of Deuteronomy are with us,
> Always with us,
> We had a Speech, our children have
>   evolved a jargon.
>   ["A"-4, 12]

Here Zukofsky appropriates the elegiac falling rhythms of *The Cantos* to give voice to the aged, exilic Jewish consciousness. Separated from the aesthetic treasures of the Christian West, these old Jews cling instead to the beauties of the Torah. Their complaint would have been familiar to Zukofsky from an early age, for the terms "Speech" and "jargon" refer to the debate between advocates of Hebrew and Yiddish that had raged ever since the mid-nineteenth century, when Yiddish (often called "zhargon" and not only by its detractors) became the language of a secular Jewish literature. For these old men, Hebrew is *loshen kodesh,* the Holy Tongue, the only proper language of Jewish textuality. Its biblical grandeur and purity are meant solely for religious purposes, as opposed to the vernacular use to which Zionist settlers were putting it in Palestine. This was as much a modern aberration as secular literature in Yiddish: "If the speech has subsided into a jargon studded with alien expressions, as they [the old men] fear, then it no longer transmits the ancient traditions" (Ahearn 52). Zukofsky, of course, disagrees, which is why translated verses from Yehoash (famous for his Yiddish rendering of the Hebrew Bible) appear later in "A"-4.

Yet if the voice of the elders is also meant as a jab at the *Menorah* "Sanhedrin," then Zukofsky is setting up a sly analogy: the genteel Jewish humanism of *Menorah* is to Hebrew grandeur as Zukofsky's modernism is to lively, upstart Yiddish literature. Jewish culture cannot remain mired in tradition: just as Yehoash can "make it new"

through his Yiddish poetry and translations, so Zukofsky can challenge the high-minded Arnoldians of the Jewish-American intellectual elite. The Jewish difference in *Menorah*'s humanism may have been
intended to offer "the intellectual an invaluable critical perspective
on the Western world" (Alter 53), but for the young poet, this perspective was not critical enough: compared to the Poundian springs from
which Zukofsky was imbibing, the *Menorah* perspective probably
tasted stalely Victorian. As the old men say in "A"-4 (sounding more
like Eliot than Pound), "Even the Death has gone out of us—we are
void" (13).

But while it was a high-spirited gesture to defy one's Jewish hu-
manist elders, it was quite another matter to turn and embrace Pound's
cultural agenda instead. As John Tomas says of Zukofsky in his essay on
"Poem beginning 'The' ": "Like so many other Jews, he has adopted
the ways of the secular culture that surrounds him, but he has refused
to ignore the consequences of his choice. He has emphasized that his
rebellion is inevitably linked to his other revolts: political, artistic, and
cultural. Yet he admits his discomfort with his position. He has not
chosen to write in Yiddish, as had many of his contemporaries, and
his choice of English as a medium for verse means that he has committed himself to preserving and extending that poetic tradition, a
tradition that has been essentially hostile to Jews" (61). It remains
difficult to determine the extent to which Zukofsky ever reconciled
these contradictions, especially around the figure of Pound, who, for
the younger poet, always represented the tradition's cutting edge. We
know that in the early years of their friendship, their correspondence
is strewn with references to Pound as father, Zukofsky as son, sometimes in terms of literary parentage, sometimes as parody of God the
Father's relation to Christ (*Pound/Zukofsky* xix). These joking references point to what the friendship meant to both men, not only as
poets involved in a project of literary renewal, but as anti-Semite and
Jew, a dyad that cannot be neglected in any narrative of modernism.

In his encyclopedic study of Pound's fascism and anti-Semitism,
Robert Casillo argues that "Pound's constant attacks on the despised
Jews actually reveal his high and fearful estimation of their power and
that of their patriarchal god. However much Pound claims access to
the divine, Judaism and the Jews remain his most formidable enemy,
rival, and obstacle. In these terms, one might view Pound's anti-Semitism as in part a revolt against the punitive parental rival and superego,

a conflict between the religion of the forbidding father Jehovah and that of the messianic son" (287). Pound saw himself as a messianic son of the father-religion, an Oedipal antagonist whose attempt to restore a pagan worldview would ultimately lead to his sacrifice at the hands of the vengeful Jews. At the same time, Pound's anti-Semitism "marks a curious fascination and even emulation" (Casillo 298) of the Jews, a fascination related in turn to his repressed beliefs that he might be Jewish and that the Jews have rejected his messianic claim. The ritualistic violence of anti-Semitism that Pound eventually espouses is thus a form of psychological projection; by projecting "repressed wishes, instincts, and desires" onto an other, "the individual feels free to attack his projected and distorted self-image in other human beings" (Casillo 207). As Casillo makes clear, Pound's scapegoating of Jews "is most likely to appear where his need for definition is as great as his ambivalence, where his distinctions collapse and his terms hover in uncertainty. For the sacrificial crisis is signalled by a failure of distinctions, the inability to clarify cultural values and boundaries" (210).

The first part of Pound's correspondence with Zukofsky begins in the late twenties and extends through the thirties, a period during which Pound became increasingly isolated from American politics and culture, while his fascism and anti-Semitism grew more extreme. Given his obsession with father-religions and son-religions, the idea of a young Jewish-American disciple must have been immensely gratifying: here was at least one Jew who recognized his paternal authority and was willing to spread the Word. As Pound's "Deerly [sic] beloved son" (*Pound/Zukofsky* 101), Zukofsky was a convert, a self-declared "shagetz" for whom Judaism meant little compared to the new modernist faith. Yet at the same time, friendship with Zukofsky stirred Pound's repressed fascination with matters Jewish, and his letters to Zukofsky are filled with ambivalent emulation in the form of his mock-Yiddish discourse.

The psychology of Zukofsky's filial role in this relationship, while having none of the vicious implications of Pound's "fatherhood," is nearly as vexed. Zukofsky's guilt at abandoning his own father's orthodoxy must have been acute; hence the bitter irony when he declares in "Poem beginning 'The,'" "Assimilation is not hard, / And once the Faith's askew / I might as well look Shagetz just as much as Jew" (*Complete Short Poetry* 17). Although Zukofsky's first important work focuses on his mother, what the poet calls the "Residue of Oedipus-faced wrecks" (*Complete Short Poetry* 9) continues to cling to him throughout the thirties. Zukofsky's typical strategy in writing about his father—and his father's faith—involves what I have identified elsewhere as a strategic use of nostalgia for an unbroken cultural tradition, which in itself is the mark of rupture (Finkelstein 130–131). In Zukofsky's case, orthodox Judaism, the figure of the rabbi or sage, and especially the figure of Reb Pinchos Zukofsky, are cast in a gentle, melancholy light (see, for example, "A"-12, 150–159), despite Zukofsky's insistence, as we have seen in his relations with the *Menorah Journal,* that modern Jewish writing depends on breaking from tradition in order to maintain its vitality. This doubleness appears throughout "*A*" and partly accounts for Zukofsky's lifelong fascination with one of the earliest in a long line of rebellious Jewish intellectuals, Baruch Spinoza.

An especially poignant instance of Zukofsky's filial dilemma occurs in an exchange of letters with Pound in 1936. Inevitably drawn into a tangled debate with his mentor over politics and economics, Zukofsky was particularly concerned that Pound's association with Italian and American fascists would destroy his already waning reputation. He continually warned Pound that his attempts to determine the Jewish role in the development of capitalism would lead to accusations of anti-Semitism, from which Zukofsky always tried to shield him. As Zukofsky bluntly tells Pound in March 1936, "If you're dead set on completely losing whatever readers you still have in America, keep it up" (*Pound/Zukofsky* 177). Three months later, Pound actually enlisted the help of Pinchos Zukofsky in his campaign by having Louis ask his father to explicate the prohibitions against usury in Leviticus chapter 25. This is especially ironic, given Pound's peculiar obsession with the Hebrew word for usury, *neschek* (literally "the bite"), which related in turn to his anti-Semitic oral aggression, a behavior he projected upon the Jews themselves (Casillo 57–59). Zukofsky consulted his father, who offered a literal explanation of Leviticus 25:36–37, emphasizing that although in the Diaspora, the religious laws against usury are relaxed, "it is a crime to make any distinctions" (*Pound/Zukofsky* 183) between Jews and Gentiles in collecting interest. As Zukofsky writes to Pound about his father, "his natural & sweet conscience troubl[es] him wherever he runs across an explicit difference, or what may possibly be interpreted as an implicit difference, btwn the rights of yid & goy" (*Pound/Zukofsky* 182).

Later in the letter, however, Zukofsky revealingly lashes out at both fathers, setting his own faith in Marxism against Pinchos's Judaism and Pound's fascism: "Where he's Messianic he's as antiquated as you sunk in an absolute which has no useful relation to the present, or a bettering of the present. Strikes me in trying to isolate the root-idea of the reprehensibility of usury—which is what you seem to be doing?—you forget that even roots grow in a soil, & that soil changes with the times. You're both suffering from cart-before-the-horseness. Serves you right for not making any effort to understand Marx's criticism of Proudhon: 'the economic forms in which men produce, consume, exchange are *transitory* and *historical*'" (*Pound/Zukofsky* 183). In this passage, the gentle, outdated natural father and the fierce, modernist poetic father receive equally harsh treatment by the rebellious son. Zukofsky could hardly have expected Reb Pinchos to embrace Marxism after a lifetime of Talmud and strict Jewish observance. But he always posed Marxist economics against Pound's advocacy of Social Credit and insisted that Pound, given his literary genius and political concern, ought to recognize the failings of his right-wing stance.

By accusing both fathers of being "Messianic" and "antiquated" in failing to grasp the material historicity of economic (and hence social) forms, Zukofsky asserts his intellectual and cultural independence. Pinchos may long for the Messiah while Pound idolizes Mussolini, but they are equally obtuse *idealists;* they suffer from "cart-before-the-horseness" because they cannot grasp the basic Marxist principle that the material conditions of society produce systems of thought and belief. According to Mark Shechner, Marxism, for Jews of Zukofsky's generation, served "as a substitute Judaism, endowed with all the powers once possessed by halakhic or Orthodox Judaism for interpreting the world, dictating principles, forming character, and regulating conduct" (8). Caught between traditional Judaism and fascist modernism, Zukofsky negotiated his Oedipal crisis and his ordeal of civility through recourse to Marxism, a Jewish modernism that provided an answer to both Pinchos and Pound.

But what does such an answer sound like when shaped into poetry? Here is one example:

> Broken
> Mentors, unspoken wealth labor produces,
> Now loom as causes disposing our loci,

The foci of production: things reflected
As wills subjected; formed in the division
Of labor, labor takes on our imprecision—
Bought, induced by gold at no gain, though close eye
And gross sigh fixed upon gain have effected
Value erected on labor, prevision
Of surplus value, disparate decision.
                    ["A"-9, 106–107]

Or perhaps more simply,

Arrived mostly with bedding in a sheet
Samovar, with tall pitcher of pink glass,
With copper mugs, with a beard,
Without shaving mug—
To America's land of the pilgrim Jews?
To buy, after 20 years in a railroad flat,
A living room suite of varnished
Mahogany framed chairs and
Blue leather upholstery,
To be like everybody, with what
            is about us.
                    ["A"-8, 83]

Works Cited

Ahearn, Barry. Zukofsky's "A": An Introduction. Berkeley: U of California P, 1983.
Alter, Robert. "Epitaph for a Jewish Magazine." Commentary 39.5 (May 1965):
    51–55.
Althusser, Louis. Lenin and Philosophy and Other Essays. Trans. Ben Brewster. New
    York: Monthly Review P, 1971.
Casillo, Robert. The Genealogy of Demons: Anti-Semitism, Fascism, and the Myths
    of Ezra Pound. Evanston, IL: Northwestern UP, 1988.
Cuddihy, John Murray. The Ordeal of Civility: Freud, Marx, Levi-Strauss, and the
    Jewish Struggle with Modernity. New York: Basic Books, 1974.
Eagleton, Terry. Criticism and Ideology. London: Verso, 1976.
Finkelstein, Norman. The Ritual of New Creation: Jewish Tradition and Contemporary
    Literature. Albany: State U of New York P, 1992.
Gilman, Sander L. Difference and Pathology: Stereotypes of Sexuality, Race, and Mad-
    ness. Ithaca: Cornell UP, 1985.
———. Jewish Self-Hatred: Anti-Semitism and the Hidden Language of the Jews. Bal-
    timore: Johns Hopkins UP, 1986.

Harshav, Benjamin, and Barbara Harshav, eds. "Documents of Introspectivism." *American Yiddish Poetry: A Bilingual Anthology.* Berkeley: U of California P, 1986.

Schimmel, Harold. "Zuk: Yehoash David Rex." *Louis Zukofsky: Man and Poet.* Ed. Carroll F. Terrell. Orono, ME: National Poetry Foundation, 1979.

Shechner, Mark. *After the Revolution: Studies in the Contemporary Jewish American Imagination.* Bloomington, IN: Indiana UP, 1987.

Tomas, John. "Portrait of the Artist as a Young Jew: Zukofsky's 'Poem beginning "The"' in Context." *Sagetrieb* 9.1–2 (Spring–Fall 1990): 43–64.

Wald, Alan M. *The New York Intellectuals: The Rise and Decline of the Anti-Stalinist Left from the 1930s to the 1980s.* Chapel Hill: U of North Carolina P, 1987.

Zukofsky, Louis. *Pound/Zukofsky: Selected Letters of Ezra Pound and Louis Zukofsky.* Ed. Barry Ahearn. New York: New Directions, 1987.

4

Zukofsky, Marxism, and American Handicraft

BARRY AHEARN

I

During the early 1930s, Louis Zukofsky was aware that the United States was undergoing economic hard times. He indicated that awareness to Ezra Pound by detailing the ways in which the national crisis affected him personally. Thus, on 2 September 1932, "Zuk fambly (favver) down to last penny—shd. get job & do something for 'em. (Where, tho?)."[1] On 8 October 1932, "At present, personal effects is $3.00." By December 1932, Zukofsky saw the possibility for financial and artistic rescue in an organization called Writers Extant (later The Objectivists Press). "We the Writers Extant, W.E., W E, should therefore engineer for ourselves, & out of *our* resources, to clarify the general mess, to centralize the marketing of our products (and so to get ourselves published without obligation to a price system) and to support the Writers Extant as much as possible with *our* limited means." A few weeks later, on 8 January 1933, with Franklin Delano Roosevelt still two months away from inauguration, Zukofsky reported that "I shall probably be penniless in another week, and perhaps salary-less in Feb." Somehow Zukofsky managed to scrape through 1933. By 1934 things were looking up, thanks to the New Deal. He wrote to Pound on 12 April 1934, "Working on a C[ivil].W[orks].A[dministration]. job, now transferred to Dep't of Public Welfare, N.Y.C.—6 hours of continual insult to the intelligence." The continual insult persisted. On 14 November 1934, he reported he was laboring "4 days a week from 9 to 5:15 on an abominable job" and that "4 people I know [are] starving." But at least *he* was not starving, thanks to the federal funds that

Zukofsky received almost without interruption from January 1934 until April 1942.

The Federal Art Project was established in late 1935. Under its auspices work began on the *Index of American Design*. It was this project that absorbed much of Zukofsky's energy during the Great Depression; he was hired as part of the research staff. How Zukofsky got the job of investigating American crafts and design is not altogether clear. He may have used his connections to people working in the arts. As far back as the late twenties he had been acquainted with one of the most important contemporary designers in America, Russel Wright. (He wrote a letter in March 1928 to E. E. Cummings, introducing himself and mentioning that they had a mutual friend in Wright.) There is another possibility, though a less likely one. In a letter of 7 December 1937, Zukofsky mentioned "a comprehensive woman here, techincal [sic] supervisor of the project (Index of Am. Design, Fed. Art.) & expert textile designer one Ruth Reeves who says she knows you, & who has read 'A'-8 with intelligent liveliness" (*Pound/Zukofsky* 193). Though Reeves may have helped Zukofsky get his job, it seems more likely from Zukofsky's account that he made her acquaintance only after he joined the research staff of the *Index of American Design*.

Although the circumstances that led to his hiring remain murky, it is nevertheless quite clear that Zukofsky resented having his talents wasted, or at least not being used as he thought they should have been. At the best of times Zukofsky considered his day job a necessary inconvenience. As he wrote to Pound on 18 January 1936, "It's tough getting up in the morning knowing what one shd. do about the rest of "A"-8 & the rest etc. etc., & having to go off immediately to the W.P.A. [Works Progress Administration] job till 6, & then [Communist] party shits etc." As this letter makes clear, Zukofsky considered that his efforts for the WPA prevented him from making faster progress with "A"-8. Furthermore, he felt he deserved to be one of the 6,000 or more writers drawing a wage from the Federal Writers' Project.[2] If Kenneth Rexroth and Harry Roskolenkier merited the opportunity to write and get paid for it, why not he? After all, Zukofsky had edited the "Objectivists" number of *Poetry*, in which Rexroth and Roskolenkier had been merely published. He wrote to Pound on 8 December 1936, "I'm on the Fed. Art Project getting up information for 'em on old gardens. Now why I ain't on a writer's project is too long a political story to go into."

Yet this wholeheartedly negative opinion of his job changed sometime during the writing of "A"-8. The job itself became part of the composition of this movement. On pages 96–97 the poem recounts a visit made in November 1936 by "the researchist in old gardens" (Zukofsky himself) to a Mr. Thomas Hicks, General Blacksmith and Toolmaker in the Bronx. The poem also records Zukofsky's salary at the time, down to the last penny: $23.86. Zukofsky earns his wages by interviewing Hicks.

> The gas station on Hicks' corner
> Had some time ago fumed out his garden.
> But could he pencil a sketch of it,
> Or draw a plan
> ["A"-8, 97]

Other bits and pieces of Zukofsky's research on American crafts dot "A"-8.

> This linen table napkin—needlework in blue
> Made in America—
> Sharecropper's or marble striker's grandmother's table napkin
> Is as good to us as Brueghel's *Harvesters*
> ["A"-8, 66]

Zukofsky borrows from the correspondence of Marx and Engels to show Marx's use of craftwork:

> It would be entirely possible to show from the development of the clock
> How entirely different the relation between theoretical learning
> And practice was in the handicraft,
> From what it is in large-scale industry.
> ["A"-8, 74]

As late as "A"-12 (256–257), Zukofsky's interest in American handicrafts appears in the list of projected works he never got to write. A short story to be called *The Hounds,* about "an early iron master," has its origin in notes on "Ironworkers and Ironmasters" made by Zukofsky on 27 August 1938 for the *Index of American Design:* "The names are isolated, as isolated as the lives of the early ironmasters seem to have been, according to 'The Legend of the Hounds,' a verse narrative by George Boker of the 18th century: the owner of Colebrook Furnace, Pa., returns from a fox hunt, enraged by the falseness of his hounds, and with whip in hand, drives the whole pack of them into the blazing tunnelhead." Another projected work, *About Some Americans,* would have considered—among others—J. K. Ingalls, author of *Work and Wealth* (1878) and *Social Wealth* (1885). This forgotten reformer came to Zukofsky's attention when he was working on the history of American quilts. In research notes dated 14 March 1940, for the projected radio broadcast on "Friendship Quilts," Zukofsky observes that a presentation quilt had been made for Ingalls by the women of his congregation in 1842, when he was a Unitarian lay preacher. Then Zukofsky's notes drop the ostensible subject of the broadcast—quilts—and go on at length about Ingalls's publications on economic reform. These research notes from 1940 contain the same Ingalls quotation used in "A"-12 in 1950.

Zukofsky saw that his work for the *Index of American Design* could contribute to his poem's concern with the labor process and with beauty, for he was studying objects that combined elements of both. Aesthetic satisfaction had been a component in their manufacture, but the other dimension, the labor process, was also important. In the script for a broadcast on "A Pair of New York Water Pitchers," Zukofsky goes into great length about indenture, noting along the way that "[i]ndenture was really a means by which the growing mercantilism of the 17th and 18th Centuries employed government sanction to transfer labor to undeveloped colonies." As the quotation shows, Zukofsky's analysis of the labor process during the thirties proceeded along Marxist lines. This comes as no surprise to anyone who has read the first half of "A"-9.

But what kind of a Marxist was Zukofsky? As Burton Hatlen says in his essay "Art and/as Labor," there has been some disagreement about the extent to which these portions of "*A*" are Marxist. He himself concludes that "Zukofsky finds a way of reconciling art and politics within an explicitly Marxist conception of labor" (Hatlen 206). I would endorse this view, with the qualification that there are varieties of Marxism and that Zukofsky's bears further examination. His work on the Index and on "A"-8 and other poems during the thirties reveals a decidedly idiosyncratic Marxism.

II

There are some important comments about Marx in Zukofsky's letters to Pound. On 11 May 1935, for example, he took issue with

Pound over the nature of commodities. "When I see you writing 'Labor is not a commodity' I think I understand your good intentions, but I also know you're wrong because I've thought about certain things, have been in contact with 'em (via my fambly and myself etc.) & read a coupla' things (How can you say you read Marx on the working day etc. & still continue as you do is beyond me)—Labor is not a commodity *to whom?*"[3] What Zukofsky defends here—the proposition that labor is a commodity—is enunciated by Marx in the portion of *Capital* to which Zukofsky refers: "The Working Day." In this, the eighth chapter of *Capital,* Marx begins, "We set out from the supposition that labour power is bought and sold at its value. This value, like that of any other commodity, is determined by the labour time necessary for its production" (Marx 230). A few pages later, Marx presents an imaginary monologue in which the typical worker addresses the typical capitalist. Here also, the worker considers the labor power he has sold to the capitalist to be a commodity (Marx 233). Zukofsky's letter to Pound emphasizes both the abstract truth he finds in Marx's treatment of labor as a commodity and the immediate and practical truth that he and his family have discovered in the American marketplace. Curiously, Zukofsky did not elaborate on the expenditure of his or his family's labor power in the marketplace. He did, however, emphasize the great pains he was taking with his art, which he regarded as his truly important labor.

In a letter of 10 June 1936, Zukofsky noted Marx's dedication to difficult, unrewarding, but necessary work. "If you refuse to read painstaking letters of Marx to Engels on money—very detailed, factual, scientific, expert analyses—usually ending with 'shit' (I take it because old Marx was not sicklied over with 'pale & viscous shimmer of spirituality,' & didn't enjoy grinding his arse on a bench over finance, economics etc.—very much yr. 'spiritual' attitude by the way—but did it for the sake of the numbskulls who needed it, & against the rot that had to be done away with)."[4] This portrait foregrounds Marx as a laborer, intent on producing analysis that, however difficult and joyless for the laborer himself, is necessary to educate others. Zukofsky thought of himself and his literary labor in the thirties in much the same way. "If I get anywhere, or am to be any influence in C. P. [Communist Party] or anywhere, I can as I see it now do it only by having enough output, written production, that will get me across as a 'figure' in the first place" (10 June 1936). Reading Zukofsky's published and unpublished letters to Pound suggests that the only communists with whom Zukofsky felt compatible were the mighty dead, especially Marx.[5]

While Zukofsky was writing poetry that he considered truly Marxist, he was submitting it to Pound for judgment. On 18 January 1936, Zukofsky noted that he had begun work on "A"-8. He had even sent Pound a sample: "You realize, of course, that the 4 pages I sent is only the beginning of A-8." In the same letter he seemingly threw in his lot with contemporary followers of Marx. "It's very simple[,] any intelligence worth anything can see that communism is the only way out—whatever he thinks of the present control of the Party." It was unwise of Zukofsky to refer to the leadership of the American Communist Party. Pound thereby assumed that Zukofsky had the ear of the Party's bigwigs, and Zukofsky had to disabuse him of this notion several times. Far from being part of the Party's inner circle, he had considerable difficulty getting along with the literary section. A letter of 12 March 1936 mentions the "nitwits on New Masses." On 10 June 1936, he expressed to Pound his disgust with communists of his acquaintance. "You want to present 'economics' to literary apes (like Mike G[old].) etc. I have tried to work with these apes for over a year now at formidable cost of time, energy etc., & I am not going to continue till my status etc. makes it more favorable. There is no use presenting anything to apes who remain apes & probably *will remain* apes." Later in the letter, Zukofsky characterized the "literary apes" as people who had joined the Party "as a last refuge in a failing order," not because they were genuinely revolutionary workers or revolutionary political leaders. Zukofsky found that the audience for his own poetry was not in the Communist Party, but in another poetic worker, Ezra Pound. And even he seemed mostly unreceptive. As Zukofsky wrote on 8 December 1936, "I will send the rest of "A"-8 when ready. But what good will that do. You haven't even acknowledged receiving the last of it—pp. 5 & 6, sent with a special letter explaining the form etc. Now it happens that you are one of only 4 people who cd. tell me—at least *maybe* tell me—something about it, if you choose to." Zukofsky's dilemma was that his preoccupation with the proper poetic form for his poetry in the latter half of the thirties fell flat with the communist literati. As far as most of them were concerned, the problem of artistic form had been mostly solved. It could be found in such poems as Maxwell Bodenheim's "To a Revolutionary Girl," which appeared in *New Masses* on 3 April 1934. An extract shows that the form presented no difficulty for its readers:

> You are a girl,
> A revolutionist, a worker
> Sworn to give the last, undaunted jerk
> Of your body and every atom
> Of your mind and heart
> To every other worker
> In the slow, hard fight
> That leads to barricade, to victory
> Against the ruling swine.

There was no room in *New Masses* for Zukofsky's most important poems of the same year, " 'Mantis' " and " *'Mantis,' An Interpretation.*" They would have been judged too complex for the understanding of the average working man. But *Capital* also was considered rather beyond the comprehension of the typical wage slave. Periodicals such as the *Daily Worker* and *New Masses* were in the business of popularizing the thinking of Marx, Engels, and Lenin. Why couldn't Zukofsky write like Bodenheim?

Perhaps the answer lies in Zukofsky's determination to remain true to the conception he had of himself. Zukofsky did not consider himself typical of the urban proletariat. Even in " *'Mantis,' An Interpretation,*" where he sympathizes with the plight of the oppressed poor, the poem makes it clear that its author is an exceptional individual. To see Zukofsky as a Marxist in the thirties is quite correct, with the qualification that his use of Marxism has little to do with the rigid doctrinal control and collective action prescribed by the Party.

Indeed, much of " *'Mantis,' An Interpretation*" opposes collectivism and Party discipline. The poem posits a materialism, but the *matter* of fundamental importance is the body of the poet. (Perhaps no poet since Byron has so seriously considered the body a source of wisdom.) " 'Mantis' " takes the form of a sestina because that shape appropriately expresses Zukofsky's inner physical dynamic. Zukofsky makes this explicit in " *'Mantis,' An Interpretation.*"

> The sestina, then, the repeated end words
> Of the lines' winding around themselves,
> Since continuous in the Head, whatever has been read,

whatever is heard,
    whatever is seen
Perhaps goes back cropping up again with
Inevitable recurrence again in the blood
Where the spaces of verse are not visual
But a movement,
With vision in the lines merely a movement.
    [*Complete Short Poetry* 69]

Zukofsky invented what we might call a corporeal Marxism.[6] It had the advantage of uniting him with the oppressed, since all are adversely and physically affected by economic conditions. In this way, Zukofsky can maintain that the "growing oppression of the poor" is "the situation most pertinent to us" (*Complete Short Poetry* 69). Yet other experiences, such as one's reading, also enter the body. And what if the body in question is that of a highly gifted poet? Doesn't that create a wide gulf between one's self and those not so gifted? Zukofsky's Marxism leaves the development of sophisticated critiques of capitalism, or of the individual's place in a capitalist society, to a few highly intelligent writers and political activists—himself among them. Only the bodies of these few are peculiarly suited to the writing of poetry or other complex forms of expression.

So corporeal Marxism is double-edged. It shows that Zukofsky has experiences comparable to those suffered by the masses of the downtrodden. ("A"-8 offers some autobiographical glimpses of early Lower East Side difficulties.) From these experiences—and from other experiences not necessarily available to everyone—he builds his poems. All the while he knows that he is one of the elite who can truly write poetry in his time. Other tasks would merely divert his genius.

III

Although Zukofsky prefers to read American handicrafts as relics of labor processes best understood according to Marxist economic analysis, there is a persistent tension between these handicrafts and conventional Marxist analysis. This tension, I believe, contributed to Zukofsky's adaptation of conventional Marxism. The most salient reason why the *Index* work led him to a different, highly idiosyncratic Marxism has to do with the objects he was sent to study. The items Zukofsky writes about in his notes for the *Index of American Design* and in his radio broadcast scripts are not products of alienated labor. When they speak they reflect the lives and loving care of the individuals who made them. As Zukofsky observes in his account "American Kitchenware," these humble objects "recall a time when men were likely to be found working on something at home, and for their homes, side by side with their wives."

In "A"-8, when Zukofsky visits Mr. Hicks, the first glimpse of his house is this:

> Darkness
> But for the flame of the belly-stove.
> And you did not see Russia in the green-blue light of the coal,
> Could faster see Lady Greensleeves
> ["A"-8, 96]

The visit to the world of Hicks, in other words, is a visit not to the future but to the past—a feudal, preindustrial past. Hicks and the values he represents do not seem able to survive in the Industrial Age. As the poem observes: "The gas station on Hicks' corner / Had some time ago fumed out his garden" ("A"-8, 97). John D. Rockefeller and his oil wells, and Henry Ford and his Model T's, have destroyed what Hicks represents.

It was precisely the passing of American handicrafts that gave them new value toward the end of the nineteenth century. They became symbols for American ideals that were supposedly endangered in the machine age: self-reliance, industriousness, and pride in one's work. Such sprawling museum sites as the Rockefeller-financed Colonial Williamsburg, Henry Ford's Greenfield Village, Electra Havemeyer Webb's Shelburne Museum, or even more modest reconstructions such as Henry Flynt's Historic Deerfield, are not just windows into the past. They are emblematic of these American ideals, with the added subtext that these ideals are best exemplified not only in a preindustrial setting but also in a setting that predates immigration from non-Anglo-Saxon countries. These reconstructed colonial and early federal sites are tantamount to a retroactive deportation. Safely free from alien contamination, they attempt to recover a past populated by decent, hard-working Americans of British descent (or, at a pinch, German).

American crafts and design can be interpreted in two markedly different ways: one treats them as totems of a pure-blooded American past, the other uses them to further cultural democracy. Zukofsky takes the latter course. As far as he is concerned, these artifacts illuminate the social and economic life of the common people. It is to the common people, not to the collector, that they should speak. "For old things are lost, destroyed, stored away in attics and cellars, sold,—accumulate the dust of antique shops and museum cases. Only an enterprise like 'The Index of American Design' can bring them back to the people" (Radio Broadcast Script, "The Henry Clay Figurehead"). Yet even as he points to the popular significance of artifacts, Zukofsky also emphasizes the artist's role. Duncan Phyfe, for example, puts into his furniture "curves so slight as to escape detection, not geometrical curves, but free hand lines based on the geometrical" (Radio Broadcast Script, "Duncan Phyfe").

The Marxism that Zukofsky invokes would allow artists greater freedom of expression because artists would have more control over the production of their works. Zukofsky endorses a future that he thought—at least in the thirties—inevitable. As Alfred Kazin recalls, he and other young New Yorkers "thought of Socialism simply as a moral idea, an invocation of History in all its righteous sweep" (Kazin 6). Although Zukofsky found American communism as it existed quite deficient, he believed it would change. He told Pound that even though "there are cliques political, poetical, etc. etc. . . . they will eventually be kicked out because the communist idea of action is the right one & won't suffer 'em" (18 January 1936). Zukofsky looked forward to the day when he and other writers could form writers' cooperatives under communism. This vision of the future seems to be all that Zukofsky had to say about it. In fact, he seems to have given little consideration to the nature of a postcapitalist society. There was not much point in his doing so. Whatever the shape of the future state, he would still be laboring on his art.

When considering the depth of Zukofsky's commitment to a communist future, it is worth noting that the common American laborer is held rather at arm's length in "A". It is as if Zukofsky felt that fundamentally he had little in common with industrial laborers. The most frequent symbol for American labor in the poem is the miner, from "A"-1's "The Pennsylvania miners are again on the lockout" ("A"-1, 3) to the Pennsylvania miners of "A"-8 ("A"-8, 83–86). But did Zukofsky ever actually meet a miner, much less visit a coalfield? Zukofsky's inside information about Pennsylvania miners came from Robert Evans, who, as a contemporary friend of Zukofsky's recalls, was not one of the proletariat, but "the retired Chief Engineer of the Lehigh Valley Coal Company."[7] It is hardly ever the case that the early movements of "*A*" address the problems of laborers in New York city. Where, for example, are vignettes comparable to those we find in the poems of Charles Reznikoff, such as "Depression" in *Separate Way* (1936)? It is odd that Zukofsky, who writes to Pound about the manifold difficulties he and his family and acquaintances are having in the struggle to stay alive, prefers to load "A"-8 with details from newspaper accounts of the Depression. So far as "*A*" is concerned, the Depression seems to be happening to everyone else.

The attraction Zukofsky finds in American handicrafts and design that predate industrial manufacture is the attraction of an artist who sees his own work as comparable to theirs. The same values he finds in their craft exist in his. "*A*" was self-consciously conceived as a poem that would be a record of its time, that would, as he says of nineteenth-century hand-made lanterns, "still have the virtue of being able to light up social currents of a past" (Radio Broadcast Script, " 'Wide Awake' Lantern and Eagle"). Or as he says of Duncan Phyfe, "[his] furniture reflects the virtues of his life and age." "*A*" itself, though it exists in an age when mass production techniques have apparently eliminated handicrafts, is an American handicraft.

Having gone out on this interpretive limb, however, let me retreat a little. Hatlen makes a serious charge against Zukofsky when he observes that "A"-8 is a poem "that ostentatiously displays its indifference to the 'common reader' and that makes no attempt to address on 'their' level those workers that "A"-8 celebrates as the agents of history" (Hatlen 233). If this is the case, then "A"-8 is markedly different from American handicrafts. Why? Because Zukofsky himself notes that these handicrafts had to please the consumer. Speaking of Duncan Phyfe, Zukofsky recognized that "like all successful craftsmen, he must have held his thumb at the pulse of public taste." Hatlen argues that public taste was the farthest thing from Zukofsky's mind: therefore, Zukofsky cannot be called a successful craftsman in the tradition of Phyfe or other, anonymous, craftsmen.

There are some indications, however, that Zukofsky did not think of "A"-8 as wholly indifferent to the common reader. He did select two portions of it for publication in *New Masses*. Whatever the mo-

mentary difficulties of the movement, there are portions not requiring critical nutcrackers and tweezers. These portions could justifiably
be designated the "popular" aspects of "*A*". When Zukofsky had the
chance to reach his largest audience on record, a portion of "*A*"-8 was
the piece he selected. As he wrote to Pound on 17 June 1937, "You
should ha' been somewhere in 'Murka on Sun. June 6, at 1 P.M. and
heard Sonny read a chunk of 'A'-8 ("the labour process"—down thru
"Socony will not always sign off on this air") over WOR, nation-wide
network." Less than a month later he proudly reported to Pound, "Got
a fan letter today, all the way from California re my 'majestic' last line
'Socony will not always sign off on this air' heard over Mutual Broad-
casting System some weeks ago." Many portions of "*A*"-8 were beyond the comprehension of the average working man, but Zukofsky
thought other parts would be plain enough to intelligent listeners.

To a great degree, then, Zukofsky saw that his own work exemplified the virtues of American handicrafts. To the extent that he did
so, "*A*" reveals itself as a poem not quite at home in an industrial era,
just as Zukofsky was not comfortable when handling machines,
whether cameras, typewriters, or automobiles. The future of "*A*", with
its withdrawal from Marxist formulas after 1940 and its return to the
Zukofsky family as the locus of concern, seems forecast in the section
of his planned broadcast on Duncan Phyfe where he speaks of Phyfe
in retirement: "He retired from business in 1846 . . . but continued to
make presentation pieces for his family, always at the bench in his own
shop, in the backyard of his home, for the remainder of his life."

Notes

1. Unless otherwise indicated, all quotations from the letters and other papers
of Louis Zukofsky are from the Louis Zukofsky collection of the Harry Ransom
Humanities Research Center of the University of Texas at Austin. Copyright
Paul Zukofsky. Zukofsky material may not be quoted from this article by third
parties without express permission by the copyright holder.

2. The definitive study of the Federal Writers' Project is Jerre Mangione's
The Dream and the Deal: The Federal Writers' Project, 1935–1943. Mangione devotes
an entire chapter ("Manhattan Hotbed") to the New York City section of the
project. Its director at the time that Zukofsky wrote to Pound was Orrick Johns.
Among the authors rescued from starvation by the New York section were Maxwell Bodenheim, Edward Dahlberg, Ralph Ellison, Kenneth Fearing, David Ig-
natow, Norman MacLeod, and Joseph Vogel. Mangione's account of the tumul-

tuous atmosphere in the office of the New York City Writers' Project suggests that Zukofsky was better off working for the Arts Project.

3. Zukofsky's contention that labor was a commodity directly opposed Pound's belief that a commodity had to be something material. For Pound, labor could only *change* value. Furthermore, as Pound indicated in his memorial tribute to A. R. Orage, "In the Wounds," "[m]ere *work* is no longer the root of power. That is to say, it is *not* the work of the living men actually employed, or concerned in doing a given job, that contributes most to its performance" (*Selected Prose* 444). Pound noted that modern laborers could do so much more than their ancestors because of technical knowledge accumulated over the ages. It was this "increment of association" that was the basis for modern labor power. This increment was universally available and therefore could not be restricted, embargoed, or hoarded in the way that material goods (commodities) could be.

4. Zukofsky emphasized Marx's skill at handling the physical in a letter to Pound on 30 June 1936. "Marx who knew sumpn about *physical & mathematical* (calculus etc.) (not *metaphysical* damn yr. prejudices) systems of *measurement,* the need for 'em if you're gonna have any science, order, statistical presentation of facts—did the job, if you will only *read.*" Furthermore, Zukofsky adds, "I even suspect he anticipated some of yr. linguistic awareness in explaining the concrete situations, facts, etc. out of which words grow."

5. In a letter of 9 May 1936, Zukofsky listed six books he thought it important for Pound to read. He then said, "If you want to *find* out about Communism, please read in the order listed—in fak, read *only* the first 4 books." The four books Zukofsky thought essential to an understanding were the *Communist Manifesto,* Marx's *Value, Price and Profit,* and Lenin's *Imperialism* and *Teachings of Marx.*

6. Zukofsky's relations to the Communist Party parallel those of Waldo Frank. He, too, thought communism was destined to change the world for the better. He, too, found himself at odds with the methodologies of the Party. He, too, created his own brand of Marxism. "I could not join the Party; but I accepted its professed fundamental aim, the creating of free persons; even if its doctrines of the contingent nature of man and necessity of monolithic industry, and its practice, barred free persons and suppressed them. I invented the term *integral Communism* and first used it in 1931 in my *America Hispana*" (Frank 185). Frank persuaded no one else to adopt integral Communism.

7. Jerry Reisman, letter of 28 May 1993 to the author.

Works Cited

Frank, Waldo. *Memoirs of Waldo Frank.* Ed. Alan Trachtenberg. Amherst, MA: U of Massachusetts P, 1973.

Hatlen, Burton. "Art and/as Labor: Some Dialectical Patterns in A-1 through A-10." *Contemporary Literature* 25.2 (Summer 1984): 205–234.

Kazin, Alfred. *Starting Out in the Thirties.* New York: Vintage, 1980.

Mangione, Jerre. *The Dream and the Deal: The Federal Writers' Project, 1935–1943*. Boston: Little, Brown, 1972.

Marx, Karl. *Capital*. Trans. Eden Paul and Cedar Paul. 1930. London: Dent, 1974.

Pound, Ezra. *Selected Prose, 1909–1965*. Ed. William Cookson. New York: New Directions, 1973.

Zukofsky, Louis. *Pound/Zukofsky: Selected Letters of Ezra Pound and Louis Zukofsky*. Ed. Barry Ahearn. New York: New Directions, 1987.

5

Poetry and the Age
Pound, Zukofsky, and the Labor Theory of Value

ALEC MARSH

> But in England now, in the age of Gosse as in the age of Gosson
> we are asked if the arts are moral. We are asked to define the re-
> lation of the arts to economics, we are asked what position the
> arts hold in the ideal republic. And it is obviously the opinion of
> many people less objectionable than the Sidney Webbs that the
> arts had better not exist at all.
> —Ezra Pound, "The Serious Artist" (*Literary Essays* 41)

WHAT IS THE STATUS OF the poet in the age of corporate capitalism?
In a period saturated by the discourse of political economy and the
authority of economists, the fate of the "serious artist" is to be toler-
ated as, at best, an investment opportunity.[1] Because of the elevation
of economic discourse to the status of science in our century, poets,
like other artists and intellectuals, have been asked to justify themselves in economic terms. For society at large, there seems to be no
other way of determining their usefulness; that is to say, economic
justifications carry with them a hidden morality, and that morality, in
turn, hides within an aesthetic.

For Louis Zukofsky and others whose political antennae were sensitive, the discourse of economics, intensified by the moral polemic
of the Left and its puritanical ideology of use, sacrifice, and struggle,
became the basis for a political program. In the United States, left-
wing publications like *New Masses* exercised a powerful influence on
coming poets and set the terms for serious literary discussion throughout the thirties. An economic morality of modernism in poetry, evi-

dent in its jagged edges, severe diction, impatience with formal restraint, and a contempt for "rhetoric," can be read as the manifestation of a new kind of economic awareness. By the 1930s the usefulness of the artist had become a burning question in the United States as the Great Depression brought home the savage power of the economic. One result was that economic theory—and especially that article of faith behind all theorizing about industrial society, the labor theory of value—began to surface explicitly and consistently in American poetry.

The argument I am going to try to make here proposes that the irruption of frankly economic discourse into the poetry of Louis Zukofsky in the 1930s continues, in Marxist terms, that defense of poetry for which Pound had seen the need even before the First World War. This defense, like Pound's, is based on an appeal to the discourse of political economy—specifically economics proper—*not,* primarily, on an appeal to literature or culture. To argue that Pound and Zukofsky defend poetry in economic terms is both to particularize what Michael Davidson noticed when he observed "the fatal pact between modernist objectivism and materialism" (521) and to place his claim in context. It was not just Objectivism but poetry itself that seemed to require a material foundation.

Any economic defense of poetry is necessarily materialistic; it implies that poetry is a form of labor that is primarily an expression, or symptom, of concrete historical conditions. When historical conditions moved from the intolerable to the catastrophic—as they did at the beginning of the Second World War—this pact with history would indeed prove "fatal" to the economic defense of poetry; instead of conferring authority upon poetry, a materialistic theory of poetry sharply limited poetry's moral power—one reason why, in the postwar poetry of both Pound and Zukofsky, ethical systems have pride of place and economics is relegated to the wings. After the war we see an attempt by Pound to transcend the economic, to make people see that "beyond civic order" must be "l'AMOR" (*Cantos* 648); he devotes great energy in this period to translating Confucius. Meanwhile Zukofsky, turning away from his reliance on Marx, completes the first half of "A"-9, which he had suspended in 1940, by invoking the figure of Spinoza and moralizing that "[a] wise man pledging piety unguarded / Lives good not error" ("A"-9, 110): there is no more talk of Marx's labor theory of value but instead, as in Pound's postwar poems, an appeal to ethical love.

But the postwar turn in these poets' work cannot be appreciated unless their fierce faith in their different economic poetics is understood. Any economic defense of poetry in the age of corporate capitalism accepts the idea that production—meaning both the mass production of commodities and the new social relations of production, distribution, and consumption that must accompany this process—has become the key conception through which Western civilization in the twentieth century defines itself. The economic argument between Pound and Zukofsky that culminates in Zukofsky's translation, in "A"-9, of Pound's version of Cavalcanti's "Donna mi prega" into Marxian language, can be read as part of an argument between the poets over the proper place of poiesis and production in a modern industrial economy.

For Pound as well as Zukofsky during the 1930s, the power of political economic discourse is (sometimes grudgingly, always ambivalently) conceded. Both poets see it as their duty to civilize society and to save it from the contradictions of capitalism. Because he bases his critique of capitalism on natural processes, Pound sees the industrialized world as trapped by "unnatural" Usura, speaking the perverse and artificial language of finance, evidenced in a corrupt monetary system. Pound's critique is, in fact, steeped in the traditions of American populism. For Zukofsky, like other Marxists, the "money question" is part of the larger, purely social illness he ascribes to capitalism, an illness to be cured by social revolution—nature has nothing to do with it. In each poet, however, we find an explicit message forming a "metermaking argument" in the poems themselves. The highly politicized economic consciousness characteristic of modern life has made a distinct mark that takes the form of a new kind of self-consciousness within their poems. This new sort of poetry is capable—or so the poets hope—of finding immediate use in the social struggle for economic justice. As a result they write poems that are explicitly economic and political, accepting the discourse of political economy with the same solemnity once reserved for that of literature. In Pound and Zukofsky's poetry—especially in the thirties—in "A"-8 and -9, as in many Cantos, good poetry is sound economics and good economics should be sound poetry. Take, for example, Zukofsky's allusion to Marx at the beginning of "Song 27" ("Song—3/4 time [*pleasantly drunk*]") of *29 Songs* (1934):

Right out
    of
        Das Kapital

    vol.I
        chap. 3
            2.
                A
                [*Complete Short Poetry* 58]

This allusion refers the reader to the section of *Capital* entitled "The Metamorphosis of Commodities" (*Capital* 198). Zukofsky's purpose—he then goes on to quote a confection of passages—is to show that Marx is reminding us that the economy is by its nature a poetic business and, therefore, that Marx's allusion to Ovid (and thus Zukofsky's reference to Marx) is both good economics and perfectly poetic. Just as Marx imagines the circulation of commodities sweating "money from every pore" (*Capital* 208, *Complete Short Poetry* 61), so Zukofsky implies that poetry is "sweated" from texts and thus that surplus value (profit) is akin to meaning because, like money, it is derived from labor—here the labor necessary to chase down allusions, to find a copy of *Capital,* look up the citation and ponder Marx's words as one does Zukofsky's. The difference between extracting surplus value and making the poem mean may be that meanings do not exploit anybody—instead, we have an unalienated "song." Still, the poetic process Zukofsky wants us to undertake is, one could say, the equivalent of a revolutionary transformation of the capitalist system of commodity circulation. Zukofsky has temporarily achieved a circulation of texts (which are in one sense commodities) through the honest use of the reader's labor without exploitation.

This method—a sort of poetic labor theory of value—is how a Marxist might argue that the meanings in *The Cantos* of Ezra Pound are produced. In 1934, the same year as Zukofsky's "Song 27," Pound wrote C. H. Douglas's "A + B Theorem," the heart of Douglasite economics, into Canto 38—which is otherwise devoted to an exposé of what we now call the "military-industrial complex." Like Zukofsky's, Pound's purpose is not lyrical, or "poetic" in the usual sense. As word music the passage appears to be deliberately made ineffective, as it consists of Douglas's prose chopped into verse form. It begins:

> A factory
> has also another aspect, which we call the financial aspect
> It gives people the power to buy (wages, dividends
> which are power to buy) but it is also the cause of prices
> or values, financial, I mean financial values.
>   [*Cantos* 190]

The reader is perfectly right—indeed compelled—to ask, "Yes, but is this poetry?" Pound, who had once advised neophytes not to "imagine that a thing will 'go' in verse just because it's too dull to be prose" ("A Retrospect," 1918, *Literary Essays* 6) might refer us to a statement he made about Provençal song in another early essay: "It is my personal belief that the true economy [in composing] lies in making the tune first" and then adding the words (*Selected Prose* 37). Here, Pound clearly means economy to refer to a savings of imaginative labor, but when we juxtapose this statement with the later, explicitly "economic" passage of poetry above, we see more. Pound now believes that the economy (in the large sense) calls the tune underlying and giving form to modern life. In this sense, the passage from Canto 38 is deeply poetic because it is the notation of the economic score being played in industrial society circa 1930. The difference for the poet in composing to the economy as opposed to Provençal song is that now the poet must correctly transcribe a tune *already* being played. Pound's attempt to fit Douglas's words to the industrial song being played so badly out of tune in the Great Depression, his attempt, in effect, to play the conductor of the modern industrial orchestra, is an attempt to be a modern Orpheus. Unfortunately, Pound must fail, because the poem is never identical to the history it sings and because the poet himself (unlike Orpheus) is in history, not insulated from it by myth, so he cannot hear the whole song.

One purpose behind the poems quoted above is a defense of poesy, an argument for the social value of poetry. Without the explicit invocations from the discourse of economics, the poets' ruminations on the state of society run the risk of committing them to anachronistic political economy, one which denies the importance of social labor by expressing—as the romantics had—the efforts of the individual. For, economically speaking, poiesis is an artisanal mode of production, and the poet is figured as a "craftsman," as in Eliot's dedication to Pound in *The Waste Land:* "il miglior fabbro." Such a traditional defense of poetry threatens to become an attack on modern life, because it suggests that modernity itself is the worship of the false god of mass commodity production. In the 1930s, Zukofsky, who had been deeply involved in writing about American artisans and artisanal modes of production in the entries for the *Index of American Design* he had been preparing for the Works Progress Administration, attempted to reach beyond that craftsman aesthetic, revising his modernist poem *"A"* into a form of social labor by invoking specifically Marxist terms. His poem could then move beyond the "poem including history" that was Pound's model for the epic (a model to which *"A"* had hitherto been more or less adhering) to become more like *The Communist Manifesto,* a work with both historical and visionary dimensions. By invoking social labor as the means of poetic production, as he does in the opening of "A"-8 where "labor" is invoked "as creator" ("A"-8, 43), Zukofsky hoped he was launching his poem into a Marxist future that he believed to be inevitable.

Pound sustained a somewhat different vision, not, I believe, because he was "elitist," as many have argued, and certainly not because he was a fascist but because he was, in the economic discourse of the 1930s, reactionary. A Jeffersonian in political economy, Pound was committed to eighteenth-century agrarian and mercantilist approaches to the problem of production and labor, while his Douglasite money radicalism encouraged him to solve the problems of modern mass production—the problems, that is, of overproduction and underemployment that *were* the Great Depression—through reforms to the money system that seemed to be impeding the flow of goods to those who needed them.

Despite these clear differences in economic doctrine, Pound's openly "economic" poems, like Zukofsky's, self-consciously enact the circulation of texts and therefore implicate reader and poet in a network of transactions that mime the circulation of commodities. The frankly economic subject matter engaged by both poets indicates their renewed concern with the action of production and distribution and the massive social phenomena of the modern, industrialized economy, phenomena supposedly beyond the pale of poetry.

The political differences between Pound and Zukofsky came to a head in the mid-1930s at a time when Pound's social credit money radicalism was taking a sharp right turn toward Mussolini's brand of state capitalism; Zukofsky, meanwhile, was himself becoming more dogmatically Marxist. Their argument, most noticeable in an exchange of letters in 1935, had important poetic consequences. By the time he began "A"-8 that same year, Zukofsky had veered away from Pound's position by dropping a favorite allusion of Pound's—Spinoza's appeal to nature as creator and created—which he had himself quoted in "A"-6 (22–23), for a specifically Marxist claim for the priority of labor. There he offers "Labor as creator, / Labor as creature" ("A"-8, 43), and both "A"-8 and the first half of "A"-9 are written under the sign of labor and labor time as the measure of value.

Zukofsky's rebellion against Pound's influence culminates in his translation of Cavalcanti's "Donna mi prega" in the first half of "A"-9. This spectacularly perverse effort has less to do with the medieval poet than with Zukofsky's economic disagreements with Pound, whose own version of Cavalcanti's " 'philosophical canzone' in Canto 36 is one of the great set pieces" of *The Cantos* (Kearns 82). Zukofsky tries, in the first half of "A"-9, to declare his independence from Pound's *Cantos* by setting the canzone on a soundly Marxist footing, substituting a pastiche of Marx's own language (from *Capital* 176–177) for the Neoplatonism of Cavalcanti's poem, to which Pound had more or less adhered in his translation. In Zukofsky's revision of Canto 36, social labor takes the part of divine love. The economic polemic between the two poets, then, not only is an agon of influence between Pound and the younger poet who called him "Papa" but also shows how the discourse of economics had become a form of literary criticism by cornering the discussion of Value and thus "values" in the 1930s.

The contrasting positions taken in Canto 36 and the first half of "A"-9 can be traced to a heated exchange of letters between the two poets in 1935 in which they wrangled over the nature of commodity; "A"-9 undoubtedly stems from this quarrel over the relative status of poiesis and production. These letters (*Pound/Zukofsky* 168–173) reveal a deep disagreement over the nature of labor and commodity. True to his Jeffersonian populism, Pound denies the Marxist position that the problems of capitalism are based on the social exploitation of labor by capital—he thinks finance capital alone does this, exploiting capitalists and workers alike by manipulating the value of money. Zukofsky, by contrast, retorts that *"you* can still read Charlie [Marx] and find out for yourself why *labor* is the *basic commodity* (if that word is to have any consequential meaning at all) and how the products of labor arc just the manifestations, and money yr. capitalistic juggling, of that commodity" (*Pound/Zukofsky* 171). The sharp tone of these letters suggests how strongly both poets felt about their quite different readings of the corporate industrial economy. They take the challenge insistently put to poets in the 1930s—that poetry must somehow be socially "useful"—very seriously.

Their argument surfaces first in a really violent letter from Pound to Zukofsky dated May 28, 1935 (its salutation reads "You bloody buggaring fool/").[2] Pound writes:

> Have you not even sense enough to USE A WORD with a meaning and let the meaning adhere to the word.
>
> A commodity is a material thing or substance/ it has a certain durability.
>
> If you don't dissociate ideas, and keep ONE LABLE [*sic*] for ONE thing or category, you will always be in a gormy mess.
>
> Labour may transmute material, it may put value into it, or make it serviceable. . . .
>
> Commoditas, latin = advantage, benefit. <all right>
>
> But commodity in english, and in econ/ used to mean WARES. not underwear.
>
> In Italian it is clear, *lavoro* non è *mercé.*
>
> The workman can't store it/ it is not a product, that he can put on [the] shelf for a month. It is not something he can dig up and keep.
>
> [*Pound/Zukofsky* 168]

Pound continues in the letter to browbeat his protégé, saying "N[ew]/ <Masses> is quite right/ my poetry and my econ/ are NOT separate or opposed. essential unity" (169). And "Don't embrace Social credit/ LEARN a little about human relations; and don't try to kid me that monetary system don't affect 'em" (169).

It is difficult to know what triggered this explosion: possibly it was the quotation from Marx on commodities in "Song—3/4 time" or the critique and caricature of American populist money radicalism in "This Fall, 1933"—a poem about the "AMERICAN BANKNOTE COMPANY" (*Complete Short Poetry* 56). It may have been *"'Mantis,' An In-*

terpretation," included in the copy of *55 Poems* Zukofsky had sent Pound in the winter of 1934. In the latter "poem," we read:

> lines 13 to 18—the economics of the very poor—the
> newsboy—unable to think beyond
> "subsistence still permits competi-
> tion," banking, *The Wisconsin Elkhorn
> Independent*—"Rags make paper,
> paper makes money, money makes
> banks, banks make loans, loans make
> poverty, poverty makes rags."
> [*Complete Short Poetry* 71][3]

Pound may well think of himself as the populist newsboy here—his grandfather Thaddeus, after all, was from Wisconsin. As a major Republican politician in the state during the heated presidential campaigns of the 1890s, he had given and published many antipopulist speeches on "the money question" in local Wisconsin papers. Some of these speeches were pasted into family scrapbooks that Pound had in his possession during the time when Zukofsky was his student at the "Ezuversity" in Rapallo in 1933; it is entirely possible that Zukofsky saw them there. In any case, the newsboy's analysis of the labor problem, "subsistence still permits competition," is true to the American populist critique of capitalism because he assumes a free market for labor and denies that labor is a commodity controlled by capitalists. Pound in his letter is adamant that "*lavoro* non è *mercé*"—work is not wares, not a commodity, not a thing apart from the worker. "The workman can't store it / [his labor] is not a product, that he can put on [the] shelf for a month": it is himself and (apparently) inalienable. The crucial question here, however, because of its aesthetic consequences, is why Pound is so insistent in denouncing the basic Marxist assumption that labor is a commodity. This letter does not supply the answers, and to find them we must jump forward in time, to Pound's pamphlet *Oro e lavoro* (1944, translated by John Drummond as *Gold and Work* [1951]).

Gold and Work begins like so many works of economics, with a short Utopian fantasy. Pound's Utopia is an agrarian republic with a simple mercantile economy in which the factory system and the financial superstructure that make industrialism possible are both absent. Usury is a crime; people use stamp scrip and so avoid other forms of taxation. The lack of factories obviates a proletariat. So in this world there is no "labor" in the sense of the Marxist collective noun; rather the Utopians "attach the importance to agricultural tasks that I attached in my youth to tennis or football" (*Selected Prose* 337). Labor is like play, a game of skill rather than toil. Since skill is, in economic terms, capital, we can see that Pound has a radically different conception of how work gets done than do such Marxists as Zukofsky. Later in the pamphlet, Pound will excoriate both liberals and Bolsheviks for their "fundamental contempt for the human personality" because they can both speak of labor as an abstraction—as in the "export of labor" to pay debts, or in the way "Stalin 'disposes' of forty truckloads of human 'material' for work on a canal" (*Selected Prose* 342).

Pound's Utopia is possible because the Utopians have the same respect for the "definitions of words" that Pound had accused Zukofsky of forgetting. Pound tells us "that by learning how to define words these people have succeeded in defining their economic terms, with the result that various iniquities of the stock market and financial world have entirely disappeared from their country" (*Selected Prose* 336).

Pound's Utopia is a Physiocratic republic that could have been dreamed by Thomas Jefferson. The Physiocrats—the first school of political economy in the West, founded by François de Quesnay in the mid-eighteenth century—did not subscribe to the labor theory of value, in part because an industrial system did not yet exist in France.[4] To the Physiocrats all wealth came directly out of the earth. Marx noted with disapproval that to them, "the land is still regarded as a part of nature which is independent of man, and not yet as capital, i.e. as a moment of labour itself. Rather labour appears as a moment of *nature*" (*Early Writings* 344). Unalienated from nature, indeed literally working in full partnership with it, farmers were *the* productive class as far as the Physiocrats were concerned.[5] The entire apparatus of capitalism and finance was not superfluous but simply "sterile," only manipulating an already existing wealth, never augmenting its value through their labor.

It seems to me that the radically anachronistic assumptions that lie at the root of Pound's ideas on political economy are one reason why Zukofsky cannot understand what Pound is talking about in that violent 1935 letter. His patient and spirited reply to Pound is soundly Marxist in its adherence to the labor theory of value and helps us put Pound's Jeffersonian sense of commodity and Physiocratic attitude toward labor in perspective:

> Dear E: Have *You* not even sense enough to know that a definition is worthless if it is so general as to include nothing?
>
> "A commodity is a material thing or substance / it has a certain durability"—E. P. May 28/35. I.e. taking you at your word, the moon, Mars, an extinct crater, man's shit [are commodities]—*not* fertilizer because *labor has been put into it,* and it *has social* value. Unmined coal is a material thing, but not a commodity. When the miner digs it up, it has a *use* value because so much labor power has been expended digging it up for a social need. Yes, what is the use of *my* trying to rehash what "Charlie" said in the first chapter of "Das Kapital" when you've never (evidently) taken the trouble to read it. . . . [6] There's more material fact and more imaginative poetic handling of fact in that first chapter of Marx than has been *guessed* at in your economic heaven. I tried to handle the matter in my song 3/4 time & maybe *I've* made a gormy mess of it—but *you* can still read Charlie and find out for yourself why *labor* is the *basic commodity* (if that word has any consequential meaning at all) and how the products of labor are just the manifestations, and money yr. capitalistic juggling, of that commodity. (That money *shd.* be just a medium of exchange is another matter, but you write as if it is to-day, when you know perfectly well it isn't. Marx put it: Commodity-Money-Commodity (what exchange *shd.* be): Money-Commodity-Money (what <the> *exchanges* are).
>
> What do you think labor *is* aside from what you say it does— "transmute material"—just automatic exhilaration in the best of all possible—to-day—economic worlds?
> [*Pound/Zukofsky* 171]

The essence of the problem here is a deep disagreement over the labor theory of value. Pound writes: "Labour may transmute material, it may put value into it, or make it serviceable." Zukofsky's correction—"labor *is* the transmutation of material"—is good Marxism, but as we have seen, Pound is writing out of a Jeffersonian, agrarian, and Physiocratic tradition which assumes that nature cooperates in the act of production: it is not the object of man's laboring subjectivity but in effect labors with us. In this tradition, value has a certain "natural" quality that precedes value in use or value in exchange. The true basis of credit, Pound claims, "was, and is, the abundance, or productivity, of nature together with the responsibility of the whole people" (*Selected Prose* 339). In such a polity labor cannot be a "basic commodity" as long as the whole people remain responsible both to nature and to each other, because it must depend on natural relations of production, not social ones. And he notes: "It should be remembered that the soil does not require monetary compensation for the wealth extracted from it. With her wonderful efficiency nature sees to it that the circulation of material capital and its fruits is maintained, and that what comes out of the soil goes back into the soil with majestic rhythm, despite human interference" (*Selected Prose* 346). Here, what the Marxist Zukofsky would call human labor, Pound calls "human interference," and an ecological "circulation of material capital" takes precedence over that cornerstone of Marxism, the analysis of the circulation of man-made commodities to which Zukofsky refers in his reply to Pound.

To Zukofsky in his Marxist phase, making poetry is just one aspect of labor and therefore part of the system of commodity production: "And of Labor: / Light lights in air" he writes in "A"-8 (making a kind of corrective allusion to Pound's echoes of the Neoplatonist philosopher Scotus Eriginas),

> on streets, on earth, in earth—
> Obvious as that horses eat oats—
> Labor as creator,
> Labor as creature
> ["A"-8, 43]

If poetry can be assigned to the economic category of labor—and the horse is a constant symbol of the poet throughout "*A*"—then poiesis must be a subcategory of production. Poetry then is, so to speak, a symptom, a commodity, one of many relations of production determined by the dominant mode of production—in this case corporate capitalism.

This is clearly a challenge to Pound, who, as we have seen, following in the Neoplatonic tradition of Scotus and, more important, the Physiocratic economics of Jefferson, maintains the role of nature in the act of creation (Kearns 78). To Pound, poiesis—poetry making—subsumes production, because only poetry, he claims, can make sense of our productions. Only poetry can make what we produce mean-ingful by reattaching it to the objective world of nature.

This position commits Pound to a vision of labor that is fundamen-tally erotic. The model of production from which Pound works is sex-ual reproduction, not—his gestures toward the factory in Canto 38 to the contrary—mass production. His site of production is not the shop floor but the sexual act; this is why, I believe, Zukofsky's economic refutation of Pound's economics focuses on the apparently uneco-nomic Canto 36, Pound's version of Cavalcanti's "Donna mi prega," rather than more obvious targets like the Douglasite Canto 38, or the anti-Semitic Canto 35. Leon Surrette has pointed out how Pound's sexual politics misreads Cavalcanti's poem in Canto 36 by attaching to its Neoplatonic sublimities the "Eleusinian" "Sacrum, sacrum, in-luminatio coitu" (*Cantos* 180). But if we read the Cavalcanti as a very high-flown sort of implicit economic program—as I believe Zukof-sky did—then we can see why the poem irritated Zukofsky into writ-ing his own knotty canzone on the labor theory of value.

As an economics, Pound's "Donna mi prega" is founded not on la-bor, but on love.

> Cometh he [love] to be
> > when the will
> From overplus
> Twisteth out of natural measure.
> > [*Cantos* 178]

Love, derived from the surplus of the will—"not by reason," but "Be-yond salvation" (*Cantos* 178)—creates something else, the poem, founded on the "natural measure" it is twisted out of, in a way sub-limely analogous to the way in which labor derives value from the raw material nature provides us. As a measure of value, love "draweth likeness and hue from like nature / So making pleasure more certain in seeming" (*Cantos* 179). Like other measures of value, love is able to establish commensurability by drawing out likeness from like nature in the same way that prices, say, in a crude mockery of the poem's sublime balances, allow us to equate a tweed jacket with a long week-end in Maine because they "cost the same."

If that sounds far-fetched, consider the opening of Zukofsky's "A"-9, his version of Cavalcanti:

ALEC MARSH

An impulse to action sings of a semblance
Of things related as equal values,
The measure all use is time congealed labor
In which abstraction things keep no resemblance
To goods created; integrated all hues
Hide their natural use to one or one's neighbor.

    ["A"-9, 106]

The "integration" Zukofsky is complaining about here is precisely the particular differences in use values—as of a jacket or junket to Maine—that prices, that is, abstract "exchange values," repress. This first, Marxist, half of "A"-9 concerns alienation, and most of it, as Barry Ahearn reminds us, is "spoken," as it were, by the alienated commodities themselves (Ahearn 101). What is repressed in Zukofsky's poem (as well, we might add, in the Marx from which the poet derives his diction) is the erotic lushness that gives Pound's poem its music; here we have the clicking of an analytical machine. "A"-9 is alienated from its sensual sources, and perhaps, since its subject is alienated things, this is what Zukofsky wanted. Such alienation is not possible in Pound's version of the poem, however, because his poem's "economics" are finally based on "love," and the primal economic act within the Canto is the act of sexual reproduction—"inluminatio coitu" (*Cantos* 180). Any vision of the social in Pound's poem is linked to the biological—and thus, finally, to nature.

Zukofsky's counterpoem in "A"-9 is a Marxist insistence on the social as defined by labor. Following a moment of Marx's own rhetorical exuberance at the end of his chapter on "The Commodity" (*Capital* 176–177F), the first part of "A"-9 is spoken by things endowed with a kind of consciousness because they embody labor: "hands, heart, not value made us," they say. "Lives worked us slowly to delight the senses, / Of their fire shall you find us" ("A"-9, 107). This "fire" is quite a different thing from the "diafan from light to Shade," which "cometh from the seen form" in Canto 36 (177). They are both, of course, mystifications,[7] but they are not of equal value in allowing poetry to get written.

Zukofsky's Marxist poem, laid aside in early 1940, became *First Half of "A"-9,* a "brochure" that would include, Zukofsky wrote Pound, "your text of Donna Mi Prega; Extracts from Marx—Capital Chap. 1–13 & value, Price and Profit; several notes from modern physicists;

your two translations of Guido's canzone" and Zukofsky's own version of the poem, which he called "a sublime failure" (*Pound/Zukofsky* 203). Buttressed by the authority of Marx, Zukofsky's packet may be read as a kind of "refutation" of whatever theory of value Pound had elaborated in his own version of Cavalcanti.

The outbreak of war between Italy and the United States in 1941 broke off the correspondence between the two poets. If their argument continued to work inwardly on them it only expressed itself obliquely, as in Pound's *Oro e lavoro*. Most fundamentally, the crime and horror of the war made both poets reconsider whether value might not be more safely and more permanently located in the potentially transhistorical realm of ethics rather than the brutally material theater of history, where labor and labor value could become purely destructive force. Love, not labor, might be the source of poetry after all. The second half of "A"-9, composed between 1948 and 1951, tries to make love and labor interchangeable:

> An eye to action sees love bear the semblance
> Of things, related is equated,—values
> The measure all use who conceive love, labor
> Men see, abstraction they feel, the resemblance
> (Part, self-created, integrated) all hues
> Show to natural use
>   ["A"-9, 108]

We can see that Zukofsky is still struggling with the problem of value. If labor is not the measure of value, as classical economists from Adam Smith to Ricardo and Marx have assumed, then how is value to be measured? It is here that the frontier between political economy and ethics begins to become problematic. If labor is the common measure of all value, then any value beyond the necessities for biological survival is purely social. We can, of course, as marginalist economists do, measure value (including the value of poetry) as the "margin of utility" by transferring the site where value is conferred from the scene of production to the site of consumption, the marketplace; but by doing so we completely sever economics from its moral and ethical responsibilities. Few poets, Pound and Zukofsky least of all, can afford to let their work be judged by its market value. The difficulties the labor theory of value poses for the poet, the impossibility of adequately measuring its use value by "time congealed labor," makes a poetics based on the labor theory of value impossible to sustain. Concerning "A"-9, Zukofsky ruefully notes in a letter to Pound that "I don't suppose anyone will be anxious to print the canzone—& 2 years actual labor on it plus 7 years thought (?) and study won't, in any case, be rewarded with even nominal compensation" (*Pound/Zukofsky* 203).

Pound and Zukofsky, like Marx and Douglas before them, always understand that the true function of political economy (and poetry) is not only to describe how an economy works but to use economic analysis to create social justice. If economics has an ethical component, then it may be necessary to accept that value may be based on something prior to labor, and therefore prior to society or even language, something like nature or the divine. Believing this, we have moved from the social relativism that permits us to speak about "values" to truth and natural right and what Emerson calls "natural facts." Zukofsky's return to Spinoza's ethics—the return, that is, to divinity and love—is absolutely necessary if he is to continue "A"-9 and his epic project.

The eight-year hiatus in the composition of "A"-9 might have something to do with the limitations of a defense of poetry based on a labor theory of poetic value—that "fatal pact" between poetry and materialism. Zukofsky's return to Spinoza in the second half of "A"-9, and thus to eternal values prior to labor, like Pound's increasing reliance on Confucian ethics in the later *Cantos,* suggests the inadequacy of the discourse of political economy as a basis for poetry. It is only through a return to "love," which combines the "labor / Men see" with "the abstraction they feel," that poetry can be sustained. Poiesis, not production, must be the master idea in a poet's Utopia.

Notes

1. The concept and periodization of "corporate capitalism" come from William Appleman Williams, *The Contours of American History.* In a note to *The Corporate Reconstruction of American Capitalism,* Martin J. Sklar, one of Williams's most important students, notes: "[I]t may be fairly said that William A. Williams established the concept of corporate capitalism as an essential periodization of United States political, social, and intellectual, not only economic, history, since the 1890's. Williams's phrase (*Contours* 343–478) was 'The Age of Corporate Capitalism,' and he dated the period from 1882 to the 1960s (and presumably beyond)" (18n.). If Sklar is right, then the social and intellectual, and therefore

cultural, manifestations of the new corporate age ought to be evident in American poetry.

2. Barry Ahearn, who has edited the Pound/Zukofsky correspondence, doesn't remember any antecedent to this letter. This fact suggests that Pound may be reacting not to a letter but to something in Zukofsky's poems.

3. For a different reading of these lines, see Davidson 526.

4. The labor theory of value gained general currency through *The Wealth of Nations* (1775). Benjamin Franklin had formulated a labor theory of value in his pamphlet, *A Modest Inquiry into the Nature and Necessity of a Paper Currency* in 1729. If Quesnay or Mirabeau knew of this work it did not affect them. See Ronald Meek, *Studies in the Labor Theory of Value* 40–41.

5. Pound is directly in the Physiocratic tradition when he says, "The artist is one of the few producers. He, the farmer and the artisan create wealth; the rest shift and consume it" ("The Renaissance," 1914, *Literary Essays* 222).

6. Zukofsky was probably wrong. According to Redman, Pound "had acquired the Italian edition of *Capital* in the early thirties and his markings and annotations show that he studied it with unusual care"—including chapter 1 (Redman 147). Still, it would be nice to think that Pound went through *Capital* as a result of Zukofsky's letter.

7. In *The Mirror of Production* (1975) Jean Baudrillard deconstructs not only the "labor theory of value" but also finally the concept of labor itself with all of its ethical baggage, revealing both to be ideological manifestations. See chapter 1, "The Concept of Labor" (21–51).

Works Cited

Ahearn, Barry. *Zukofsky's "A": An Introduction*. Berkeley: U of California P, 1983.

Baudrillard, Jean. *The Mirror of Production*. St. Louis: Telos, 1975.

Davidson, Michael. "Dismantling 'Mantis': Reification and Objectivist Poetics." *American Literary History* 3.3 (Fall 1991): 521–541.

Kearns, George. *The Cantos*. Cambridge: Cambridge UP, 1989.

Marx, Karl. *Capital*. Vol. 1. New York: Vintage, 1977.

————. *Early Writings*. New York: Vintage, 1975.

Meek, Ronald. *Studies in the Labor Theory of Value*. 1956. New York: Monthly Review P, 1976.

Pound, Ezra. *The Cantos*. London: Faber & Faber, 1975.

————. *Literary Essays of Ezra Pound*. Ed. T. S. Eliot. 1935. New York: New Directions, 1968.

————. *Pound/Zukofsky: Selected Letters of Ezra Pound and Louis Zukofsky*. Ed. Barry Ahearn. New York: New Directions, 1987.

————. *Selected Prose, 1909–1965*. Ed. William Cookson. New York: New Directions, 1973.

Redman, Tim. *Ezra Pound and Italian Fascism*. Cambridge: Cambridge UP, 1991.

Sklar, Martin J. *The Corporate Reconstruction of American Capitalism, 1890–1916: The Market, the Law, and Politics.* Cambridge: Cambridge UP, 1988.

Surette, Leon. *A Light from Eleusis.* Oxford: Clarendon P, 1978.

Williams, William Appleman. *The Contours of American History.* Cleveland: World, 1961.

6

"A Precision of Appeal"
Louis Zukofsky and the *Index of American Design*

IRA B. NADEL

> Emphasize detail 130 times over—or there will be no poetic object.
> —Louis Zukofsky, " 'Recencies' in Poetry" (21)

In 1856 Walt Whitman challenged America's new poets by asking two lengthy questions:

> Have you studied out the land, its idioms and men?
> Have you learn'd the physiology, phrenology, politics, geography,
> pride, freedom, friendship of the land? its substratums and
> objects?   [477][1]

Among American modernists of the 1930s, only Louis Zukofsky could answer in the affirmative. For four years (1936–1940) he assiduously studied the history of American arts and crafts through his work for the *Index of American Design*. Organized in the spring of 1935 by the Works Progress Administration (WPA) and the Federal Art Project, the *Index* became a national effort to illustrate and record the tradition of American crafts—or in Zukofsky's words, the preparation of "a graphic survey of American decorative arts and crafts from the earliest Colonial days to the beginnings of large-scale production" ("Crolius Stoneware" [1]).[2] The historical research on the manufacture of American crafts, he added, "supplements the thousands of paintings of objects vividly rendered by artists on this project" ("Stoneware" [1]).

Under the initial direction of the textile designer and painter Ruth Reeves and under the editorial direction of biographer Constance

Rourke, the *Index* was to be an accurate visual account of the tradition of American craftsmanship and culture. It was to contain a pictorial record of America's artistic past, employing hundreds of artists, in the words of the overall director, Holger Cahill, to "clarify our complex heritage for the expert" and "recreate the past in human symbols for the average citizen" (quoted in McKenzie 135).

A pamphlet on the *Index* prepared by the Federal Art Project of the City of New York, a branch of the WPA, lists four aims for the program:

1. to record pictorially "material of historical significance" previously neglected and in possible danger of being lost.

2. to gather "pictorial records of a body of traditional material which may form the basis for an organized development of American design; that is, to discover a usable American past in this field."

3. "to make source records of this hitherto unavailable material accessible . . . through the publication of portfolios of authenticated historical native design."

4. "to give work to artists, photographers and others who . . . are unable otherwise to find employment for their skill, and who through the Federal Art Project are making the cultural benefits of its programs available to the public."

[*Index* 1–2]

In short, the *Index* was to provide for the first time "a pictorial record of objects of indigenous American character in the decorative, provincial and folk arts" from the seventeenth to the nineteenth centuries (2). Theoretically, the *Index* rested on the ideology of the everyday: "the past of a nation is to be reconstructed from the humble articles of utility no less than from the record of great events," reads a passage from the eight-page pamphlet (2).

The ambitious goals of the *Index* soon required detailed essays that would present a historical survey of a given category such as furniture or glassware. Between August 1938 and April 1940, Zukofsky completed four of these comprehensive essays and prepared eleven radio scripts on objects listed in the *Index*. Political and financial considerations prevented the completion and publication of the *Index*, however, and curtailed the proposed radio broadcasts on WNYC in New York. Most of the 17,000 drawings and essays by contributors like Zukofsky remain unpublished.

In the tradition of Henry Adams, William Carlos Williams, and Ezra Pound—the relevant texts being *Mont St. Michel and Chartres, In the American Grain,* and *Guide to Kulchur*—Zukofsky's contributions to the *Index* provide a guide to American culture of the colonial past and the New Deal present. In addition, his essays illustrate a principle he outlined in "An Objective": "writing occurs which is the detail, not mirage, of seeing, of thinking with the things as they exist"; eyes always measure the "thing thought" (*Prepositions* 12). In his analyses of ironworks, kitchenware, friendship quilts, stoneware, furniture makers and carpenters, Zukofsky not only satisfies his own desire to repossess American culture but enacts his own aesthetic of the particular, as expressed in "A"-12:

> A precision of appeal—
> Let no one think it
> Unnatural.
> As Spinoza said in this line—
> If they understood *things*
> My arguments would convince them[.]
> [184]

"Things," of course, dominate Zukofsky's work, from "Ferry" in *29 Poems* to the horses of "A"-7 and the eighty flowers of *80 Flowers.* In "*A*", of course, objects range from the opening violins playing Bach ("A"-1, 1), to the found texts of Henry Adams in "A"-8 or William Carlos Williams in "A"-17. Things, in fact, are the text of "*A*", as Zukofsky states in "A"-12:

> Texts: Things
> Axiom: He composed—or
>   hunted, sowed and
>   *made things*—
>   with hand or bent—
>   is matter and thinks
>   [164]

It is no surprise, therefore, to discover that one of the largest entries in the index made for "*A*" is for "thing" and that we ourselves become things "like a quantum of action / defined product of energy and time" ("A"-9, 108), a reflection of Zukofsky's stress on the individuality of detail and its importance for confirming the texture, not only of his poem, but of our lives. "Our restlessness," he later explains, " is for what things—any / We are and are not—that rule us" ("A"-12, 238).

The significance of Zukofsky's work on the *Index of American Design* is manifold: it immersed him in American history; it confirmed the method initiated by the Objectivist "movement"; it underlined the value of citation and keen observation; it united a poetics of detail with the plot of history; it clarified Zukofsky's emerging social and political thought; and finally, it reflected an aesthetic that required the proximity of lost or forgotten objects—if not in actuality, then by reproduction. Walter Benjamin observed this development two years before Zukofsky began work on the *Index:* "every day," he wrote, "the urge grows stronger to get hold of an object at very close range by way of its likeness, its reproduction" (Benjamin 223). In a 1937 letter to Lorine Niedecker, Zukofsky expressed the same opinion but from a different angle. Technology and machinery could provide a clue to reading his texts, "once they [readers] learn the poet's machinery. It's like finding out about any other piece of machinery or doing a specific job on the belt system" (quoted in Ahearn 240). The study, research, and description of American handicrafts provided an entree into the machinery of America for Zukofsky, which also provided a means to continue with "*A*". Between 1938 and 1940, in fact, he composed the first half of "A"-9, which reflects the historical/research nature of the *Index*. The section (in its first publication as *First Half of " 'A'-9"*) is the first and only time in the entire poem when Zukofsky supplied annotations and commentary and thus is evidence of his determination to historicize and particularize his text.

In America in the thirties, the need to study the cultural past and in detail was intensified by a dual awareness of the sudden loss of an earlier America and the immediate desire (no doubt encouraged by governmental support) to restore it. And for one motivated by Objectivist principles, with their focus on particulars, employment to re-create such a past would be understood as essential. As Zukofsky suggested in a 1931 address at the Gotham Book Mart, published as " 'Recencies' in Poetry" in *An "Objectivists" Anthology*, "The desire for what is objectively perfect, [is] inextricably the direction of historic and contemporary particulars—A desire to place everything, every-thing aptly, perfectly, belonging within, one with a context.—A poem. The context based on a whole" (15). What Zukofsky seeks he summarizes as "the desire for an inclusive object," which is what he discovers in his investigations of American folk art for the *Index* (" 'Recencies' " 15). What he learned from his reading of individual objects, and how his method paralleled that of his predecessors, in particular Henry Adams and William Carlos Williams, as well as from the composition process of "*A*", occupies the remainder of this dis-cussion.

Zukofsky's fascination with American culture is well known: his 1924 master's thesis on Henry Adams, his 1930 (or 1931) proposal for a book on the prose of Thomas Jefferson ("*How Jefferson Used Words,*" "A"-12, 257), his 1934 collaboration with William Carlos Williams on the abortive opera *George Washington, [The First President],* his pro-posal for a book entitled *"About Some Americans"* ("A"-12, 256) all attest to this absorption. "A"-8, of course, represents many of these concerns and contains references to all three American heroes; his ex-periences in America—from his youth on the Lower East Side, to his uptown education at Columbia, to his teaching at the University of Wisconsin and later jobs in the metropolitan New York area and travel across the country—renewed in him the determination to understand not so much the making of Americans, as Stein phrased it, as the mak-ing of America itself (see "A"-12 [168] and "A"-13 [282–3] where, in a Whitmanesque manner, he recalls the New York of Melville, Lanier, Irving, Twain, and James [283]).

In the thirties, however, even before his employment by the WPA, Zukofsky sensed the analogies between handicrafts and poetry. Writ-ing in 1931, he compared the job of writing to cabinetmaking, where "certain joints show the carpentry not to advantage, certain joints are a fine evidence; [and] some are with necessary craftsmanship in the object" (" 'Recencies' " 22). Earlier in the essay he focused on "a desk as an object" and the "process of making it" (14), which requires an act of history: "the taking over of the deep observation of past time so that a desk made to-day may yet be a desk to-day and to-morrow" (15). In this way, the desk—and by analogy poetry—becomes "as [an] object including its value" (18). Zukofsky expanded his interest in American handicrafts through his research for the *Index,* discovering that materiality and its preoccupation with making is the very heart of a craft. Furthermore, he quickly recognized that in the art of making things there were analogies not only to the country's history and ethos but to the craft of poetry. In November 1937, while employed at the *Index,* he prepared a four-page outline for a book "on American Arts Design," cited in "A"-12 as "A History of American Design" (257, see also Henderson 150).[3]

The *Index of American Design* provided Zukofsky with another pleasure: making not a survey, sample, or chronicle but an index. The completed study was to be a compass of American culture, ordering and structuring a mass of critical material from the past. Zukofsky, of course, had a long-standing fascination with indexes, most concretely (and grandly) represented by his detailed indexes to "*A*" and to *Bottom: On Shakespeare* but anticipated in the source and line notes preceding "Poem beginning 'The,' " and culminating in the index to "A"-24. The value of indexes for Zukofsky is that they permit—actually visualize—recurrencies for the reader; that is, the reader can reenter the text he or she has just finished (or perhaps has yet to start) but in a manner other than reading the lines sequentially. An index reassembles and permits access to the details of the text in a new and often unexpected fashion, while establishing categories and structures of value in the work.

More than a list for Zukofsky, an index becomes another tool of expression, and with its mathematical meanings of a ratio of one dimension of a thing to another, or a number or symbol associated with another to indicate a mathematical operation to be performed, indexes contain the simultaneity of meaning Zukofsky sought. Furthermore, Zukofsky realized that indexing was disclosing as well as ordering and was to that extent equivalent to language's becoming a showing as well as a saying—or, as he explained in a citation preceding the index of *Bottom,* "in . . . indexes, although small pricks / To their subsequent volumes, there is seen" (*Bottom* 445).[4] Creating an index permitted the poet or writer to reexperience his own text but in a different and sometimes whimsical manner; the index entry for "eye(s)" in *Bottom,* for example, reads "*passim,* 9–443," while the entry for "Culture" reads "a graph, 33–443." But as Zukofsky writes in "A"-14, "No / index was whole" (337), realizing the fundamental incompleteness of any index, an incompleteness which the index to "*A*" itself reveals, the work initially prepared by Zukofsky and first consisting only of entries for "a," "an," and "the." Celia Zukofsky expanded it; Louis Zukofsky then revised it (Quartermain 207–208 n.18). Nonetheless, that the project to record the principal examples of American crafts and decorative arts was conceived of, and titled as, an "index" was of no little importance to Zukofsky, who noted in his essay on kitchenwares that his purpose was in large part to relate "an overwhelming number of disconnected facts" ("Wares" [18])—in short, to create an index.

Zukofsky's contributions to the *Index* began with a thirty-three-page single-spaced typescript entitled "American Ironwork, 1584–1856," completed on 27 August 1938. He continued with an eight-page essay on chalkware in September 1938 and then a thirty-four-page typescript on American tinware in January 1939. His major essays ended with a sixty-four-page essay on American kitchenware, 1608–1875, completed in March and April 1939. All of these essays exist in typescript, supplemented with detailed footnotes and sometimes specific descriptions of the objects cited. The prose is generally descriptive, although Zukofsky often feels motivated to provide a cultural commentary extending beyond America's shores, as the third paragraph of "Chalkware" (26 September 1938) demonstrates: "The chalkware are genre objects and their designs are easily traceable to the genre ornaments and miscellaneous 'image toys' popular in peasant and working class households in England, France and Germany, beginning about 1700 and lasting thru Victorian times. The English Staffordshire ware (1700–1850) embracing various porcelain—stoneware or salt-glaze, brown and white earthenware figures—cast in a mold and fired, found a ready market in America" (1).

While the syntax of the prose is straightforward, the texture is rich and detailed. In describing the subjects of Staffordshire ware, Zukofsky supplements the broad categories of animals, birds, rustic, allegorical, and historical figures with specifics: "two cranes with candle-stick or flower-holder; a pair of hawks; jugs in forms of owls; stags; a grotesque ox; horses; sheep; elephants; a postillion on horse-back; a woman in form of a bell; musicians; a Dutch boy and girl; actors; sailors; shepherds and shepherdesses; Diana; Charity; Voltaire; Washington; King George III" (2). History, in the form of newspaper accounts, business documents, or occasionally poems, often interrupts the historical narratives to supplement his descriptive surveys. In his essay on American tinware, for example, he quotes the nineteenth-century American poet Emma Hart Willard and a Connecticut poet, Hugh Peters.

The radio broadcasts were different in style as well as in content. Preparing them for a series on WNYC Radio entitled "The Human Side of Art," a series sponsored by the *Index,* Zukofsky wrote the scripts and provided commentary. Using an interview format, he struck an informal tone. The announcer on the first broadcast introduced the *Index* project as "a monumental history of American handicrafts": "the whole field of manual and decorative crafts in America will be summed up in colored and black and white plates together with written descriptions of the objects rendered" (*"Henry Clay"* [1]). Zukofsky's first words reflect the ethos of the project and introduce an important motif: touch. "In objects which man made and used, people live again. The touch of carving to the hand revivifies the hand that made it" (*"Henry Clay"* [1]). The passage echoes a section of Williams's *In the American Grain* in which Williams laments the reliance of society on "science and invention—away from touch" (179). Machines, he complains, "increase the gap between touch and thing *not* to have contact" (177). Completed on 16 November 1939, the script was the first of eleven prepared for broadcast; their subjects ranged from the furniture maker Duncan Phyfe to friendship quilts. Of most interest, Zukofsky is cast as the expert, the knowledgeable source of detail, history, and information regarding manufacture. Ironically, the files and logbooks of WNYC contain no record of any of these broadcasts ever being made; 80 percent of the broadcasts exist in manuscript only, the remainder in typescript.

"The *Henry Clay* Figurehead," however, reveals another element of Zukofsky's unfolding aesthetic of the particular. The title refers to a carved figurehead of the American politician and three-time presidential hopeful Henry Clay (1777–1852), who lost to John Quincy Adams, Andrew Jackson, and James K. Polk. At the outset, Zukofsky explains the reason for one's involvement with objects from the past: they revivify the past. Despite their loss, objects can be restored through an aesthetic that recognizes the universality of art:

> As pictures, yet, and as facts. They still exist, because they existed. And because rendering the truths they were to the people who made and used them becomes part of the factual material of the artist's drawing.

A drawing of a ship's figurehead becomes a guide not only to all ship's figureheads that preceded it, but a reason for creating sculpture in our time. It ceases to be a museum piece or a collector's item as soon as the form and color of the drawing help to circulate its image among people. They *must* admire, and demand an effort from contemporary art that will yield a comparable pleasure to the living.

["*Henry Clay*" 2]

Re-creation through art, which for Zukofsky is through language, establishes the simultaneity of time, purpose, and meaning of the object. Re-creating the object charges it with meaning for the present. From observing and studying the past, which is precisely what Zukofsky does in the *Index,* a new and powerful art will emerge, for in seeing past art, the public will demand successful objects in the present. In this process, nothing is lost, since all art coexists, as Zukofsky explains in a letter to Lorine Niedecker that is included in "A"-12:

> Each writer writes
> one long work whose beat he cannot
> entirely be aware of. Recurrences
> follow him, crib and drink from a
> well that's his cadence—after
> he's gone.
>
> [214]

What Zukofsky celebrates in the *Henry Clay* passage is the power of art to renew its value, something that he experienced directly through his detailed research on the *Index* and that may have been initiated in 1935 through his activity of locating poetic selections and surveys at Columbia for what would become *A Test of Poetry* (completed 1940, published 1948). Reproduction, whether in a drawing or in an anthology, reclaims art; and when such re-creation occurs through language, language achieves its goal of directly transmitting experience or fact. As words become presences in Zukofsky's poetry, historical art objects become images of immediacy influencing artists and viewers in the present. This illustrates Pound's dictum that "*all* ages are contemporaneous *in the mind*" (quoted in Perloff 138) while supporting Williams's view that words only become liberated when they are accurately tuned to the facts that supply their reality (*Imaginations* 150).

Equally fascinating is Zukofsky's narrative of the *Henry Clay* figurehead, which interprets the carving as an icon embodying Clay's character. Clay's political disappointment is a clue to the figurehead's origin; Zukofsky suggests that the carving might actually be the "totem" of a "Henry Clay Club" from Poughkeepsie, New York, the birthplace of Clay's running mate, Talmadge. A tragic accident on the Hudson River in July 1852, however, was the source of the figurehead's name: in a race with another ship, the steamer *Henry Clay* caught fire, resulting in many deaths and the destruction of the boat, although the figurehead survived. Yet the figurehead itself remains a mystery: is it a political totem or ship's figurehead? It can only be decided finally, Zukofsky states, when all the facts are known, although "the imagination may favor one or the other" (*"Henry Clay"* 6).

A detailed description of the actual figurehead ends the talk, supplemented by a dramatic re-creation of the recovery of bodies and the scene on the riverbank in the aftermath of the disaster. Zukofsky also notes that the dead included Nathaniel Hawthorne's sister and that Hawthorne's story "Drowne's Wooden Image" (1846) evokes a figurehead as powerful as that which survived the river disaster. The first of the radio broadcasts, "The *Henry Clay* Figurehead" reveals the methods Zukofsky would elaborate in sections of *"A"*: research, documentation, definition, history, and fact, vying with each other in poetic statement.

Zukofsky's most notable predecessors in writing American cultural criticism were Henry Adams in *Mont Saint Michel and Chartres* (1904) and William Carlos Williams in *In the American Grain* (1925). Pound's *Guide to Kulchur* (1938) is a work coterminous with the *Index* but less influential on Zukofsky, since it appeared while his writing for the *Index* was under way. More important, from Adams, Zukofsky drew the verbal confidence and focus on particulars found in the *Index;* chapter 9 of *Mont Saint Michel,* dealing with the stained glass windows of Chartres, is representative. There objects are seen as signs, and the enthrallment of the thirteenth-century glass artist with the Virgin is no mystery: "all this is written in full, on every stone and window of the apse, as legible as the legends to anyone who can read," Adams states with assurance (154). Attention to detail provides the wider cultural and analytical view, anticipating the confident tone and assertion of artistic value Zukofsky duplicates in his essays on American handicrafts.

But Adams goes further. In his discussion of the windows, he focuses on their minutiae, encouraging visual inspection to experience the art that is, he notes in 1904, almost wholly lost (155). The drive to reclaim the past through verbal representation equals Zukofsky's determination to provide accurate artistic detail to rescue disappearing American art forms. Ornament, decoration, and detail, as well as subject matter, treatment, influence, and color, are important to both Adams and Zukofsky. Furthermore, the history of the windows of Chartres is of as much interest to Adams as the manufacture of American tinware is to Zukofsky, because both accounts reveal essential elements of cultural construction (157). Adams's careful reading of the Window of Saint James, for example, donated by the Merchant Tailors, "whose signature appears at the bottom" (158), recounts the lengthy narrative of Saint James in a series of panels, followed by a paragraph of interpretation and is succeeded by a wonderful discussion of what was thought to be the best of the thirteenth-century windows, the one that represents the Chanson de Roland (159–161). Following a lengthy description, Adams concludes that this window and that of Saint James "are pure art, as simply decorative as the decorations of the Grand Opera," embodying "decorative perfection" (162). Zukofsky, of course, worked with lesser material—but not lesser in terms of its value to American culture. But in Adams's treatment, he saw what attention to detail could reveal, and in chapters from *Mont Saint Michel* like "Towers and Portals" and "Twelfth Century Glass," especially with its passages on glass as art and on the techniques of production (126–128), Zukofsky found an articulate and persuasive model.

In *In the American Grain,* of which Zukofsky owned an inscribed copy, Williams provided a more contemporary and specifically American engagement with history through wide-ranging essays on Christopher Columbus, Cotton Mather, Washington, Poe, and Lincoln. Detail and observation are again fundamental. Of Samuel Champlain, for example, Williams relates his "energy for detail—a love of the exact detail" and offers an incisive comment that applies to Zukofsky himself and his career: "Is it not clarity itself? The man absorbed in his work, eager, riding ahead of his plans—and fate dogging him behind" (70, 72).

In *In the American Grain,* Williams attempts to define a broadly conceived yet precise account of influential figures and events in the shaping of America, based on "its signs and signatures" (iv). Sources are the book's concern, from the first-person narrative of Red Eric to the description of Columbus or the life of Aaron Burr. But through it all:

detail, from the flora and fauna recorded by Columbus on a beach at San Salvador to the testimonies at the Salem Witch trials and, surprisingly, the specifics of Williams's six-week visit to Paris in 1924—all of which construct the narrative of America in the work (25–26, 85–100, 105).

Williams's goal, which was also Zukofsky's, was to "seek the support of history" in making it "SHOW itself" (116). The easiest way was through things and individuals, demonstrating the process of what D. H. Lawrence in his review of the book called "the Americanization of the white men in America" and not the "Europeanizing of the American continent" (Lawrence 413–414). Like Zukofsky, Williams stresses the indigenous culture that defines America. If Adams wanted to educate Americans about their European roots, and Williams wanted Americans to discover their own indigenous origins, Zukofsky sought to combine both through his contributions to the *Index*, itemizing the American folk past while indicating its historical record. And both antecedent texts, like their successor, were highly researched works. The use of old documents in both Adams and Williams clearly anticipates the documentary nature of Zukofsky's essays. In his assessment of American history, Williams notes that "the most confusing thing . . . is the nearly universal lack of scale" (75). The use of documents by Williams, however, overcomes this confusion; in Zukofsky, the careful analysis of American culture through its handicrafts serves a parallel function.

Adams in *Mont Saint Michel* and Williams in *In the American Grain* prepare us for the *Index of American Design;* each work is a prelude to its successor. The three works move from the European origins of American culture and art (Adams) to the formation of the New World (Williams) and to the stamping of that world by individual craftsmen of the colonial and federalist periods (Zukofsky). But while Adams and Williams return to European origins, Zukofsky remains centered in America for aesthetic as well as cultural beginnings, immersing the reader in the finest of America's crafts, from the "Caswell Carpet" of 1835 (now in the Metropolitan Museum of Art in New York) to American kitchenware. The engagement with these objects and the need to express clearly their history and importance reaffirms Zukofsky's obligation to see clearly and write precisely, which Pound declared to be *the* touchstone of art in "The Serious Artist" (*Literary Essays* 48). In addition, Zukofsky's centering on the objects of the

American past corroborates a position Williams—and implicitly Adams—supports: to counter the loss of America's past, we must reconstruct what it had been. "The unstudied character of our beginnings" must be replaced by detailed knowledge of our sources (*American Grain* 109). As Williams proclaimed, "what has been morally, aesthetically worth while in America has rested upon peculiar and discoverable ground" locatable in records, books, and art : "[W]hat we are has its origins in what *the nation* in the past has been" (109). In these studies, Williams wrote, "I have sought to re-name the things seen" (v). Zukofsky's goal was similar, although the experience also taught him to question the validity, fact.

When he discussed the *Henry Clay* figurehead, Zukofsky concluded that imagination would finally determine whether or not the object was a political totem or ship's figurehead, since fact alone was inconclusive. This acknowledgment registers Zukofsky's skepticism toward fact and resistance to reading it as symbol (see " 'Mantis,' An Interpretation," *Complete Short Poetry* 70). "The 'fact' / is not so hard-set as a paradigm," he announces in "A"-12 (215). In "An Objective," he writes that "the combined letters—the words—are absolute symbols for objects, states, acts, interrelations, thoughts about them" (*Prepositions* 14). Presentation in detail does not guarantee the truth, despite its appeal to a rational mind. Language, not logic, structures history. The reevaluation of fact and its purity originates in Zukofsky's historical work for the *Index* and finds its expression in the first half of "A"-9, which begins with the reconsideration of fact:

> An impulse to action sings of a semblance
> Of things related as equated values.
>   ["A"-9, 106]

Things are not of equal value; they only appear to be so because "singing" makes them so. "Labor takes on our imprecision," he adds (106). Coincidentally, Zukofsky completed the first half of "A"-9 in November 1939, as he was preparing his radio broadcasts for the *Index*.

The history of American design that Zukofsky wrote provided him not only with a means to repossess a fading American culture but also with a corroborative epistemology that reconfirmed the value of sight over intellect recorded in the second half of "A"-9: "An eye to action sees love bear the semblance / Of things, related is equated" (108), which he earlier enunciated in " 'Recencies' in Poetry" in a sentence that reads, "poems are only acts upon particulars, outside of them" (25). The *Index* completed a decade devoted to exploring the value of sight, detail, particulars, and fact—and the conclusion that it is impossible "to communicate anything but particulars—historic and contemporary—things" (" 'Recencies' " 16). Through his work for the *Index,* work that taught him to see history as things, not names, and to see writing as seeing, not feeling ("A"-22, 511; *Prepositions* 12), Zukofsky achieved what Williams identified as "this want, in America" for "aesthetic satisfaction," that "can only be filled by knowledge, a poetic knowledge, of that ground" (*American Grain* 213).

Notes

1. This particular poem is "By Blue Ontario's Shore," which Zukofsky cites in "A"-8 (65).

2. Zukofsky adds that "research in the historical background and manufacture of American costume, ceramics, glassware, furniture, metal work, woodcarving and textiles, supplements the thousands of paintings of objects vividly rendered by the artists on this project" ("Stoneware" [1]). In referring to Zukofsky's contributions to the *Index of American Design,* I will indicate the page or pages in the individual essays, all of which are unpublished and exist either in typescript or manuscript. Zukofsky's contributions to the *Index* are described in Booth 227–229, MSS I4–I18. Unless otherwise indicated, all quotations from the papers of Louis Zukofsky are from the Louis Zukofsky collection of the Harry Ransom Humanities Research Center of the University of Texas at Austin. Copyright Paul Zukofsky. Zukofsky material may not be quoted from this article by third parties without express permission by the copyright holder.

3. In 1946 Zukofsky reiterated his analogy between poetry and handicrafts when he cited a weaver and architect as examples of craftspeople whose actions achieve "constructions apart from themselves, [and] move in effect toward poetry" ("Poetry," *Prepositions* 8). In a 1969 interview with L. S. Dembo, Zukofsky returned to carpentry: "[P]eople are free to construct whatever table they want, but if it's going to be art, you had better have some standards. I at least want a table that I can write on and put to whatever use a table usually has" (Interview 268).

4. See Heidegger, as quoted in Fredman 77. The *Bottom* passage is from *Troilus and Cressida,* I.iii.343.

Works Cited

Adams, Henry. *Mont Saint Michel and Chartres.* Intro. Raymond Carney. New York: Penguin, 1986.

Ahearn, Barry. *Zukofsky's "A": An Introduction.* Berkeley: U of California P, 1983.

Benjamin, Walter. "The Work of Art in the Age of Mechanical Reproduction." *Illuminations.* Trans. Harry Zohn. New York: Schocken, 1969. 217–251.

Booth, Marcella. *A Catalogue of the Louis Zukofsky Manuscript Collection.* Austin: Humanities Research Center, U of Texas, 1975.

Fredman, Stephen. *Poet's Prose: The Crisis in American Verse.* 2nd ed. Cambridge: Cambridge UP, 1990.

Henderson, Cathy. "Supplement to Marcella Booth's 'A Catalogue of the Louis Zukofsky Manuscript Collection.' " *Lawrence, Jarry, Zukofsky: A Tryptich.* Ed. David Oliphant and Gena Dagel. Austin: Humanities Research Center, U of Texas, 1987. 107–181.

Index of American Design. New York: Federal Art Project, W.P.A., n.d.

Lawrence, D. H. "American Heroes." *Nation* 122 (14 April 1926): 413–414.

McKenzie, Richard D. *The New Deal for Artists.* Princeton: Princeton UP, 1973.

Perloff, Marjorie. *Poetic License: Essays on Modernist and Postmodernist Lyric.* Evanston, IL: Northwestern UP, 1990.

Pound, Ezra. *Literary Essays.* Ed. T. S. Eliot. New York: New Directions, 1968.

Quartermain, Peter. *Disjunctive Poetics: From Gertrude Stein and Louis Zukofsky to Susan Howe.* Cambridge: Cambridge UP, 1992.

Whitman, Walt. *Complete Poetry and Collected Prose.* New York: Library of America, 1982.

Williams, William Carlos. *Imaginations.* Ed. Webster Schott. New York: New Directions, 1971.

———. *In the American Grain.* Intro. Horace Gregory. 1925. New York: New Directions, 1956.

Zukofsky, Louis. *First Half of "A-9."* New York: Privately printed, 1940.

———. "Index of American Design," MSS I4-I18. Louis Zukofsky Manuscript Collection, Harry Ransom Humanities Research Center, U of Texas, Austin.

———. Interview with L. S. Dembo ["Sincerity and Objectification"]. *Louis Zukofsky: Man and Poet.* Ed. Carroll F. Terrell. Orono, ME: National Poetry Foundation, 1979. 265–281.

———. " 'Recencies' in Poetry." *An "Objectivists" Anthology.* Ed. Louis Zukofsky. Var, France: TO Publishers, 1932. 9–25.

II.

Toward the Postmodern
Zukofsky's Life of Writing

7

A "no man's land!"

Postmodern Citationality in Zukofsky's "Poem beginning 'The'"

MING-QIAN MA

The "present" essay is but a tissue of quotations.
— Editor's note from *Critique* (1969) for the first version of Derrida's text, reproduced in *Dissemination*

The text is a tissue of quotations drawn from the innumerable centres of culture.
— Roland Barthes, *Image, Music, Text*

LOUIS ZUKOFSKY, COMMENTING IN HIS essay "American Poetry, 1920–1930" on the imagistic diction employed by his modernist precursors Pound, Eliot, Williams, Moore, and H. D., makes the following observation: "Whatever one's preferences, the diction of these poets remains their fully varied material." But he quickly adds, "which includes quotations from sources apparently useful in preserving poetry wherever it is found" (*Prepositions* 146). Zukofsky's description of modernist poetics as a poetics of quotations, teleologically selective and artistically mimetic, points toward, among other things, his own rethinking of modernist praxis. If, as Rainer Nägele proclaims, "[r]adical thought emerges from the deepest immersion into tradition . . . [and] is never a creation ex nihilo, but the effect of translation and interpretation" (19), then Zukofsky, himself a "brilliant disciple" of the Pound tradition (Hatlen 21), is also, and to no lesser degree than Pound or his contemporaries, an ambitious innovator. With his own poetics "rooted in Pound's 'Grand Collage' " (Hatlen 21), Zukofsky's critical insight into the modernist tradition—a tradition that Michael André Bernstein describes as "carrying" a "load of embedded quotations," the interaction of which "constitutes a central thematic concern and narrative convention" ("Bringing" 177, 178)—foregrounds a concomitant inquiry beyond the parameters of modernism, an inquiry articulated in his poetry through an exploration of what Hugh Kenner describes as the "strange possibility" that "whatever is sayable has already somewhere been said" ("Foreword" ix). "Poem beginning 'The,'" in this sense, marks Zukofsky's departure from the modernist poetics of citation oriented toward "a conceptual reorganization and a new linguistic encoding of the real world" (Zacchi 105), to a postmodernist poetics of "generalized citationality" (Johnson xxx) featuring, in the poet's own words, "chorals out of random input" ("A"-14, 354), or "assemblage of naught" ("A"-22, 509).

I

In his *ABC of Reading,* Pound begins the section titled "Exhibits" with a statement that might be read as an encapsulated and yet systematic theorizing or rationalizing of the modernist use of quotations: "The ideal way to present the next section of this booklet would be to give the quotations WITHOUT any comment whatever. I am afraid that would be too revolutionary. By long and wearing experience I have learned that in the present imperfect state of the world, one MUST tell the reader. I made a very bad mistake in my INSTIGATIONS, the book had a plan, I thought the reader would see it" (95).[1] The issue at stake here is not *what* but *how* to quote. Designed primarily to educate, to enlighten, to communicate, Pound's poetics, however he may describe or define it, is intended in the light of this passage to be the poetics of "exhibits." In the Poundian project of "MAK[ING] IT NEW," in which the antecedent for "IT" points, as Leonard Diepeveen observes, to "the past poetic/political tradition" (64), to exhibit is to quote; for ideally for the poet, quotation is the most eloquent form of articulation bodying forth a built-in "plan." Semantically self-evident and communicatively self-sufficient, quotations constitute, in the Poundian scheme of things, the methodological underpinning of the imagist aesthetic. Not only do quotations, for instance, provide the most viable (i.e., the most direct) routes to Pound's "[d]irect treatment of the 'thing' whether subjective or objective," but they also satisfy the need "[t]o use absolutely no word that does not contribute to the presentation" (*Literary Essays* 3). For economically, quotations, through their concreteness and precision, help to achieve what Pound calls the "maximum efficiency of expression" by saving the moderns from the burden and embarrassment of "saying the same thing with less skill and less conviction" (*Literary Essays* 56, 11); rhetorically, they establish for the poet "a strategic position" in a given context, functioning as "luminous details" (*Selected Prose* 26); and ideologically, quotations "[bear] true witness" (*Literary Essays* 44) to cultural and historical manifestations, thus presenting what Diepeveen describes as "a formalist, atemporal version of originality" (60). Such a description seems even more apt in light of Pound's conception of the nature of poetry. For one thing, "Logopoeia," asserts Pound, "does not translate, though the attitude of mind it expresses may pass through a paraphrase" (*Literary Essays* 25). For another, poetry, "the most concentrated form of verbal expression" (*ABC* 36), will not allow the verbiage of paraphrase. Commenting on "how complete is Mr. Eliot's depiction of our contemporary condition" in *Prufrock and Other Observations,* for instance, Pound emphatically draws one's attention to Eliot's "method of conveying a whole situation and half a character by three words of a quoted phrase" (*Literary Essays* 419). "Great poets," Marianne Moore recalls Pound saying, "seldom make bricks without straw. They pile up all the excellences they can beg, borrow, or steal from their predecessors and contemporaries and then set their own inimitable light atop the mountain" (272).

Somewhat similar is Eliot's theorizing of the modernist use of quotation, whose aesthetic premises consist of two principles: a "historical sense [as] a perception, not only of the pastness of the past, but of its presence," as he writes in "Tradition and the Individual Talent," and a "conception of poetry as a living whole of all the poetry that has ever been written" (784, 786). Such a diachronic trajectory opens, by its all-embracing "oneness," a synchronic field in which a new synthesis takes place.[2] "When a poet's mind is perfectly equipped for its work," remarks Eliot in "The Metaphysical Poets," "it is constantly amalgamating disparate experience; . . . in the mind of the poet these experiences are always forming new wholes" (532). Equally amalgamated into new constellations are quotations, and how this is done, according to Eliot in "Philip Massinger," suggests a poet's quality: "One of the surest of tests is the way in which a poet borrows. Immature poets imitate; mature poets steal; bad poets deface what they take, and good poets make it into something better, or at least something different. The good poet welds his theft into a whole of feeling which is unique, utterly different from that from which it was torn; the bad poet throws it into something which has no cohesion" (125).

Much, however, of what Pound has originally envisioned as the poetics of exhibits remains, to a great extent, only ideal or "too revolutionary." When applied "in the present imperfect state of the world," such "directness of presentation" (*Literary Essays* 33) must be modified; that is, the poetics of exhibits, of showing, of presentation, must be supplemented by and, in turn, subordinated to, a poetics of commentary, of telling, of representation.[3] Pervaded by what Michele J. Leggott calls "[t]he spirit of breezy opinionation" (99), the modernist use of quotations in Pound and Eliot follows, by necessity, a quadruple formula characterized by the "coincidence" of what Meir Sternberg labels as the four "universals" defining quotations: "representational bound, structural framing, communicative subordination, and perspectival montage or ambiguity" (109).

To quote, first and foremost, is to serve a purpose. The referential function of the quoted material is appropriated in a given text to illustrate, to prove, to argue, or to annotate and exemplify, in which case "the evocation of the past always occurs in such a way as to illuminate the present"; as Herbert Grabes points out, "[t]he situation presented in the poem forms the common meeting-point for all the levels and phases of reality evoked by quotations" (146–147).[4] As a means of achieving Pound's "triumph of total meaning over detail . . . the new synthesis" (*Guide to Kulchur* 92, 95), a quotation circumscribes a representational bound at two mutually reciprocal levels: local/microcosmic and universal/macrocosmic. While functioning as what Jennifer Clarvoe calls a "local, small scale introduction to the dynamics of the poem as a whole" (328), a quotation also asserts, by the same token, that "the particular and local bears universal significance without forfeiting its concreteness" (Grabes 151). At the center—whether thematic or structural—of Canto XIII, for instance, is posited the Confucian ethics of order, an idea that, according to Albert Gelpi, "speaks for the side of Pound which is conservative, traditional, sexist, mandarin, rationalist" (203) and an idea that Pound, expediently enough, summarizes from *The Great Digest* (Gelpi 202) in order to articulate his own sociopolitical concerns:

> If a man have not order within him
> He can not spread order about him;
> And if a man have not order within him
> His family will not act with due order;
>   And if the prince have not order within him
> He cannot put order in his dominions.
>   [*Cantos* 59]

All of the poem's quotations pertain to this Confucian social philosophy, each articulating "order" from a different angle and each urged
by a strong, individual sense of authority and responsibility, regardless
of one's sphere of application or social position (Gelpi 203). Tesu-lou's
personal view of "I would put the defences in order" is juxtaposed
with Khieu's royal standpoint: "If I were lord of a province / I would
put it in better order than this is"; and Tchi's emphasis on humble-
ness—"I would prefer a small mountain temple, / With order in the
observances, / with a suitable performance of the ritual"—is en-
dorsed and further specified as moderation by Kung himself: "Anyone
can run to excesses, / It is easy to shoot past the mark, / It is hard
to stand firm in the middle" (*Cantos* 58–59). However one approaches
it, to restore and maintain the order that has dominated Pound's own
thinking, one must, as Kung's reprimand of Yuan Jang goes, "Get
up and do something useful" (59); this becomes, Gelpi observes, "an
early formulation of Pound's maxim of translating 'ideas into action' "
(203). In this sense, Lawrence Rainey is right when he claims that in
The Cantos "the new culture is presented as a ritual recovery of quotations. New culture and new poem are consecrated in a ceremony
that ratifies and is ratified by quotation, as if citation were the discursive counterpart to the theme of human and cultural regeneration"
(57).

The modernist preoccupation with quotations as representational
bond entails, in turn, a structural patterning, an interaction between
two kinds of texts that have been named host and found (Clark and
Gerrig) or frame and inset (Sternberg). Though they are presented as
the component parts of the host texts, quotations as found texts maintain their own status nonetheless and must be identified and acknowledged in one way or another. In other words, "[t]heir boundaries—
their beginnings and ends—must be clear" (Clark and Gerrig 766):

What you have done, Odysseus,
    We know what you have done . . .
And that Guillaume sold out his ground rents
(Seventh of Poitiers, Ninth of Aquitain).
"Tant las fotei com auzirets
"Cen e quatre vingt et veit vetz . . . "
        [*Cantos* 21, ellipses in original]

The image for quotations thus employed in the modernist praxis becomes, rather fittingly, that of an immigrant: a permanent resident
with an alien registration number, documented by, as the case may be,
quotation marks, italics, duplications of foreign words, or various
forms of notes and indexes. For the modernists, to maintain such a
distinction or boundary is a psychological imperative, for their use of
quotations, as Michael André Bernstein contends, "does not so much
draw upon a canonic tradition as seek to establish one" ("Bringing"
178), one that is based on what Pound believes to be "a return to
origins . . . a return to nature and reason" (*Literary Essays* 92). This
return, however coherent in content, also needs a visual or formal
manifestation to buttress its sense of literalness or actuality. If, as
Diepeveen argues, "for most quoting poets the quotation is a fact, not
a symbol" (xv),[5] modernist poetry, by its grand "synthesis of hetero-
genous 'origins' " (Bernstein, "Bringing" 187–188), demonstrates that
it not only makes history anew but, more important, makes history.
    Yet for the modernist message to emerge, quotations have to forfeit
their independence in use in order to facilitate a textual hierarchy. In
this respect, the modernist use of quotations takes on an explicitly
Emersonian overtone.[6] "Whatever the formal autonomy conferred by
[the frame]," argues Sternberg in the same vein, "[t]he inset is communicatively subordinated to the frame" (131). Hence the paradox:
the inset's textual territory is acknowledged in the frame only to be
invaded, its sovereignty recognized only to be violated, and its original
context accepted only to be recontextualized. "The supreme control
lies with the frame," with its specific "norms and premises," writes
Sternberg, for "[t]o quote is to mediate, to mediate is to frame, to
frame is to interfere and exploit" (125, 144, 145). Successful communication in modernist poetry comes, then, from the successful coloni-
zation of the found texts by the host texts.
    Out of this communicative subordination emerges the perspectival

montage or ambiguity. The modernist montage, however, is hardly an entirely random mosaic; in Pound the selection and arrangement of quotations, never arbitrary to begin with, constitute in fact what Andrew Kappel describes as the poet's "vast programmatic shuffling and sifting of world literature into a usable selective order" (288). Nor is the ambiguity completely opaque, for a quotation, once colonized, "[exhibits] an intrinsic integrity in a new context provided by Pound's poem," and its original context, now exploited, helps the quotation "[make] its point as it stands" by offering "the missing links that make the [host text] intelligible" (Kappel 230, 231, 235).[7] Take Pound's portrait of Henry James in Canto VII:

> And the great domed head, *con gli occhi onesti e tardi*
> Moves before me, phantom with weighted motion,
> *Grave incessu,* drinking the tone of things,
> And the old voice lifts itself
> weaving an endless sentence.
> [*Cantos* 24]

This passage corresponds almost word for word to Pound's personal memories of the novelist in his essay "Henry James" (*Literary Essays* 295); later in the essay Pound exalts James as a literary figure of global significance: "As Armageddon has only too clearly shown, national qualities are the great gods of the present and Henry James spent himself from the beginning in an analysis of these potent chemicals; trying to determine from the given microscopic slide the nature of the Frenchness, Englishness, Germanness, Americanness. . . . We may rest our claim for his greatness in the magnitude of his protagonists, in the magnitude of the forces he analysed and portrayed" (*Literary Essays* 300–301). The image Pound paints here of James is, "only too clearly" indeed, that of a classical literatus dealing with his subjects from a transnational or transcontinental perspective, an image the magnitude of which finds its articulation in the canto not only in James's stylistic grandeur—"drinking the tone of things, / And the old voice lifts itself / weaving an endless sentence"—but also in his physical massiveness: "And the great domed head . . . / Moves before me, phantom with weighted motion." A context as such naturalizes, so to speak, the two quotations from Dante and Virgil. Originally referring to Sordello, for instance, "con gli occhi onesti e tardi" (with eyes honest and slow) (Terrell 31) adds to and completes, in physical as well as moral terms, James's otherwise faceless image; "Grave incessu" (solemn movement), which describes "Homer, Horace, and Ovid, three of the four great shades of antiquity approaching Dante and Virgil (Virgil himself being the fourth)" (Terrell 31), identifies James as one of them, accepting him into the historical procession. With their original contexts providing matching physical attributes and appropriate occasions, both quotations become, in a way, Pound's mouthpieces, identifying James with and recontextualizing him as part of that grand tradition.[8] In what Sternberg terms "transpacity," then, "mimetic and perspectival interference go together" (144, 109), which in turn renders quotations "specific" or even "self-explanatory" (Grabes 148); such is the case with Canto VII. In this version of modernist poetics, quotations thus employed, as Clarvoe notes, "anchor the poem to implied confirmation" (329).

II

In contrast to Pound's practice, in which quotations are used as stage lighting for "the dance of the intellect among words" (*Literary Essays* 25), Zukofsky's "Poem beginning 'The' " presents itself as an exemplar of a postmodern citationality in which quotations are themselves the dance, occupying center stage of the poem. Zukofsky's ontological treatment of quotations is theorized in the poet's definition of poetry itself, which is "precise information on existence out of which it grows, and information of its own existence, that is, the movement (and tone) of words" (*Prepositions* 20). Zukofsky's departure from modernism is suggested in this statement by a shift of emphasis: from message or meaning to information, from history or tradition to existence, from poetry as a referential entity always in closure to poetry as a physical movement forever in progress and, most germane to our topic, from precision in terms of a teleologically controlled selection of quotations to precision in terms of objectively recorded contingencies of occurrences.

To equate poetry with information is, as Charles Bernstein would argue decades later, to deny "the self as the primary organizing feature of writing" (41) and to return poetry to the general flux of existence. For the term "information," according to Norbert Wiener, "is a name for the content of what is exchanged with the outer world as we adjust to it, and make our adjustment felt upon it. The process of receiving and of using information is the process of our adjusting to the contingencies of the outer environment, and of our living effectively within that environment" (17–18). It is, as N. Katherine Hayles puts it in her discussion of Claude E. Shannon's work, "a statistical measure of uncertainty" (270) or, in William Paulson's words, "a measure of a quantity of possibilities" ("Literature" 39). Information as such does not constitute meaning; rather, it concerns "the formal conditions of transmitting messages and not the eventual meaning or significance of messages that might be actually sent" (Paulson, *Noise* 54). Viewed from this perspective, poetry, for Zukofsky, does not encode existence into what Paulson describes as a "uniquely defined, in a sense expected . . . specific message of given quantity" (*Noise* 57); instead, it presents itself as an adjustment to, and, at the same time, as part and parcel of, the dynamics that is existence, with all its uncertainties and possibilities.

In this sense, Zukofsky's definition of poetry presupposes a particular kind of temporal relationship between writing and its material. If, on the one hand, poetry grows out of information on existence, the poem's material exists prior to its own coming into being and takes on the status of found object when used in the poem. If, on the other, poetry is information of its own existence, its form and content—that is, "the movement (and tone) of words"—become, then, synchronous, thus defying any attempt at finding an inherent, logical arrangement of details. In other words, poetry (Poem) occurs when writing fuses both the "simultaneousness" (beginning) and the "priorness" ("The") of its material (Poem beginning "The"), which in turn demands a structure or an objectification "committed," as Charles Altieri argues, "to composition rather than interpretation" (15). "Good poetry," therefore, "does not argue its attitudes or beliefs," contends Zukofsky: "It exists independently of the reader's preferences for one kind of 'subject' or another" (*Prepositions* 20).

"Poem beginning 'The,' " then, unfolds a world in which the poet, according to Zukofsky, "lives with the things as they exist . . . , thinking with the things as they exist" ("Interview" 217). The three-word title of the poem, for instance, recapitulates Zukofsky's Objectivist rendering of poetry or information as found texts. Featured prominently in the title is, of course, the word "The," the definite article whose semantics and function are, in general, "controlled by the basic notion [of] 'a previously recognized, noticed, or encountered' " person, object, and so forth (*Webster's* 1473). To illustrate further its denotative "previousness," the definite article is itself put in quotation marks, the awkward redundancy of which suggests, as Robert Duncan notes, "a kind of self-consciousness in which not the poet but the act of writing was this 'self' " (425). Since poetry is "precise information on existence out of which it grows," it always begins with what has already begun, thus designating itself as a composite of found texts.

Zukofsky further emphasizes his conception of the poem as a structure of found texts by prefacing the poem with an elaborate dedication, one that is as much an index to the sources of the poem as it is an acknowledgment. In either case, however, this text is intended not so much to highlight a controlled, purposeful selection of source materials pertinent to a certain message conveyed in the poem as to acknowledge, apologetically indeed, its own lack of comprehensiveness: "Because I have had occasion to remember, quote, paraphrase," the poet writes, "I dedicate this poem to Anyone and Anything I have unjustifiably forgotten" (*Complete Short Poetry* 8). In fact, the poem's indebtedness to preexisting information is such that whatever is not named, the poet feels obliged to mention, should be otherwise "Obvious—Where the Reference is Obvious" (8). Coupled with this lack of comprehensiveness, one finds a pervasive lack of specificity that takes diverse forms; in contrast to Pound's and Eliot's concrete, explicit indexes and notes oriented to "use-context" (Rainey 53), this lack of specificity makes a definite statement. The index's vagueness ("*The Bible*—1–3, 9, 313, 314"), pointlessness ("The French Language—31, 33, 51, 292"), and all-inclusiveness ("Power of the Past, Present, and Future—Where the reference is to the word Sun") seem to insist that this index will seek to attain neither the roots nor the routes of the poem's references (in contrast to Pound—see Rainey 69), but a "rested totality," a "complete appreciation . . . , the apprehension satisfied completely as to the appearance of the art form as an object" (*Prepositions* 13). Whether a "travesty" (Byrd 165) or a "parody" (Dembo 298) of the Poundian tradition, the poet's dedication as index presents a direct reversal of modernist textual practice. In beginning the poem with an all-encompassing index, Zukofsky destabilizes his own text by calling into question its host status and, in so doing, privileges a postmodernist poetry that is a found text, an ontological entity, a quantitative measure of existence, over a modernist poetry that is a message, a teleological construct, a "qualitative intuition" (Paulson, *Noise* 57) of existence.

But poetry is also a quantitative measure of its own existence, synchronous with its "movement (and tone) of words." "The care for the detail" demands, at each passing moment, "the structure" (Zukofsky, "Interview" 222), a structure that is not, to use Altieri's words, a "controlling imposition" but "a mode of attention" (15). As such, sincerity and objectification merge into a single act of writing that is "the detail, not mirage, of seeing, of thinking with the things as they exist" (*Prepositions* 12) and that, treating cultural facts as physical movements rather than intellectual stases, creates an open field of undifferentiation. Altieri writes, "Sincerity is usually not self-expression. Rather it involves insistence on the surface of the poem as concerned primarily with direct acts of naming as signs of the poet's immediate engagement in the areas of experience made present by conceiving the act of writing as a mode of attention. Sincerity involves refusing the temptations of closure—both closure as fixed form and closure as writing in the service of idea, doctrine, or abstract aesthetic ideal" (15). "Poem beginning 'The' " resists closure, either thematic or structural, by its insistence on its own surface, which is, as Michele J. Leggott puts it (in a slightly different context), "the unearthing of contingencies, those places where one voice had been, or seemed to have been, listening to another" (55):

1	The
2	Voice of Jesus I. Rush singing
3	in the wilderness
4	A boy's best friend is his mother,
5	It's your mother all the time.
6	Residue of Oedipus-faced wrecks
7	Creating out of the dead,—
8	From the candle flames of the souls of dead mothers
9	Vide the legend of thin Christ sending her
	out of the temple,—
10	Books from the stony heart, flames rapping
	the stone,
11	Residue of self-exiled men
12	By the Tyrrhenian.
	[*Complete Short Poetry* 9]

All the elements here, be they quotations or movements (and tones) of words, are threaded together in what the poet, in a letter to Pound, calls "a matter of sequential statement" (*Pound/Zukofsky* 79). Yet it is—as Zukofsky's punning on the word "matter" seems amply to suggest—a sequence of "facts as order" (*Prepositions* 18) rather than ordered facts. Although the word "mother," for instance, the "Symbol of Our Relatively Most Permanent Self, Origin and Destiny" (*Complete Short Poetry* 8), either appears or is implicated in most of the lines I have quoted, it nevertheless does not create thematic cohesion or structural patterning. The movement from line 1 to line 12 presents a physical line up of cultural artifacts in which "mother" is figured, but that movement is neither a logical structuring nor a chronological development of a theme. Zukofsky's numbering of his lines is also illustrative. While seemingly guiding the poem forward in an ordered, linear progression, these numbers demonstrate a remarkable disrespect for their own designated positions in the sequence by allowing themselves to be rearranged, thus turning the poem from a sequential ordering to a spatial configuration. With a pace of their own, they "enumerate themselves, write themselves, read themselves. . . . By themselves" (Derrida, *Dissemination* 290),[9] totally indifferent to each line's—or entry's—plea for a textual as well as contextual maneuver, proposing, as a result, what Robert Duncan calls "neither tradition nor past but immediate presentation" (424). Indeed, for Zukofsky, this "number anomaly," as Marjorie Perloff comments concerning "the often illogical numbering" of propositions in Wittgenstein's *Tractatus,* "is . . . a kind of clinamen, a bent or swerve where logic gives way to mystery" (30), a mystery of existence, with all its uncertainties and possibilities.

III

Pound's regret about being unable to use the ideal mode of presentation, one consisting of quotations without any commentary (*ABC* 95), raises another issue germane to modernist praxis: context. His extensive, repeated exposition of this subject throughout his critical writings suggests that modernist poetry is fundamentally context dependent or context sensitive.[10] For Pound, any serious art work embodies a "total perception of relations" (*Selected Prose* 268),[11] which functions, in a way, as "a sort of energy, something more or less like electricity or radioactivity, a force transfusing, welding, and unifying" (*Literary Essays* 49). In poetry, "the more highly energized" (*Literary Essays* 49) form of verbal expression, this total perception of relations is established and specified by what Grabes calls "a controlling perspective" (141), one that determines not only its own contextual circumference but that of its material, including quotations. In order that poetry "[bear] true witness" and "[be] most precise" (*Literary Essays* 44), the poet, accordingly, must choose "words for their 'meaning,' " meaning that is not "a set, cut-off thing" but "comes with roots, with associations, with how and where the word is familiarly used, or where it has been used brilliantly or memorably" (*ABC* 36). For a poet engaged in "the dance of the intellect among words," this emphasis on context appears even more crucial, in that logopoeia "employs words not only for their direct meaning, but it takes count in a special way of habits of usage, of the context we expect to find with the word, its usage concomitants, of its known acceptances, and of ironic play. It holds the aesthetic content which is peculiarly the domain of verbal manifestation, and cannot possibly be contained in plastic or in music" (*Literary Essays* 25). The same holds true for choosing quotations. So determinant, in fact, does context become in the modernist praxis that "[i]f there is anything about justice," one hears Pound announce with regard to the use of quotations in a specific reading of Seneca, "[i]t must be in the context, not in the two lines quoted" (*Selected Prose* 396).

Pound's theorizing of context helps us to formulate the text-context dichotomy undergirding the modernist use of quotation. Directed by a controlling perspective, to quote is to contextualize other texts into a new synthesis so as to initiate a communicative context, one that is, as Alan Durant describes, "translated, updated, for a new historical moment" (32). The establishment of a critical resonance across time and space then requires that both the context of the host text and the original context of the found text be impregnated with a certain conceptual overlap, a sort of "echo chamber" in which the untranslatability of logopoeia in the texts becomes translatable in the contexts that "converge and interact through quotations" (Rainey 57).[12] In other words, between these two contexts there must be "a simultaneously commemorative and projective bond" (Michael Bernstein, "History" 21). As such, the subordination of the found text to the host text in modernist poetry becomes a theatrical gesture, for the former's willingness to give up its autonomy and the latter's capability of appropriating it result from the fact that they share a stable, identical, and universal context. Viewed from this perspective, the relationship between the frame and the inset becomes, to be more exact, "a ruse, a *mise-en-scène* by which the belated writer establishes the worth of his discourse," as Claudette Sartiliot puts it, "a form of complicity" (11, 20) the Platonic nature of which massively reduces the modernist "field of equivocality" (Derrida, *Margins* 310).[13]

Moreover, for the effective "acquisition and transmission of knowledge" (Pound, *Literary Essays* 61), a poet has to select quotations on the basis not only of kind or quality but also, and perhaps more importantly, on that of amount or quantity. The presence of a certain number of found texts proportional to the quantitative scope of the host text contributes to the latter qualitatively as an organizing, hierarchical system. Properly maintained and manipulated, the ratio between these two texts helps sustain a textual as well as conceptual space where the two different contexts are engaged in a communicative conspiracy, generating as a result what Paulson calls "a contextual redundancy," which "implies a certain degree of expectability or predictability built into its structure" (*Noise* 60, 64). This contextual redundancy provides the host text with a "capacity for self-correction" and the "margin of intelligibility" (*Noise* 64).[14] The failure to achieve and maintain such a ratio invites "entropy of message" (*Noise* 57).

Although it is generally considered more fragmented and ambiguous than others of the cantos, Canto LXXIV exemplifies Pound's creation of contextual mosaics at the point where, as Diepeveen puts it, "Control occurs only through a seeming lack of control" (103). The overall context of the poem, given the autobiographical backdrop of the Pisan detention camp in which Pound was imprisoned, is the poet's own psychological complexity, a complexity articulated through the sharp juxtaposition of a mind still engaged in political debate and a consciousness ruthlessly bombarded by its futility and irrelevancy. The tension between his impulse to continue his argument and his forced acceptance of reality is such that the poet has to resort to a textual strategy as a self-defense mechanism to pull himself out of either situation before he is hurt. The result throughout the poem is a constant thought rupture by inserted alien details, interruptions that suggest the poet's increasing self-doubt.

Several pages into the canto, for instance, one finds the following lines:

Les Albigeois, a problem of history,
and the fleet at Salamis made with money lent by the state to the
                    shipwrights
            Tempus tacendi, tempus loquendi.
Never inside the country to raise the standard of living
but always abroad to increase the profits of usurers,
            dixit Lenin,
and gun sales lead to gun sales
        they do not clutter the market for gunnery
            there is no saturation . . .
                [429]

The entire passage here, except for the quotation in the middle ("Tempus tacendi, tempus loquendi"), is the continuation of the poet's passionate exposition of the issue of money in relation to the state, which can be traced back to Cantos XLII, XLIII, and XLV. While Pound, in the section preceding the quotation, uses "the fleet at Salamis made with money lent by the state to the shipwrights" as an example to "illustrate a major thesis of Social Credit, that the extension of credit should be the prerogative not of private banks but of the state, which should benefit from the interest" (Terrell 369), in the part following the quotation he condemns current corruption through the mouth of Lenin. The quotation intrudes halfway through the poet's otherwise consistent argumentative trajectory.

Translated as "A time to be silent, a time to speak," "Tempus tacendi, tempus loquendi" is, according to Terrell, "the personal motto of Sigismundo Malatesta" (120), whom Pound admires for his achievements and identifies as "a constructive and self-constructive force": Malatesta is a persona "for Pound's questing ego" (Gelpi 200, 201). The motto's context takes shape in Malatesta's love for Isotta degli Atti, which "disclosed his highest and noblest self" (Gelpi 201) and becomes crystallized when he inscribed the motto on her tomb in Rimini (Terrell 120). Against its context as such, and in a very few words, "Tempus tacendi, tempus loquendi" expresses eloquently a sense of nobility transcending the mundane, a heartfelt inadequacy of language and absence of understanding in the face of the irretrievable loss of one's love.

Pound's use of the quotation here forms a contextual juxtaposition, a variation of what Hugh Kenner identifies in *The Pound Era* as the poet's "heuristic device" in the form of the "subject-rhyme" (423). Vis-à-vis Pound's passionate pursuit of a political issue, his loss of any prospect of putting it to use, and his painful sense of alienation, there is Malatesta's noble love for Isotta degli Atti, his loss of her through death, and his stoic awareness of forced silence. As they contextually inform each other, Pound's canto transplants into its structure Malatesta's motto, which in turn bespeaks the poet's state of mind in quiet desperation, struggling to remind itself that "beauty is difficult" (444). "Good writing," Pound remarks, "is perfect control" (*Literary Essays* 49). It is a control rendered possible by "detailed specifications of context and circulation" (Durant 32), by the "precise sense," whether of words or of quotations, "as understood at that particular epoch that one would like to have set before one" (*Literary Essays* 162).

IV

To the modernist "leitmotif" of contexts, "Poem beginning 'The' " is, as the poet himself puts it, "a direct reply" (*Pound/Zukofsky* 79, 78). If the modernist qualitative intuition of existence is always dependent on context, and if, as Alison Rieke asserts, "[p]oems are, by definition, specific kinds of contexts" (117), Zukofsky's poem is one in which the established text-context dichotomy collapses and the conventional function of context is subverted. The compositional strategy the poet resorts to lies in being "more discursive" (*Pound/Zukofsky* 79), so much so that the modernist concepts of texts, contexts, and their relations are thereby pushed to each's ultimate limit, thus exposing, by default, their working mechanism as nothing but the logic of self-referentiality.

The form of the poem dramatizes a Baudrillardian critique of modernist binary thinking, in that the aggregate of found texts challenges, rather overtly, the text-context distinction as a structuralist formula based on Saussure's theory of the sign. By "an artificial separation" of a text and a context, the poem argues, at least by analogy, the modernists are able to posit "an equivalence" between "the signifier as form" and "the signified and the referent, which are registered together as content—the one of thought, the other of reality (or rather, of perception)—under the aegis of the signifier" (Baudrillard 78, 81, 83). With this separation, they succeed in putting together a system of signification in which "its second term [context as signified and referent] acts as the satellite and alibi for the first [text]" (Baudrillard 81) and becomes, in due course, the operational prerequisite for modernist poetic license. "This discretion," Baudrillard recapitulates, "is thus the very principle of the sign's rationality," whereby what begins as "a fiction" "leads to a science fiction" (Baudrillard 81, 84), turning into the cause what is in actuality the effect (Derrida, *Dissemination* 323).[15] For "the 'context' of any given text," as Branham and Pearce argue, is nothing but "the perception of it" (20), one that is, in Baudrillard's words, "carved out and projected as [the text's] function . . . reflection . . . effect . . . shadow . . . its 'pantographic' extension" (83, 84). It follows, in this way, that the context of any given quotation "is never replaced or subsumed but only imaged" by the host text, as Sternberg points out, "where the image takes the form of an inset version" (130).

Zukofsky's critique of the context as the perception and projection of the text leads to the radical formal innovation in his use of quotations, one that Pound has conceived of earlier (for an entirely different purpose, of course) but perceived (therefore) as "too revolutionary."[16] The method could be described as "crowding-out." By a *coup d'état* of excessive found texts, "Poem beginning 'The' " enacts a self-efface-ment, allowing the quotations to succeed in a complete takeover and, in so doing, erasing its own textual space. With the physical disappearance of a text as the projective agency, the poem deactivates the otherwise concomitant context, the controlling perspective that "pretends or is presumed to be exterior and external," and refuses to "reach outside of the boundaries of the writing which constitutes" itself (Polletta 88–89). What is left to environ the poem now is, literally, the half-dozen movements (and tones) of words, which form, as Hayles phrases it, a "context of no context" (275)—or, in Derrida's words, a context "without any center of absolute anchoring" (*Margins* 320).

The absence of a text armed with a contextual bond then frees the quotations from an array of conceptual assertions into an orgy of texture, of clusters of words devoid of any qualitative intuition.[17] Consider, for instance, the following lines:

45   For it's the hoo-doos, the somethin' voo-doos
46   And not Kings onelie, but the wisest men
47   Graue Socrates, what says Marlowe?
48   For it was myself seemed held

49   Beating—beating—
50   Body trembling as over an hors d'oeuvres—
51
52   And the dream ending—Dalloway! Dalloway—
53   The blind portals opening, and I awoke!
            [*Complete Short Poetry* 10–11]

Zukofsky's dedication as index makes the reference of each line clear: "College Cheer—45," "Christopher Marlowe's *Edward II*—46, 47," "The French Language—51," and "Virginia Woolf's *Mrs. Dalloway*— 52"; as for line 48, 49, 50, and 53, they must be "Obvious—Where the Reference is Obvious" (*Complete Short Poetry* 8).[18]

What Zukofsky does with these references is to push the generality of each to the extreme, a generality that is otherwise measured and adjusted by a controlling perspective in relation to other references' "different kinds and degrees of generality" (Scharfstein 187) so that each entry or quotation here is capable of relating to others: a generality, in other words, that is not only extensive enough to allow a quotation to become, as Michel Serres puts it, "independent of its empirical realizations" (69) but strict enough for a quotation to retain its "metaphorlike" function (Diepeveen 76). Once abused, this extreme generality takes a paradoxical turn: it essentializes, rather than popularizes, the quotation, insisting on its idiosyncrasy, its empirical denotations, its textual as well as contextual narcissism, which favors isolation over relation. As a result, these quotations each in its own way hearken back to contexts too exclusive to be shared and point to spheres of application too restricted to allow any trespassing.

All the reference can offer for line 45, for instance, is a college setting. Although the colloquial expression and its tone indicate a certain juvenile mischievousness, nothing else is specified. Questions such as "Cheer for what?" or "What do the 'voo-doos' refer to?" or "What is this 'somethin'?" remain unanswered. Having failed to suggest what can be expected, the ambiguity or generality then forces one's attention back to its source as the sole point of reference: the college setting. This contextual self-love or self-sealing embodied by line 45 cuts any conceptual tie with lines 46 and 47, from Marlowe's *Edward II*. Even if one identifies these two lines as offering a glimpse of a court episode in which King Edward II's relationship with his minion Gaueston is viewed philosophically by Mortimer Senior from a historical perspective (Marlowe 29), and even if one might argue that such a relation-ship is a kind of "voo-doo," which relates to the "voo-doos" back in line 45, the incompatibility between line 45 and lines 46–47 in terms of setting (college vs. court), magnitude of the issue (students' pranks vs. national interests), and attitude toward that issue (cheer vs. serious analysis) refuses any negotiations between the two parts. Furthermore, lines 48–50, purportedly "Obvious," are in fact far from it. Beginning with an adverbial clause of reason ("For it was myself seemed held"), these lines immediately throw one in medias res, confronting one with an overwhelming sense of emotional and psychological self-involve-ment or self-indulgence ("Beating—beating— / Body trembling as over an hors d'oeuvres—"), which circumscribes a world too private and too personal to be anyone's business.

Each anchoring itself firmly and rigorously in its own vague con-text, these quotations become, as Scharfstein writes, "utterly unique, which is to say, absolutely incomparable" (60). As their "referential context shrinks" to zero, "their sphere of application grows ambigu-ous" (Goodman 308). Mutually isolated and extremely fragmented, quotations in "Poem beginning 'The' " are busily engaged in a civil war, claiming simultaneously each's textual-contextual boundaries, only to be further "dismembered, reduced to decontextualized for-mulas," making themselves unable, in Zacchi's words, "to testify to the identification / identity principle of the cultural system" (107). At the same time, each quotation's relentless insistence on its own context in isolation becomes as much redundant as self-defeating, disarming the quotation of its status as a statement and reducing it further to a mere group of words. What the poem presents, then, is a writing that "does not comment," as Zukofsky writes in *A Test of Poetry,* a com-position that "does not linger to embroider words around a subject" (84, 89). Once freed from a contextual bond, quotations in "Poem beginning 'The' " cease to assert themselves as texts of messages and become merely the texture of words.

Zukofsky's critique of the modernist text-context dichotomy in "Poem beginning 'The' " creates a textless text, a "no man's land" (*Complete Short Poetry* 15, line 182), and his radical employment of quotations finds its most eloquent (if unwitting) explicator in Derrida. Since "the tree" onto which these found texts are supposed to be grafted "is ultimately rootless," writes Derrida, quotations as scions in such a text as "Poem beginning 'The' " "eventually [come] to be grafted onto [themselves]" (*Dissemination* 356). But "at the same time," Derrida continues, "everything is a root, too, since the grafted shoots themselves compose the whole of the body proper, of the tree that is called present" (*Dissemination* 356). As such, quotations or citations do not imply stasis or origin; they mean, to use Derrida's words again, "both 'setting in motion' . . . and . . . solicitation, i.e., the shakeup of a whole" (*Dissemination* 357). In this sense, "Poem beginning 'The,' " while presenting itself as a "no man's land," independent of "whatever political or religious persuasions [there may be] outside the poem" (Duncan 427), finds in this "no man's land" "the promise of 'shall be' " (*Pound/Zukofsky* 79). For Zukofsky's quotations do not represent, as John Taggart notes, "a group of discrete texts which will read the rewoven text for us" (208); rather, they suggest a reconstructive potential in the poem as texture out of which one composes one's own song, gesturing, perhaps, toward what Edward Schelb calls "a new ordering of sensibility outside of the circumference of Modernism" (32), toward what Zukofsky himself describes in "A"-12 as "Pinprick of contents, but an assemblage / of all possible positions" (174).[19]

A powerful manifesto for a new poetry, Zukofsky's "Poem beginning 'The' " is more than just "an exemplar . . . for writing yet to come in 1937" (Duncan 423). It embodies in embryo a postmodernist poetics that, as Zukofsky himself sees it, "might even bear fruit of another generation" (*Pound/Zukofsky* 79). In many ways, "Poem beginning 'The' " anticipates the later postmodern praxis exemplified by John Cage. Perhaps, even, it is Zukofsky's 1920s version of Cage's 1960s statement that "[e]veryday life [or existence for that matter] is more interesting than forms of celebration" (291).

Notes

1. See also Pound's "The Approach to Paris, v," in which he describes poetry as the "constatation of facts. It presents. It does not comment" (662).

2. See Rosalind Krauss, "Re-presenting Picasso," in which she argues that the use of the past in the modernist praxis "allows for the rewriting of succession (diachrony) as system (synchrony), thereby producing the ahistorical object" (92–93). Also cited in Diepeveen 60.

3. Michael André Bernstein makes a similar point when he writes, "Pound's language presents, represents, and invents all at once, and it does so *without privileging any single mode or trivializing essential distinctions between categories*" ("History" 17, emphasis added).

4. See also Diepeveen 65 and Zacchi 101–109. Although Zacchi emphasizes that "[o]nly transformative and regenerative operations on the original are possible" (104), and that "[q]uotations can acquire generative functions" (109), his theorizing remains largely modernist in that the "textual clash" and the corollary "new birth" from the "co-existence of the two codes" (104) contribute to, rather than call into question, a predetermined and discernible narrative line with an identifiable theme.

5. Richard Sieburth, similarly, argues that to quote is more than just to mime: "It is a mode not merely of copying or reflecting but of including the real. . . . To quote is thus to adduce words as facts, as exhibits, as documents" (121).

6. Emerson writes, "We cannot overstate our debt to the Past, but the moment has the supreme claim. The Past is for us; but the sole terms on which it can become ours are its subordination to the Present" (204).

7. Sieburth points out that Pound's "extensive and multifaceted use of quotations in the *Cantos*" presents "a logical development of a modernist aesthetic that can be traced back to those techniques of constatation and subversive juxtaposition that Flaubert applied at almost every level of his art." However, Sieburth argues, while Flaubert uses cinema-like montage as "vehicles less of metaphor or revelation than of destructive irony"—a use approximating, rather, that of Zukofsky—Pound adopts the technique for a constructive end, "ideogrammatically 'presenting one facet and then another until at some point one gets off the dead surface of the reader's mind onto a part that will register" (Sieburth 121–122, quoting *Guide to Kulchur* 51).

8. See also Diepeveen 73–74.

9. Derrida's critical commentary on Philippe Sollers's novel *Numbers* can be read as an extended punning on the word "number," which has an illuminating application to Zukofsky's use of numbers here in "Poem beginning 'The.' "

10. For a detailed discussion of the terms "context sensitive" and "context free," see Fischer.

11. See also Dasenbrook, who argues that for Pound the "essence of any situation is a relation" (108).

12. Diepeveen makes a similar argument: "Pound's emphasis on the universal implies that the disparate objects (often both historically and culturally disparate) of the quoting poem must relate to each other; they must be translatable. Eliot and Pound moved to a formal concept like pattern as the central term to support their argument about translatability and originality" (59–60).

13. For an insightful discussion of communication as a game or a complicity between two interlocutors (or between two texts, for that matter), see Michel Serres, "Platonic Dialogue" (*Hermes* 65–70).

14. Henri Atlan defines "redundancy" as "a kind of generalization of repetition," as "the existence of constraints between elements, so that knowledge

about one of them provides automatically knowledge about another." For more details, see his "Disorder, Complexity, and Meaning."

15. See also Paulson, *Noise* 61.

16. See also Leggott 99.

17. Diepeveen defines "texture" as asserting "the idiosyncratic rather than the interchangeable. Texture does not just define the sounds of a group of words, it has consequences. It shows how these sounds point to and are part of those words' individual, nonparaphrasable meanings. Texture also implies a quotation's history, its past, 'original' use and this original use's earlier appropriations by culture" (3). Diepeveen's definition, as the subtitle of his book indicates, focuses on the "formal properties" of quotations, which highlights the importance of their original contexts. While agreeing with him in all of these observations, I also use the word "texture" here to refer to quotations as raw material in the sense that, without a contextual framing by a text's controlling perspective, quotations are simply words in cluster to be used or reused.

18. In his "Portrait of the Artist as a Young Jew: Zukofsky's 'Poem beginning "The" ' in Context," John Tomas writes that "[s]uch references . . . ensure that nobody will take these notes seriously" (44). His own reading of the poem is, as the title of his article indicates, based on a serious consideration of references and contexts that he locates elsewhere, as a replacement for the references provided by the poet. What seems to have been overlooked in Tomas's approach is, perhaps, the possibility that it is precisely Zukofsky's lack of seriousness that makes the point here.

19. Critics have already started working on this aspect of Zukofsky's poetry. Michele J. Leggott, in her discussion of "A"-22 and -23 as the poet's attempt to condense "six thousand years of historical record" into "a persistent sound rather than names," describes the condensing process as follows: "Texts ingested into Zukofsky's system of notebooks have had their links with other kinds of historical reality severed; from this point they are materials for Zukofsky history, to be further condensed and marshalled as plans develop" (7, 56). Taggart's reading of "A"-12 and its source material in Hasidic sayings (199–200) reveals a compositional strategy strikingly similar to that of "Poem beginning 'The.' " He argues, furthermore, that "to try to locate specific sources" for Zukofsky's poetry presents "a temptation difficult and even misleading"; for "[w]hat Zukofsky has done is to separate the words and phrases from their original contexts to provide himself with a vocabulary for composition" (208, 200).

Works Cited

Altieri, Charles. "The Objectivist Tradition." *Chicago Review* 30.3 (Winter 1979): 5–22.

Atlan, Henri. "Disorder, Complexity, and Meaning." *Disorder and Order.* Ed. Paisley Livingston. Saratoga, CA: Anma Libri, 1984. 109–128.

Barthes, Roland. *Image, Music, Text*. Trans. Stephen Heath. New York: The Noonday Press, 1977.

Baudrillard, Jean. *Selected Writings*. Ed. Mark Poster. Stanford: Stanford UP, 1988.

Bernstein, Charles. Interview. *Difficulties* 2.1 (Fall 1982): 29–42.

Bernstein, Michael André. "Bringing It All Back Home: Derivations and Quotations in Robert Duncan and the Poundian Tradition." *Sagetrieb* 1.2 (Fall 1982): 176–189.

———. "History and Textuality in Ezra Pound's *Cantos*." *Ezra Pound and History*. Ed. Marianne Korn. Orono, ME: National Poetry Foundation, 1985. 15–22.

Branham, Robert J., and W. Barnett Pearce. "Between Text and Context: Toward a Rhetoric of Contextual Reconstruction." *Quarterly Journal of Speech* 71.1 (February 1985): 19–36.

Byrd, Don. "The Shape of Zukofsky's Canon." *Louis Zukofsky: Man and Poet*. Ed. Carroll F. Terrell. Orono, ME: National Poetry Foundation, 1979. 163–185.

Cage, John. "Cagean Esthetics." *Esthetics Contemporary*. Ed. Richard Kostelanetz. Rev. ed. Buffalo: Prometheus, 1989. 290–301.

Clark, Herbert H., and Richard J. Gerrig. "Quotations as Demonstrations." *Language* 66:4 (December 1990): 764–805.

Clarvoe, Jennifer. "Quoting History, Reading Poetry." *Agni Review* (1990): 326–333.

Dasenbrook, Reed Way. *The Literary Vorticism of Ezra Pound and Wyndham Lewis: Towards the Condition of Painting*. Baltimore: Johns Hopkins UP, 1985.

Dembo, L. S. "Louis Zukofsky: Objectivist Poetics and the Quest for Form." *Louis Zukofsky: Man and Poet*. Ed. Carroll F. Terrell. Orono, ME: National Poetry Foundation, 1979. 283–303.

Derrida, Jacques. *Dissemination*. Trans. Barbara Johnson. Chicago: U of Chicago P, 1981.

———. *Margins of Philosophy*. Trans. Alan Bass. Chicago: U of Chicago P, 1982.

Diepeveen, Leonard. *Changing Voices: The Modern Quoting Poem*. Ann Arbor: U of Michigan P, 1993.

Duncan, Robert. "As Testimony: Reading Zukofsky These Forty Years." *Paideuma* 7:3 (Winter 1978): 421–427.

Durant, Alan. "The Language of History in *The Cantos*." *Ezra Pound and History*. Ed. Marianne Korn. Orono, ME: National Poetry Foundation, 1985. 23–35.

Eliot, T. S. "The Metaphysical Poets." *Criticism: The Major Texts*. Ed. Walter Jackson Bate. Enlarged ed. New York: Harcourt Brace Jovanovich, 1970. 529–534.

———. "Philip Massinger." *The Sacred Wood: Essays on Poetry and Criticism*. New York: Knopf, 1930. 123–143.

———. "Tradition and the Individual Talent." *Critical Theory Since Plato*. Ed. Hazard Adams. New York: Harcourt Brace Jovanovich, 1971. 784–787.

Emerson, Ralph Waldo. "Quotation and Originality." *Letters and Social Aims*. Boston: Houghton Mifflin, 1904. 175–204.

Fischer, Andreas. "Context-Free and Context-Sensitive Literature: Sherwood Anderson's *Winesburg, Ohio* and James Joyce's *Dubliners.*" *Reading Contexts.* Ed. Neil Forsyth. Swiss Papers in English Language and Literature, vol. 4. Tübingen: Gunter Narr Verlag, 1988. 12–31.

Gelpi, Albert. *A Coherent Splendor: The American Poetic Renaissance, 1910–1950.* Cambridge: Cambridge UP, 1987.

Goodman, Lenn E. "Context." *Philosophy East and West* 38.3 (July 1988): 307–323.

Grabes, Herbert. "Deliberate Intertextuality: The Function of Quotation and Allusion in the Early Poetry of T. S. Eliot." *Multiple Worlds, Multiple Words.* Ed. Hena Maes-Jelinek, Pierre Michel, and Paulette Michel-Michot. Liège, Belgium: English Department, U of Liège, 1987. 139–152.

Hatlen, Burton. "From Modernism to Postmodernism: Zukofsky's 'A'-12." *Sagetrieb* 11.1–2 (Spring–Fall 1992): 21–34.

Hayles, N. Katherine. *Chaos Bound: Orderly Disorder in Contemporary Literature and Science.* Ithaca: Cornell UP, 1990.

Johnson, Barbara. Translator's Introduction. *Dissemination.* By Jacques Derrida. Chicago: U of Chicago P, 1981. vii–xxxiii.

Kappel, Andrew J. "The Reading and Writing of a Modern Paradiso: Ezra Pound and the Books of Paradise." *Twentieth Century Literature* 27.3 (Fall 1981): 223–246.

Kenner, Hugh. Foreword. *Prepositions: Collected Critical Essays.* By Louis Zukofsky. Expanded ed. Berkeley: U of California P, 1981. vii–x.

———. *The Pound Era.* Berkeley: U of California P, 1971.

Krauss, Rosalind. "Re-presenting Picasso." *Art in America* (December 1980): 90–96.

Leggott, Michele J. *Reading Zukofsky's 80 Flowers.* Baltimore: Johns Hopkins UP, 1989.

Marlowe, Christopher. *Marlowe's Edward II.* Ed. William Dinsmore Briggs. London: David Nutt, 1914.

Moore, Marianne. "The Cantos." *The Complete Prose of Marianne Moore.* New York: Viking, 1986. 268–277.

Nägele, Rainer. "Benjamin's Ground." *Benjamin's Ground: New Readings of Walter Benjamin.* Ed. Rainer Nägele. Detroit: Wayne State UP, 1988. 19–37.

Paulson, William R. "Literature, Complexity, Interdisciplinarity." *Chaos and Order: Complex Dynamics in Literature and Science.* Ed. N. Katherine Hayles. Chicago: U of Chicago P, 1991. 37–53.

———. *The Noise of Culture: Literary Texts in a World of Information.* Ithaca: Cornell UP, 1988.

Perloff, Marjorie. "Toward an Avant-Garde Tractatus: Russell and Wittgenstein on War." *Common Knowledge* 2.1 (Spring 1993): 15–34.

Polletta, Gregory. "Textuality, Actuality, and Contextuality: The Example of

Gravity's Rainbow." *Reading Contexts.* Ed. Neil Forsyth. Swiss Papers in English Language and Literature, vol. 4. Tübingen: Gunter Narr Verlag, 1988. 83–101.

Pound, Ezra. *ABC of Reading.* New York: New Directions, 1934.

———. "The Approach to Paris, v." *New Age* 13 (2 October 1913): 662.

———. *The Cantos of Ezra Pound.* New York: New Directions, 1986.

———. *Guide to Kulchur.* New York: New Directions, 1970.

———. *Literary Essays of Ezra Pound.* Ed. T. S. Eliot. New York: New Directions, 1935.

———. *Selected Prose, 1909–1965.* Ed. William Cookson. New York: New Directions, 1973.

Rainey, Lawrence S. *Ezra Pound and the Monument of Culture: Text, History, and the Malatesta Cantos.* Chicago: U of Chicago P, 1991.

Rieke, Alison. "Words' Contexts, Contexts' Nouns: Zukofsky's Objectivist Quotations." *Contemporary Literature* 33.1 (Spring 1992): 113–134.

Sartiliot, Claudette. *Citation and Modernity: Derrida, Joyce, and Brecht.* Norman: U of Oklahoma P, 1993.

Scharfstein, Ben-Ami. *The Dilemma of Context.* New York: New York UP, 1989.

Schelb, Edward. "Through Rupture to Destiny: Repetition in Zukofsky." *Sagetrieb* 9.1–2 (Spring–Fall 1990): 25–42.

Serres, Michel. *Hermes: Literature, Science, Philosophy.* Baltimore: Johns Hopkins UP, 1982.

Sieburth, Richard. *Instigations: Ezra Pound and Rémy de Gourmont.* Cambridge, MA: Harvard UP, 1978.

Sternberg, Meir. "Proteus in Quotation-Land: Mimesis and the Forms of Reported Discourse." *Poetics Today* 3.2 (Spring 1982): 107–156.

Taggart, John. *Songs of Degrees: Essays on Contemporary Poetry and Poetics.* Tuscaloosa: U of Alabama P, 1994.

Terrell, Carroll F. *A Companion to 'The Cantos of Ezra Pound.'* Berkeley: U of California P, 1980.

Tomas, John. "Portrait of the Artist as a Young Jew: Zukofsky's 'Poem beginning "The" ' in Context." *Sagetrieb* 9.1–2 (Spring–Fall 1990): 43–64.

Webster's New World Dictionary of the American Language. 2nd college ed. New York: Simon & Schuster, 1982.

Wiener, Norbert. *The Human Use of Human Beings: Cybernetics and Society.* New York: Da Capo, 1954.

Zacchi, Romana. "Quoting Words and Worlds: Discourse Strategies in *Ulysses.*" *James Joyce Quarterly* 27.1 (Fall 1989): 101–109.

Zukofsky, Louis. "Interview." *The Contemporary Writer: Interviews with Sixteen Novelists and Poets.* Ed. L. S. Dembo and Cyrena N. Pondrom. Madison: U of Wisconsin P, 1972. 216–232.

———. *Pound/Zukofsky: Selected Letters of Ezra Pound and Louis Zukofsky.* Ed. Barry Ahearn. New York: New Directions, 1987.

8

Writing and Authority in Zukofsky's
Thanks to the Dictionary

PETER QUARTERMAIN

There will have to be a
Redefinition of writing
— Louis Zukofsky, "A"-13 (292)

I

IN CONSIDERING ZUKOFSKY'S POETICS of procedural composition, as the following notes on the writer's authority must, I have in mind something along the lines of Joseph Conte's notions of "a procedural order that is proteinic and predetermined," and one that is "aleatory," random, and "protean" (11), but I make no sharp distinctions between the two, for it appears to me that Zukofsky frequently combines them. Much of the general drift especially of the later parts of my discussion draws upon the English poet J. H. Prynne's remarkable essay *Stars, Tigers and the Shape of Words*.

I take as key and starting point (my italics), Zukofsky's 1966 comment "That's Herrick: I want to *deduce* something as good as that" in the *Poetry U.S.A.* film about him,[1] and his repeated determination to be a writer "representative" of his age. Zukofsky's friend the English poet Basil Bunting admired Spenser for abandoning *The Faerie Queene* after finishing only six of the poem's projected twelve books because neither the poem nor its author could keep pace with the rapidly changing late sixteenth-century world. This is but one way of saying that the poet must be representative of his time, and that Spenser had the wit to recognize his poem's increasing inability to be so representative. It is a common artistic ambition, of course: Théophile Gautier pursued it avidly, and surely it is one of the great driving forces behind Ezra Pound's enormous economy of literary energy. Zukofsky repeatedly admired the representative quality of writers he admired (like Whitman, say, Adams, or Apollinaire) and affirmed it as his own intention: "I don't want to falsify my time," he told an audience in London in 1969, "so I get it down" (*Prepositions* 170). As Zukofsky well knew,[2] it is an extremely difficult thing consciously to achieve, and the difficulty is compounded if you believe—as did, for instance, Pound or Eliot, Bunting or Zukofsky—that the poem must approximate the condition of music, that its most important feature is its sound, the form rather than the purport of the saying and doing. The connection of the poem to music is of course very ancient indeed, as is that between music and mathematics.

Notions of the mathematical basis of the arts have a long history, reaching back through Dryden and Spenser to Alberti and Piero della Francesca to Plato and beyond; none of us needs reminding that "number" and "measure" and "metre" are terms shared by mathematics and prosody. But they enjoyed something of a revival in the twenties and thirties, John Rodker in 1926 suggesting that the "mathematical preoccupation" of futurism "has lately touched all the arts in some degree. In music Schoenberg, . . . and in literature Miss Stein" (11). Edith Sitwell quoted with approval Eugene Jolas's praise of Stein's "mathematical" lucidity (217), and Zukofsky himself pointed in the early sections of "*A*" to Bach's and Mozart's "calculus." Sometime in 1937 Zukofsky remarked in a letter to Niedecker that Newton was discovering the calculus at the same time Bach was writing mathematical counterpoint, and he specifically linked Bach and Mozart's calculus to that of the just completed "calculus" section of "*A*"-8. Such considerations of form necessarily redraw the relationship between the writer's motives and his or her desires for the finished work. Eliot thus formulated writing, in perhaps the most widely read literary essay of the century ("Tradition and the Individual Talent"), as an escape from personality.

In the early 1930s George Kingsley Zipf, an assistant professor of German at Harvard, taking a number of languages as his database (Chinese, English, German, Latin), attempted to show through "the direct application of statistical principles to the objective speech phenomena" (xi) that "the length of a word is closely related to the frequency of its usage." The statistical method, he said, "may well prove itself of considerable service in studying objectively the otherwise highly subjective phenomena of meaning, value, and experience" (12), and in what he called "a cautious inspection of the problems of meaning, emotion, and mental phenomena in general," his book *The Psycho-Biology of Language: An Introduction to Dynamic Philology* (1935) explicitly aimed "through the discussion of meaning and emotion to bring our new linguistic data into a rational perspective with the rest of human behavior." Noting that in all languages under analysis "the most frequent word in any sample will occur on the average once in approximately every 10 words, the second . . . in every 20 words," and so on, Zipf concluded that the distribution of words in any sample "approximates with remarkable precision an harmonic series" (xii). Acknowledging that "speech-phenomena cannot be isolated from the content of speech, nor from the personal, social, and cultural backgrounds of the speaker" (6)—that is to say that people use language for expressive and communicative purposes, and try to say what they mean—Zipf suggested that the speaker's control of meaning was more apparent than real, subject as it was to "dynamic laws of speech with general applicability in any language" (3). Those laws, of which Zipf argued the speaker is unaware, are impersonal and highly ordered "underlying forces which impel linguistic expression" (3). How, then, be representative of your age?

It is a truism, not to say trite, to remark that time and space diminish the precision of expressive or communicative utterance and with their passage render increasingly imperfect the expressive and communicative power of a given utterance. The expressive and communicative aspects of language are so dependent upon the circumstances that produced utterance, on the tones and gestures accompanying it, that our recollection of something someone else said lasts a matter of hours or even minutes. We have each of us in the small hours written notes to ourselves that were totally incomprehensible some few hours later. Zukofsky himself a shade ruefully talks in "A"-12 about old work,

> Much of it in pencil—blurred—other
>   notes written over it
> I can't read back thru the years—
>   ["A"-12, 251]

And there is a wonderful instance of Charles Olson at Goddard College in April 1962 reading a poem he'd written less than three months earlier: "I don't know, I don't even know what the hell I'm referring to—wait a minute. . . . Can you help me? What am I talking about there? Do you know what I'm talking about?" (24–25). As the semantic theorist John Lyons puts it, "there is much in the structure of languages that can only be explained on the assumption that they have developed for communication in face-to-face interaction" (637–638).

Yet if the passage of space and time may be seen to diminish the precision of utterance, it is equally true that their passage enlarges its scope and range by radically decontextualizing and recontextualizing it. Immense labors of scholarship have been devoted to determining whether a particular phrase in Catullus is lascivious or not, but no debate reckons the poems (or the phrase) worthless; there is sharp disagreement about the meaning of key passages of (say) *Billy Budd,* but there is no disagreement either that the passages are key or that *Billy Budd* is worth attending to. This is but another way of saying that such works stand the test of time and of translation, and that they do so by rather paradoxical, if not baffling, means. It also, I believe, reinforces Bunting's persuasion that the meaning of poetry "lies in the relation to one another of lines and patterns of sound, perhaps harmonious, perhaps contrasting and clashing, which the hearer feels rather than understands" (2).[3] So how can the poet be representative of the age? To point to Herrick—presumably "representative" of his age—and want "to deduce something as good as that" is to point to the poem as an intellectual construct, subject to a form of analysis that can strip the poem down to its essentials.

And to do *that* is to point to composition by procedure. The 1930s were a decade of intense and astonishingly varied literary activity for Zukofsky[4]; one of his multifarious projects involved exploring the means by which the poem can achieve such "objective" status. Stated perhaps too simply, his concentration on procedure is an investigation into meaning by deliberately obscuring the motives of utterance, yet without, I think, relinquishing the personal in ways that Eliot had seemed to call for. I want to list three of these procedures, I shall mess up the chronology in doing so, and I shall discuss only one of them in any detail. Between them they combine certain aspects of Conte's "aleatory" and "predetermined" procedures.

1. *Counting and letter distribution.* During the 1930s Zukofsky un-

dertook a series of statistical and sequential analyses of letter distribution in a number of canonical English lyric poems. Used in "A"-8, "A"-9, and indeed, elsewhere. Sufficiently well known to warrant no discussion here,[5] but closely connected to:

2. *Transliteration*. In answer to the question "What sound effects are you conscious of using or seeking?" in 1973 Zukofsky answered simply: "Transliteration (as in C. & L. Z. *Catullus*)" ("On Rhythm" 66). Adopted as a compositional principle in "A"-15 and later works, transliteration has a long history in Zukofsky's poetics, reaching back possibly as far as "A"-7 or "A"-9 but taking a much more central place in later work, with transliterations (in alphabetical order) from Greek, Hebrew, Latin, Ojibway, and Welsh as well as (possibly) French and German.[6] Counting and transliteration procedures are both close to Zipf; the next is not, and seems in its assumptions to work against them.

3. *The aleatory and random*. *Thanks to the Dictionary*, in retelling a well-known story, by arbitrarily and even randomly determined means introduces major disruptions that severely break conventional narrative and reference while by and large observing syntactic propriety; such behavior both diminishes the preciseness of utterance and enlarges its scope. This strategy, that is to say, both undermines and enlarges the significance of the story this "novel" tells. It explores, in J. H. Prynne's phrase, "the meaning-bearing nature of system violations"—an activity Zipf had himself pointed to (though in different terms) in *The Psycho-Biology of Language*[7]—for it enables Zukofsky, by means of disruptive processes, to explore the implications of his comment in 1931 that "the sound and pitch emphasis of a word are never apart from its meaning. In this sense each poem has its own laws" (*Prepositions* 17).

Each of these methods may be considered accidental; each is an attack not only on le mot juste but on most forms of authorial control, and each may turn out to be a source of iridescence (an accidental color), for the words, as Prynne puts it, act both as agencies of expression and as narrative "substrate for smelting and re-working into new forms" (30).[8]

II

Zukofsky started work on *Thanks to the Dictionary* in July 1932; it would occupy him on and off until 1939, when (16 August) he at last settled on a sequential order for the piece, signed and dated it, and sent it to a friend to be typed. The actual writing (as opposed to arrangement) was probably pretty much complete by December 1934, when he sent an extract entitled "from *Thanks to the Dictionary*" to Kerker Quinn's magazine *Direction*.[9] In 1935 he sent a quite differently ordered (and much shorter) selection, with the title "Parts of a Novel," to Basil Bunting,[10] and in 1951 he went through the text yet again, making extracts for a projected (and aborted?) magazine somewhat ironically titled *Possibilities*. Cid Corman's publication of *"A" 1–12* in 1959 encouraged Zukofsky to turn to *Thanks to the Dictionary* yet again, making further extracts, and the complete work was eventually published by Corman in Japan in 1961, almost thirty years after its inception, as the final section of *It Was,* in an edition of 250 copies.[11] Off and on, then, the book engaged Zukofsky's attention for close to thirty years.

So far as we can tell, other productions of the 1930s did not, even though they too remained unpublished or remained as unobtainable as *Le style Apollinaire,* published (1934) in Paris in a small edition mostly destroyed in a warehouse fire. Zukofsky seems not, that is to say, to have attended persistently to the fate of other works long unpublished and exactly contemporary with *Thanks to the Dictionary,* if he attended to them at all. The filmscript of *Ulysses,* written 1932–1935 with Jerry Reisman, and his compilation *A Workers Anthology,* completed in 1935 and then abandoned, are (like the four lengthy articles and eleven radio scripts of the *Index of American Design,* written 1938–1940) still unpublished half a century after their completion. Even *Arise, arise,* completed in 1936, seems to have languished in neglect until Zukofsky submitted it to Kerker Quinn's magazine *Accent* in the summer of 1953,[12] but it would remain unpublished until Lita Hornick printed it in *Kulchur* in 1962; it was then directed by Jerry Benjamin for the New/Kinda Theater Company in August 1965. The 1973 Grossman edition was early remaindered and has long been out of print.[13]

Why did *Thanks to the Dictionary* so engage Zukofsky's attention? No one besides Michele Leggott and Barrett Watten seems to have paid it any attention whatsoever, and by conventional standards it is no doubt to be counted a rather unsuccessful literary experiment. It is among the most puzzling of Zukofsky's texts, extremely difficult to read, utterly resistant to paraphrase. Even if you already know the story of King David it seems to make no sense whatsoever.

About 10,000 words long, *Thanks to the Dictionary* retells the story of David, the second king of Israel, 1055–1015 B.C.E., as recounted in the Bible (I and II Samuel–I Kings). It consists of twenty-nine un-numbered sections (though in manuscript drafts they were numbered) and a preface (270). The preface consists of a somewhat baffling itali-cized sentence: "*And what will the writers do then, poor things.*"[14] Devoid of any immediately intelligible context, it not only starts things off in medias res, its anaphoric (backward pointing) *then* perhaps echoing the opening of Pound's *Cantos* ("And then went down to the ship"), but also points to what is to come—a somewhat puzzling episodic narrative organized according to no immediately discernible principle.

Five of the twenty-nine sections have a title: "Young David" (271–272); "Thru the Eyes of Jonathan" (277); "David and Michal" (282–283); "David and Bath-sheba" (286–287); and "Degrees" (290–291). Each of the twenty-nine sections draws much of its vocabulary from a page from one of two dictionaries, a 1930 *Funk and Wagnalls Practical Standard Dictionary,* and a 1917 *Webster's Collegiate Dictionary.*[15] The page determining the vocabulary of each episode was as a rule estab-lished—as the twenty-fifth section tells us—by a throw of dice. It is difficult to say how strictly Zukofsky stuck to his procedure, since the opening section draws on the opening page (page 1) of *Funk and Wag-nalls.* "Degrees," the twenty-sixth section and at one time no doubt the actual preface to the work, tells us not only about the dice, but also that the dice chose page 327 (of *Webster's*), which apparently begins with the entry for *Dib,* with *Dickson City,* a borough in East Pennsyl-vania, among its entries.[16] The closing words of this section, in telling us that the dictionary page for the next (twenty-seventh) section was deliberately chosen (and thus a violation of procedure), hints at the possibility that this section was itself chosen because it includes the entry for *dictionary:* "on page 303, the hand has turned back, there is David" (291).

David is the subject of section 27 (291–298). Almost 3,000 words, this section is the longest of *Thanks to the Dictionary.* It is also, after its opening paragraph, the only straightforward piece in the whole work, a condensation of the biblical history of David mostly in a single ur-gent paragraph of great narrative drive. Where the other sections of *Thanks to the Dictionary* rely upon the inclusion of apparently irrele-vant subject matter seemingly designed to block referentiality or at least seriously impede it, this section (after its opening paragraph) relies

PETER QUARTERMAIN

for its urgency on the omission of detail in the interests of lucidity—there are many gaps, much white space on the page, sometimes simply a direct omission: "David came to Saul. He became his   . David took a harp and played" (291); "David fled from   , and came and said to Jonathan, —what have I done?" (293); "David also took   , and they were both of them his wives" (294). In his letter of 1 December 1934 Zukofsky told Quinn that the gaps separated episodes in the story, but this particular telling, clear and urgent as it is, full of names though it is, seems nevertheless rather to point toward Zukofsky's words in "A"-22, "History's best emptied of names' / impertinence" (511).

Zukofsky's compositional procedures interest me here and the ends to which they seem to be put. Section 27 (the story of David) opens with a paragraph that draws on page 303 of *Webster's,* working (but not in alphabetical order) from "Date" to "Dauphin" to "Dative" to "Dauber" to "Daughter" to "Datum" until it reaches what appears to be the terminus ad quem, "David," whereupon it then settles into telling David's story in a single paragraph that is over six printed pages long.[17] In the opening paragraph (291), as in the rest of the work, Zukofsky varies his recourse to the dictionary, though not in any apparent pattern, sometimes using a term in isolation ("Dates! dates! dates!"), sometimes giving the term and its definition ("Who paints coarsely or cheaply—a dauber, a dabber"), sometimes transcribing or citing a definition without identifying or using the term ("a conceded fact"—the definition of "datum"). I cannot even guess what determined Zukofsky's choices here—a further throw of the dice? impulse? an idle casting of the eye down the page? To the reader it seems almost randomly determined, so that although at times reading *Thanks to the Dictionary* may, at the local level of the episode or the sentence, feel a bit like reading something like Clark Coolidge's *The Maintains,* with which its deployment of dictionary formulas seems to have something in common, it is by no means as tightly structured a work as Coolidge's.

For at the global level *Thanks to the Dictionary* is equally puzzling, equally a skirting of chaos: after the first (which begins on page 1 of the dictionary) the sections follow no identifiable sequence. Indeed, Zukofsky's seven- or eight-year tinkering with the order of the sections seems to have culminated in a principle of *dis*order, almost as though he felt the need to demonstrate the truth of Bunting's comment, in an essay he sent to Zukofsky on 1 May 1935, that "cacophany is at least as intricate an art as harmony" ("Lion and Lizard" 30). An examination of the manuscripts suggests that Zukofsky did something like this: writing the story of David in its customary chronological sequence, cast the dice, turn to the dictionary page thus selected, incorporate what terms and/or definitions are to be incorporated, and when you've finished, start the next episode of the story in a new section, casting the dice again to find a new page, and so on. Reading *Thanks to the Dictionary*, I might add, it is difficult to determine exactly what constitutes an "episode" or how its parameters are determined. When he'd finished the first draft of the whole work (sometime in 1934) Zukofsky seems initially to have ordered the narrative approximately in the sequence of the dictionary pages used, so that the *alphabetical dictionary order* would determine the narrative sequence.[18] Such a procedure severely disturbs the chronological or "logical" sequence of the story's events, the sequence of historical narrative, reconfiguring perhaps our notion not only of story and of plot (of what happened and why) but also of how narrative meaning is constituted. Over the next half-dozen years or so (1934 to 1939 or 1940), he tinkered with the order, in the extract he sent to Bunting omitting the preface and first section altogether and starting with what is now section 28: "There was a horse, its face bauson" (298). Though the final chronological version does seem vaguely indeed to follow a chronological approximation of the story (from youth to age, at any rate) Zukofsky seems in determining the final order of *Thanks to the Dictionary* to be bent on ensuring that the work follow no clearly identifiable sequence, whether chronological in the narrative, alphabetical from the dictionary, whatever. Hence, as section 25 puts it,

> —Design!
> —Who wants a design?
> . . . .
> —Hey, this novel wants a design!
> —Okay! — says David—you find it!
>   [289–290]

Words immediately followed, in the final version, by "Degrees," the section that seems most properly fitted to be the work's preface.

There are, then, two major sources of confusion, both derived from Zukofsky's application of a single procedure: the throw of the dice. In the published version the global disorder, a rupture of sequence and thus of intelligibility or at least of narrative harmony, echoes and mirrors the local disorder within the sentence, a kind of dislocution of utterance producing a species of semantic cacophony. "Who wants a design?" asks section 25. And section 26 answers, "Thanks to the Dictionary, this book will be prefaced. As against any dictator, there is that book containing the words of a language, modes of expression, diction" (290). As against *any* dictator? Thanks to my dictionary I know that a dictator is a person who speaks words aloud for someone else to write down, and/or a person whose pronouncements on some subject are meant to be taken as the final word, and/or a ruler with absolute power and authority. David the second King of Israel "became," one reference book tells me, "the pattern and standard by which all succeeding rulers were measured, the prototype of the last perfect ruler, the Messiah."[19] Here, in *Thanks to the Dictionary,* the dice and the dictionary together are now dictator, with the Bible a triumvirate (I shall return to this observation later). Following *their* dictates, Zukofsky-amanuensis tells a very strange story indeed, comic, grave, mad, lyrical, labored, prankish, reflective, grotesque, dramatic, horrific, ludicrous, yearning. So in section 3, "after the winter everybody in Bethlehem had the flu," David journeys (I Samuel 17) to supply his brothers and the army with such circumlocutions as "the ground and bolted substance of wheat," and such anachronisms as blancmange and vermouth (instead of parched corn, bread, and cheese) (272). Recourse to the dictionary tells us he carries *flour* and *flummery* and the *fluid extract* of wormwood.

But recourse to the dictionary does not make the passage any more intelligible, even though it ends telling us "it was that way he met the Philistine" (274). What happens instead is that recourse to the dictionary provides additional and nonbiblical material for the narrative, blocking reference through a series of ambiguations and seeming irrelevancies. "The dense head-like clusters of the sessile florets lined up a passage for display," says one sentence in this episode (272), in its staggering ambiguity sounding remarkably like an inept translation into English. Insofar as the Bible is itself a translation, Zukofsky's activity is parodic if not emblematic, in this instance of the translation from Hebrew to English. The sentence immediately following, though it starts out more or less intelligible, quite rapidly turns into a vaguely suggestive gibberish composed of definitions culled from the dictionary by an imperfect speaker of American English, cursed with literary pretensions: "The stream was one issue, the flow-moss rising and falling with the water, and not forming a bog: imperfectly fluid, and a deformation of a solid body, but a gliding of interglobular movement such as might be rendered with an easy, gentle movement of speech— the brightest, finest, choicest of a period" (272–273). A scene impossible to visualize, and with only the vaguest associative connection— through the definition of *flower* with which it closes—to King David the Psalmist, whose story this purports to be.

Or does it. Is it not rather a *flourish,* which in music (the dictionary tells us) is "an elaborate but unmeaning passage for display, or as preparation for real performance." Is *Thanks to the Dictionary,* then, a sort of psalm, or the rehearsal of one?

The preface, *"And what will the writers do then, poor things,"* is a poor excuse for a preface; not until we reach the twenty-fifth section (290–291) do we find something that claims to be preface. Yet the diversionary tactics with which *Thanks to the Dictionary* abounds are such that, all this flummery to the contrary, the opening of *Thanks to the Dictionary,* drawn from page 1 of *Funk and Wagnalls,* tells us a great deal and is, indeed, a perfectly adequate preface. " 'A'. Quoting the dictionary" it begins (270). "Remembering my sawhorses, my little a.'s abbreviated for afternoon, perhaps for years, this afternoon." A little masterpiece of seeming misdirection and non sequitur, after five more sentences it ends, "But David who resists all its agents is free from iridescence, and without accidentals. If there is iridescence, it will be at his toes. His name, these words till now, are almost his story." *Almost* history?

So far as the dictionary is concerned, the whole paragraph is pretty straightforward (it is only 155 words long), the only words likely to give us pause in the intervening sentences being *Ab* and *Abad,* and these perhaps because they have fallen out of most dictionaries. *Abad* is familiar to most of us as a suffix in Indian place names; it is Hindi for—as Zukofsky tells us—peopled, cultivated, an inhabited place, especially a city. *Ab* is the eleventh month of the Jewish calendar, in which falls the holy day commemorating (with fasting) the Destruction of the Temple. Zukofsky puts it a little differently: "[W]hen the fast will not commemorate a Temple in ruins, Aaron's rod, the serpent to blossom, will grow, goldenrod." *Ab* usually falls in July and August, when goldenrod flowers; page 1 of the dictionary tells us not only that goldenrod is one name for Aaron's Rod, but also, as Michele Leggott reminds us in *Reading Zukofsky's* 80 *Flowers*, that "the first mention of Aaron's rod, before it budded and flowered, appointing Aaron and his brothers keepers of the tabernacle (Num. 17:8, 18:3), occurred when he cast it down before Pharaoh and it turned into a serpent which swallowed up the rods-also-turned-serpents of the Egyptian enchanters (Exod. 7:10–12)" (312–313)—hence "the serpent to blossom." All this is pretty straightforward and is, if not more or less common knowledge, at least pretty generally available in a public way.

But two other features of the first section of *Thanks to the Dictionary* deserve notice. While much of the information in this prose comes from the dictionary—a public source—some of it does not, but is completely personal. Who, among Zukofsky's readers in 1932, would recognize the sawhorses of "A"-7, or recognize "my little a.'s"? Who, for that matter, would in 1932 notice that personal Zukofskian interjection in the identification of *Ab*, "when the fast will *not* commemorate a Temple in ruins"? Only, perhaps, the reader already familiar with "A"-4, with its lines:

> We had a speech, our children have
> evolved a jargon.
> We prayed, Open, God, gate of Psalmody,
> . . . .
> Deafen us, God, deafen us to their music,
> Our own children have passed over to the ostracized.
> ["A"-4, 12–13]

When Zukofsky wrote *Thanks to the Dictionary,* the whole of "A" 1–7 had just—almost, indeed, at the very moment he started writing these words—been published in *An "Objectivists" Anthology.* It is worth noting that Zukofsky would virtually suspend work on "*A*" until he had completed *Thanks to the Dictionary,* starting "A"-8 on 5 August 1935 and finishing it on 14 July 1937. One thread running through *Thanks to the Dictionary* like a patterning of tropes is a more or less private and personal discourse that refers to Zukofsky's own work, in the form of horses, flowers, leaves, music, and so on. These are his little a's.

Then, too, there is the fine distinction made about David, "on his page, *not* like a slab forming the top of a capital"—which is an abacus—yet who is "not *unlike* . . . a reckoning table," which is an abacus (270; my italics). To "reckon," says *Funk and Wagnalls,* is to tell over by particulars, to enumerate, count, to esteem, to come to a settlement of one's differences with another. David, on *his* page "not unlike a reckoning table telling its sums will embrace all the words of this novel." But what, then, is to be reckoned? Perhaps Zukofsky's phrasing, which is to say his use of the dictionary, including of course his use of pun: "His name, these words till now, are almost his story." Which words are *these* words—and when is *now?* The play of possibility, in which *these words* can refer exophorically, outside the text, to the dictionary or the Bible, is echoed in the exophoric play in which *now* can be not this stage in the telling of the story but this stage of human history (i.e., 1932 or even the now in which the reader reads the story). There is a great deal to do with time in *Thanks to the Dictionary.* A dictionary, the dictionary tells us, is a word book containing all the words in a language—in which case, then, section 25's "prefatory remark" that "as against any dictator, there is that book containing the words of a language" (290) opposes the dictionary, its words, its language, not only against Hitler or Mussolini (rising to power in 1932) but also against David, second king of Israel, risen to power in 1055 B.C.E., and against Zukofsky himself, writing to power in 1932. "These words" may be *almost* his story, but they cannot be the whole thing.

III

That they cannot be the whole thing has to do not only with the nature of story (as contrasted, let us say, with the nature of "event") but with the nature of Zukofsky's sources and of the authorship of *Thanks to the Dictionary,* a fiction that raises important questions about the nature and identity of authority. If we consider where the actual words of *Thanks* came from—a question frequently and indissolubly linked in the interpretive critic's mind to the problem of what a work means—if we consider the question "who wrote this work?"—we are obliged to point to three possible authors, that triumvirate I mentioned earlier, the dice, the dictionary, and the Bible, which collaboratively dictate this quite unusual tale. This, of course, brings us back to the preface: if other sources write the text, then what *will* the authors do then, poor things?

The dice, by whose agency the (selected) vocabulary of any given section of the story is determined. The Bible, by whose agency the story in all its recorded detail is already known. The dictionary. "A dictionary," Basil Bunting would write in 1938, talking about translation, "puts difficulties in the way" ("Verse Translations" 558). There is also of course Zukofsky himself. (That there is some interference from Zukofsky-amanuensis need not argue that this transcribed text is thereby corrupt; I shall consider his role shortly.) The Bible is, of course, to many readers not only an unimpeachable authority and source of ethical, moral, and spiritual value, telling you what you *ought* to think, but also a great narrative storehouse of great instructional worth. The story of David is of central significance not only in the Jewish tradition, but in the Christian. For David, whose name traditionally means "the beloved," is the ideal king, the prototype of the Messiah; so, too, just "as Moses completed the law of Israel for all time before the people entered Canaan, so David completed the theory and contents of Temple psalmody before the temple itself was built."[20] He is, then, a figure of great historical and cultural significance within the Judeo-Christian framework, within, that is to say, "a traceable history of interpretation" (Prynne 14).

So *Thanks to the Dictionary* plays one authority against another, plays with patterns of authority: David the prototype human model; the Bible the template of sensibility and intelligibility; the dictionary the book of words as Bible; the dice, chance as decisionmaker and arbitrator. Writers, of course, work by chance, they are the habitual editors of serendipity; but then so is thought. What a thinker thinks depends on what gets put in the hopper in the first place.

But the words I quoted about David came not from a dictionary but from yet another kind of authority, the encyclopedia.[21] Now the salient feature of a dictionary is that it is a word book. It lists all (or most) of the words in a given language in an arbitrary (i.e., alphabetical) order, with definitions or explanations of meaning. It does not give details of usage, nor of context, save in the simplest ways, and it does not (in the case of most dictionaries) provide much in the way of illustrative quotation or usage. In the case of the two dictionaries Zukofsky drew upon in writing *Thanks to the Dictionary,* there is minimal information about synonyms and antonyms. The dictionary is the repository of lexical meaning; it is the repository of a vocabulary; it tells us the words for things, but it does not tell us their history or their significance, and it does not (in I. A. Richards's term)[22] "interinanimate" them. An encyclopedia does. Its etymology[23] tells us that an *encyclopedia* is the circle of the sciences, a general system of instruction. In the pedantic and somewhat solemn blather of flat-footed dictionary definition, an encyclopedia is—as we all know—"a work in which the various topics included under several or all branches of knowledge are treated separately, and usually in alphabetical order" (*Century*, s.v. "Encyclopedia"). Above all else the great virtue of the encyclopedia is that it is, as James Russell Lowell observed, a place "where one may learn without cost of research what things are generally known" (90). The encyclopedia is the repository of general culture, it is an acculturating tool. Unlike the dictionary, but like the Bible, it is a storehouse of received ideas, it teaches the tradition.

Now language, and especially "literary" language, is a system of meanings and of meaning relations more or less (in Prynne's phrase) "inflected by semantic and cultural history" (11). But Zukofsky's book, of course, is *Thanks to the DICTIONARY*, not to the encyclopedia, and the astonishing culling of odd words and unusual definitions challenges the reader to make some sense of what is being said by destroying the preordained linkages.

The very form of *Thanks to the Dictionary* is indeed crucial, for it plays the long straightforward section (section 27), which condenses at high speed and with great lucidity the story of David as recounted in I and II Samuel, against the other twenty-eight sections, with their more or less private and personal discourse (referring to Zukofsky's work) and their randomly chosen vocabulary. *Thanks to the Dictionary* plays, then, the sacred text of public virtue against the secular text of personal accomplishment and private signification against the profane vocabulary of chance. It thus plays a narrative with preexistent meaning against a writing that invites the reader to make meaning; a narrative the meaning of which we already know (for we have a traceable history of its interpretation) against a narrative whose meaning is not known. The writing of one text over another, however (and of course the very act of reading), seduces the reader into assuming that the aleatorically determined text is as coherent, as articulate, as the sacred; and the title, *Thanks to the Dictionary*, suggests that *its* meaning too is accessible, for it is already there, preexistent and recoverable from the dictionary. The dictionary thus becomes an agent of recovery, by which we excavate a set of more or less related elements—except that once we've uncovered them they still don't tell us why they're there, and the words become opaque. The dictionary thereby becomes a means by which to position the writer outside the culture, outside the tradition (and not, therefore, subject to it), and even (especially if we bear Zukofsky's much later working of *Catullus* in mind) outside the language.[24] In such "insistence on the constant display and play of language" (Zukofsky and Taupin 22), words approach the condition of *things,* and one might observe that *Thanks to the Dictionary,* insofar as it exploits the relationship of local pockets of clarity to a larger global sense, theme, structure and environment, one long work whose beat the writer "cannot be entirely aware of" ("A"-12, 214), is an anticipatory gesture towards work by such writers as Bruce Andrews, Clark Coolidge, David Melnick, or Steve McCaffery. *Thanks to the Dictionary,* however, avoids the acute semantic inertia characteristic of these writers.

One drama *Thanks to the Dictionary* affords, then, is that between what words *actually* mean (in the narrative) and what we think they *ought* to mean. The work exploits the tension between two views of language: language as arbitrary (in which meaning is in the system and the context) and language as motivated (in which meaning is in the words). Either words have "real" meanings (Adam was the perfect man because he knew the real name of things), or they don't. Either there is a necessary and inherent "natural" connection between the word and its meaning, so that words *of themselves* tell you something of what they say, or there isn't. Either the disruption of meaning is sense bearing, or it is not. *Thanks to the Dictionary* thus points to the theme of Plato's *Cratylus,* which concludes that the two views can only be reconciled by recourse not to words but to things; it also points to the difference between ordinary language, which treats words more or less as transparencies, as counters for communicative and expressive purposes, and literary language, which, using defamiliarizing techniques, develops system violations that make sense, disruptions that are sense bearing, thereby treating words as objects for meditative and exploratory purposes.

All of this is parallel to that larger social and public drama, between what one thinks and what one ought to think: the moral imperative of Authority here becomes a drama encapsulating the moral imperative of Authorship. That there is some interference from Zukofsky himself in the telling need not argue that this text is "corrupt." But of course that is entirely the wrong way of putting it, since the notion of corruption entails a prior condition of "purity." Whether we add Zukofsky's name or not to the authorial triumvirate of Bible, dice, and dictionary, it is quite clear that Zukofsky's procedural strategy in compiling this text is designed to obscure its origin; that in so doing it undercuts the divine origin of the sacred text is incidental. More to the point is that the originary motives for this text, and indeed for all texts and for language itself (to say nothing of meaning), are irrecoverable, lost, not only to readers but also to writers. In opposition to the dictatorial intent that would "overleap all particulars" (including David, including Zukofsky, including the reader) "and fasten on the *end itself*"[25] (that end itself a mental construct, a logical construct, standing in dualistic relation to the material world), stands the language itself and the arbitrarily-ordered dictionary, which indeed, as Bunting said, "puts difficulties in the way." It may or may not be an accident, but it is certainly remarkably fitting that Zukofsky carried his "original" outline and plan of "*A*" around with him in his pocket for so long that the words literally wore off the paper.[26] Such literal undoing of the origins is, surely, a trope for Zukofsky's enterprise. "To begin a song," says "A"-12,

> if you cannot recall,
> Forget.
> ["A"-12, 140]

Notes

1. Filmed 16 March 1966. I am indebted to WNET for providing a dub of the soundtrack in September 1966.

2. Witness the passage from Gibbon he quotes toward the end of "A"-15: "The poet or philosopher illustrates his age and country by the efforts of a *single* mind; but these superior powers of reason are but rare and spontaneous productions; and the genius of Homer . . . or Newton would excite less admiration if they could be created by the will of . . . a preceptor" ("A"-15, 373).

3. Reinforces, yes. But as this essay I hope shows, Bunting's view requires enlargement. The stress in my formulation would be on *patterns* rather than, with Bunting, on *sound*.

4. Work of the 1930s includes: 1930: "A"-5, -6, -7; 1931: editing the "Objectivist" issue of *Poetry;* 1932: completing (19 April) *The Writing of Guillaume Apollinaire;* July–16 August: *Thanks to the Dictionary* (first draft); *An "Objectivists" Anthology;* 1932–1935 (with Jerry Reisman): filmscript of *Ulysses;* 1935: completes *A Workers Anthology;* 5 August begins "A"-8 (completed 14 July 1937); begins *A Test of Poetry* (completed 1940); 1936: *Arise, arise;* 1937: 12 November proposal/outline for *Index of American Design* (four articles written in 1938, seven

radio scripts 1939, and four radio scripts in 1940). During this period, too, Zukofsky taught for a year at the University of Wisconsin (and a summer at Berkeley), collaborated with William Carlos Williams on *The First President,* acted irregularly as informal poetry editor for *Hound and Horn* and possibly *Pagany,* and wrote and published reviews, essays, and shorter poems. And of course he worked for a living, at a variety of more or less unpleasant jobs for more or less unpleasant pay.

5. A useful discussion of the letter distributions in "A"-9 is in Ahearn, 231–241.

6. For a detailed discussion of late transliterative effects in Zukofsky, see Leggott.

7. Zipf postulated (287–291) that symbols are constructed of "genes of meaning" (symbol X "means *abcde*"); since many different symbols have genes in common, he speculated, poetic and "bookish" language might result in such system violations as the seemingly arbitrary or incorrect mixing of semantic fields apparent in "dormant baby and sleeping rose-bush" (290n).

8. The first section of *Thanks to the Dictionary* reminds us (via the dictionary) that iridescence is an accidental color; in *The First Half of "A"-9* Zukofsky speaks of his "intention to have the poem fluoresce as it were in the light of seven centuries of interrelated thought."

9. Calling it a work in progress, Zukofsky originally sent Quinn some handwritten pages from *Thanks to the Dictionary* in August 1934; Quinn liked them well enough to type some, and in a letter on 1 December Zukofsky gave detailed instructions for typing the long section 27 (the sixth of this version's eleven sections) and explained that in the printed version each section should bear as title the page number of the dictionary from which the section was drawn. (Materials at the University Library, University of Illinois at Urbana/Champaign.)

10. "Parts of a Novel," a 17-page typescript in the Basil Bunting archive at Durham University, is undated, but was sent from 149 East 37th Street, an address Zukofsky seems to have used only for the first few months of 1935.

11. Louis Zukofsky, "Thanks to the Dictionary," *It Was* (Kyoto: Origin, 1961), 99–130. There are a very few misprints in this edition, principally to do with the spacing in the longest section (no. 27). Despite the fact that (occasionally quite severe) misprints were introduced into the reprint in the *Collected Fiction* (270–300), for ease of reference page numbers in parentheses refer to this edition because it is available.

12. Letter to Quinn 24 August 1953, at the University of Illinois at Urbana/Champaign.

13. "Arise, arise," *Kulchur* 6 (summer 1962): 66–100; the production of Jerry Benjamin took place at the Cinematheque Theatre, 85 East 4th Street, New York, on August 6, 7, 12, 13, 14, 19, 20, 21, and 27, 1965; it appeared as a book in 1973.

14. In the manuscript version (University of Texas) "And what will the writers do then, poor things" is followed by a pair of initials.

15. Letter to Quinn, 1 December 1934, at the University of Illinois/Champaign.

16. In the manuscript at The Harry Ransom Humanities Research Center, The University of Texas at Austin, each section after the preface is headed with a number and a code, usually "F&W" but in six instances "W.C.D." When Zukofsky sent his abbreviated but still coded version to Quinn's magazine in December 1934, he identified the dictionaries from which *Thanks to the Dictionary* is drawn (see note 15 above). The twenty-fifth section of *Thanks to the Dictionary* (270) tells us that Zukofsky is retelling the story of David using a vocabulary in part determined by casting dice to find the dictionary page number—in this case Funk and Wagnalls, page 327, which seems to cover "Dib" through "dictionary." My statement of the range of entries on the page is a guess, derived from the text, since I have not been able to examine either of the dictionaries in the edition Zukofsky used. Each section in The University of Texas manuscript also bears two or three (crossed out) numbers revising the order of the sequence.

17. In the manuscript. The breaks on pages 292 and 293 of *Collected Fiction* are not authorized in any manuscript that I have examined.

18. In the manuscript (at The University of Texas) fifteen of the sections were originally ordered in strict alphabetical sequence according to the dictionary page upon which they drew. Thus the thirteenth manuscript section drew on *Webster's* pages 327 (Dicta-Dicti), the fourteenth *Funk and Wagnalls* 342 (Dist), the fifteenth *F&W* 350 (Don-Doo), the sixteenth *F&W* 351 (dos), and so on. In the final published version these are sections 25, 4, 7, and 9 respectively.

19. *Century Dictionary and Cyclopedia 9: Century Cyclopedia of Names,* s.v. "David."

20. *Encyclopædia Britannica* 13th ed. 22: 535, s.v. "Psalms, Book of." The *Century,* entry for David, calls him "[t]he actual founder of a sanctifying, divine worship, refining and enriching it by the influence of music and psalmody."

21. In what follows, the distinctions I draw between dictionaries and encyclopedias have much in common with those made for somewhat different ends by both Prynne and Watten.

22. Chapter Three of Richards's *The Philosophy of Rhetoric* is titled "The Interinanimation of Words."

23. Greek ἐνκύκλιοσ, in a circle, circular, periodic (as in encyclic), and παιδεία, education, from παῖσ, child—an encyclopædia is, then, a general system of instruction in several or all parts of knowledge, which is to say the circle of the science (of what is known).

24. After an earlier and shorter version of this paper was delivered at "The First Postmodernists" conference at the University of Maine in Orono in 1993, Barrett Watten generously sent me a copy of his own wide-ranging unpublished paper, first delivered at the MLA convention in 1992, "New Meaning and Poetic Vocabulary: From Coleridge to Jackson Mac Low." Watten's extremely interesting

discussion of *Thanks to the Dictionary* as a "merging of cultural and linguistic texts" (22–26) arrives at conclusions akin to those reached here.

25. *Collected Fiction* 290 (Zukofsky's italics). The Dalkey Archive edition unfortunately prints "overlap" for "overleap." See *It Was* 121, and the manuscripts at Illinois and Texas.

26. The paper in question is at The Harry Ransom Humanities Research Center, The University of Texas at Austin. For a description, see Ahearn 38.

Works Cited

Ahearn, Barry. *Zukofsky's "A": An Introduction.* Berkeley: U of California P, 1983.

Bunting, Basil. "The Lion and the Lizard." *Three Essays.* Ed. Richard Caddel. Durham: Basil Bunting Poetry Centre, 1994. 27–31 (Also in *Sulfur* 33 [Fall 1993]: 73–78)

———. "Verse Translations." *Criterion* 17 (April 1938): 557–559.

Century Dictionary and Cyclopedia. 10 vols. New York: Century, 1897.

Conte, Joseph M. *Unending Design: The Forms of Postmodern Poetry.* Ithaca: Cornell UP, 1991.

Eliot, T. S. "Tradition and the Individual Talent." *The Sacred Wood: Essays on Poetry and Criticism.* London: Methuen, 1920. 47–59.

Encyclopædia Britannica. 13th ed. s.v. "Psalms, Book of."

Leggott, Michele J. *Reading Zukofsky's 80 Flowers.* Baltimore: Johns Hopkins UP, 1989.

Lowell, James Russell. "Books and Libraries." *Literary and Political Addresses: The Writings of James Russell Lowell.* Riverside ed. Vol. 6. Boston: Houghton Mifflin, 1894. 78–98.

Lyons, John. *Semantics.* 2 vols. Cambridge: Cambridge UP, 1978.

Olson, Charles. "Readings at Goddard College, 12–14 April 1962." *Minutes of the Charles Olson Society* 2 (June 1993): 17–27.

"On Rhythm: From America. A Questionnaire." Supplement to *Agenda* 11.2–3 (Spring–Summer 1973): 37, 66. (See also "Correction," *Agenda* 11.4–12.1 [1974]: 102)

Poetry U.S.A.: Louis Zukofsky. Video. PBS. 1966.

Prynne, J. H. *Stars, Tigers and the Shape of Words: The William Matthews Lectures 1992, Delivered at Birkbeck College, London.* London: Birkbeck College, 1993.

Richards, I. A. *The Philosophy of Rhetoric.* London: Oxford UP, 1936.

Rodker, John. *The Future of Futurism.* London: Kegan Paul, Trench, Trubner, 1926.

Sitwell, Edith. *Aspects of Modern Poetry.* London: Duckworth, 1926.

Watten, Barrett. "New Meaning and Poetic Vocabulary: From Coleridge to Jackson Mac Low." Unpublished typescript, 1993.

Zipf, George Kingsley. *The Psycho-Biology of Language: An Introduction to Dynamic Philology.* 1935. Cambridge, MA: MIT P, 1965.

Zukofsky, Louis. "Arise, arise." *Kulchur* 6 (Summer 1962): 66–100. (Also see *Arise, arise.* New York: Grossman, 1973)

———. *It Was.* Kyoto: Origin, 1961.

———. "Thanks to the Dictionary." *Collected Fiction* 270–300.

Zukofsky, Louis, and René Taupin. "The Writing of Guillaume Apollinaire: (II)— Le Poète Resusscité." *Westminster Magazine* 23.1 (Spring 1934): 53–86.

9

The Comedian as the Letter Z
Reading Zukofsky Reading Stevens
Reading Zukofsky

P. MICHAEL CAMPBELL

Louis Zukofsky's 1971 lecture "For Wallace Stevens" is important both for what it reveals about Zukofsky's career and ideas and for the light it casts upon recent critical constructions of the field of modern poetry. "For Wallace Stevens" works to undermine widely held notions that twentieth-century American poetry has somehow drifted into two (or *only* two) opposing camps, notions that have been both attacked and unwittingly perpetuated by critics who are partisans of the works of either Ezra Pound or Wallace Stevens. At the same time, "For Wallace Stevens," by drawing clear parallels between the poetry and thought of Zukofsky and Stevens, shows how those poetries, in particular through their use of comic tropes, break through the abstraction of rational thought or "philosophy" to the joyfully direct evidence of the senses; in so doing, they afford a more profound pleasure to a reader than a perhaps more strictly "reasonable" text might.

In the introduction to his recent book, *Wallace Stevens and the Literary Canons,* John Timberman Newcomb takes issue with Marjorie Perloff's description of a "split" in modernist poetic practice between the poetics of Wallace Stevens and those of Ezra Pound and between two competing camps of contemporary modernist criticism, the Stevens camp (headed by Harold Bloom) and the Pound camp (headed by Hugh Kenner). In challenging these "splits," Newcomb focuses his critique on Perloff's essay "Pound/Stevens: Whose Era?" which originally appeared as an article in *New Literary History* in 1982 and was later republished as the first chapter of *The Dance of the Intellect: Studies in the Poetry of the Pound Tradition.* According to Newcomb, Perloff has manufactured an antithesis between a Poundian poetics that emphasizes "newness" and "fragmentation" and a Stevensian poetics that favors "tradition" and "lyricism." Newcomb claims that Perloff's divisions represent an "ambitious attempt to establish an essential fissure between the two poets and their critical traditions, an assertion that is itself a highly debatable and complicated issue" (12).

Since Newcomb is a self-described "relativist" and a proponent of the sort of "reception theory" practiced by Jauss and McGann, it is not surprising that he finds Perloff's "evaluative," "author-centered"[1] critique simplistic and "untenable." He strives to counteract her conclusions by "complicating" the issue and by challenging Perloff's "binary oppositions": "what Perloff presents as a central ideological choice that critics have had to make between Stevens and Pound may be more usefully seen as a problem of evaluative intolerance and absolutism among advocates of both poets" (10). For Newcomb, the claims to truthfulness and accuracy of critics such as Perloff, Bloom, and Kenner are suspect, since their reputations as critics are tied inextricably to the relative canonical status of the poets they write about. Thus, Newcomb claims, they repeatedly attempt in their criticism to establish the canonical superiority of "their" poets and, in the process, belittle the importance of competing figures. Perloff, according to Newcomb, engages in precisely this sort of evaluative skirmishing when she attempts to shape critical differences into an "apparent mutual exclusivity: if you do significant work on (or if you value) Stevens, you cannot value Pound, and vice versa" (12). Newcomb claims that Perloff "has it backwards" and concludes that the "gap between Stevens and Pound, if it can be said to exist, is a function of the conditions of postwar criticism, is neither intrinsic nor necessarily permanent, and does not explain the essential questions of modernism" (12–13).

While I disagree with several of Perloff's conclusions, especially her advocacy of Pound's poetics over Stevens's (as is evident in the subtitle of her book, *The Dance of the Intellect: Studies in the Poetry of the Pound Tradition*), and while my sympathies (and indeed my own thesis here) are more in line with Newcomb's, I find myself nonetheless unsatisfied, at least in part, with Newcomb's analysis. Like it or not, Newcomb engages in the very evaluative processes he criticizes, and his conclusions are themselves "functions" of the age and culture he writes in. No matter how much Newcomb might want to shield his conclusions in the lead boxes of relativism and response theory, his own claims are by no means immune from the corrupting light of the same sort of analysis he brings to bear on Perloff. To his credit, Newcomb recognizes this shortcoming and admits that his "own study is itself an evaluative act that cannot be called disinterested or neutral" (14), though he insists that he is not claiming to be "intrinsically correct" or "beyond debate." But while Newcomb allows for his own relativism, he assumes Perloff is being "absolutist" rather than simply trafficking, like him, in a relativistic marketplace of ideas and arguments. Perloff's claims to "truth" are finally not all that different from Newcomb's own claim that Perloff is mistaken, that she has it all wrong. Despite Newcomb's criticisms, the distinctions Perloff makes, I would argue, are useful, interesting, and not necessarily "absolute." I take it for granted that "binaries" such as those that Perloff proposes are problematic, but what sort of analysis isn't problematic in the relativistic "poststructuralist discourse" (10) Newcomb describes?

Whether the "gap" Perloff posits is "intrinsic" or "permanent," whether it explains or fails to explain "the essential questions of modernism," is finally not as important as its usefulness in describing a contemporary critical phenomenon. Here I could cite a long list of critics whose work focuses more or less exclusively on either Stevens or Pound (a list Perloff proposes in her essay and Newcomb expands in his own work), or I could recount some of the reactions (ranging from puzzlement to disbelief to hostile opposition) that I received from several of my critical colleagues when I told them I was working on an essay on Zukofsky *and* Stevens. Whether such reactions are defensible or not, there is a strong sense among many in the critical community that Zukofsky belongs on the Pound side of some sort of poetic antithesis and that Stevens occupies an important position at the opposite pole.[2]

In this essay, I too hope to "complicate" and "problematize" the pigeonholing of Stevens and Zukofsky in separate poetic camps: late romantic, "Stevensian" on the one hand and "Poundian" on the other. My approach, however, will be somewhat different from Newcomb's "historical"/"receptionist" account. Instead of focusing on the critics and their evaluations of Stevens and/or Zukofsky, I will be looking closely here at a talk Zukofsky himself delivered in 1971 as the eighth annual Wallace Stevens Memorial Lecture at the University of Connecticut. (The talk, "For Wallace Stevens," is reprinted in edited form in *Prepositions: The Collected Critical Essays of Louis Zukofsky.*) This talk is of interest, and even surprising, to the extent that Zukofsky, a poet who in the past had followed the Poundian and Objectivist leads in criticizing Stevens, chooses to use the lecture as an occasion for revising his previously dismissive assessments of Stevens. (Most notably, in "American Poetry, 1920–1930," he notes drily how Stevens has "led his rather submerged intellectual excellences . . . to a versification clambering the stiles of English influence" [*Prepositions* 138].) As Alan Golding points out, Zukofsky could have satisfied the requirements of the lecture format by simply reading from his own work or by making only a few limited comments on Stevens. Instead, Zukofsky insisted on studying Stevens's work closely and developing certain affinities between Stevens's poetry and his own. In the talk, Zukofsky says of Stevens: "I deferred reading the greater part of his work after admiring the early poems of *Harmonium,* and it is this neglect that I wish to set right today. Reading him for the last three months I felt that my own writing, without being aware of it, was closer to his than that of any of my contemporaries in the last half century of life we shared together" (*Prepositions* 27). How is it that Zukofsky finds a greater affinity with Stevens's writing than with the work of "any of [his] contemporaries"? (Even, one asks, than that of Williams, Moore, or Pound?) What conjunctions and confluences is Zukofsky referring to? And how do these connections jibe with the (seemingly) obvious stylistic differences between Zukofsky's poetry (written, to use Perloff's term, in "the Pound tradition" of collage and fragmentation) and Stevens's (supposedly) more "traditional," lyrical verse?[3]

In trying to answer these questions, I will look briefly at some poems by Zukofsky and Stevens and attempt to unravel the complex narrative Zukofsky weaves in his talk. It is a narrative that teasingly proposes "influences" and coincidences, shared subject matter and experience, and finally a sort of kinship or confederacy. The key to understanding this narrative, I believe, is to be found in Zukofsky's oft-stated preference for "the clear physical eye against the erring brain" (*Prepositions* 167). It is here, I would argue, that Zukofsky's poetics most clearly intersect with Stevens's. For Stevens, "[p]oetry must be irrational" (*Opus Posthumous* 188); it "must resist the intelligence almost successfully" (*Opus Posthumous* 197). From this shared suspicion of "the erring brain," both poets devise similar comic strategies for "resisting" the dictates of a purely rational or abstract discourse. The antiphilosophy Zukofsky finds in Stevens ("[p]hilosophy is not [his po-

P. MICHAEL CAMPBELL

ems'] end, tho they seem to be philosophizing" [*Prepositions* 27])—and thereby recognizes in his own work—is, I argue, essentially comic in its reliance on surprising irrational/rational or physical/abstract congruences. Both Stevens and Zukofsky resist, or distrust, abstract meaning, even as both poets continually engage with and reject philosophy. Both are suspicious of denotative expression, and both go to great lengths to reveal the essentially figurative nature of language. Even as they often disagree with each other on what sort of balance needs to be struck between these extremes, on where to locate poetry in the larger debate, and on what form poetry should take, Stevens and Zukofsky share a defining concern with the central issue: the failure of "the erring brain" to keep up with "the clear physical eye."

For Zukofsky, this concern leads to the construction of a poetry that "resists" any straightforward "meaning," that aims instead to be a poetry of almost pure sound and music. As Golding describes, "[m]ore than any other twentieth-century poet, Zukofsky aspired to return poetry to the condition of music; and music has no 'meaning' " (136). Or as Zukofsky himself writes in a 1931 essay entitled, in its *Prepositions* appearance, "An Objective": "[t]he order of all poetry is to approach a state of music wherein the ideas present themselves sensuously and intelligently and are of no predatory intention" (*Prepositions* 18). In addition to this desire for a poetry of music, Zukofsky also aspires, almost paradoxically, to a poetry of vision, a poetry of collage and juxtaposition, in which poets "see with their ears, hear with their eyes, move with their noses and speak and breathe with their feet" (*Prepositions* 17). In an interview with L. S. Dembo, Zukofsky further develops this description, claiming that "the eye is a function of the ear and the ear of the eye" (267).[4] This instance of synesthesia (described wonderfully by Marnie Parsons in her recent book, *Touch Monkeys: Nonsense Strategies for Reading Twentieth Century Poetry*) is perhaps best illustrated in the opening section of Zukofsky's poem "I's (pronounced *eyes*)":

Hi, Kuh,

those
gold'n bees
are I's,

eyes,

skyscrapers.
[*Complete Short Poetry* 214]

As Golding, Parsons, and other commentators have noted, this poem is built on a series of puns that fuse our notions of the visual and the aural, the way the words "I" and "eye" not only share a phonic identity but also are perceptually interrelated. Parsons calls it "an example of the seen world transmitted by the ear, the joyful music of the eye, where synesthesia waylays concrete sense" (100). The poem begins with an elaborate aural joke: the equation of the visual poetry of haiku with the greeting "Hi, Kuh," which, as Golding points out, is "not just a self-consciously bad pun" (136) but also a reference (*Kuh* is German for cow) to a mass culture artifact: "You remember Elsie, Borden's cow?" Zukofsky asks in the Dembo interview. "That's what I meant, and I greeted her up on the sign there: 'Hi, Kuh' " (229). As this somewhat obscure joke suggests, and as most critics are all too willing to concede, Zukofsky's "difficult" poetry seems designed to frustrate conventional abstract explication or, in Stevens's terms, "to resist the intelligence almost successfully."

Stevens's poems, on the other hand, are somewhat less obvious in their evasions. In fact, Stevens is often read, even by his most perceptive commentators, as a poet who stresses meaning over form.[5] This way of reading Stevens, however, is inconsistent with many of Stevens's poems and poetic pronouncements. In his essay "The Noble Rider and the Sound of Words," for example, Stevens sounds a lot more like Zukofsky than he does like the philosopher-poet he is often portrayed as: "Above everything else, poetry is words; and . . . words, above everything else, are, in poetry, sounds" (*Necessary Angel* 32). There are countless other instances in Stevens's poems and aphorisms that similarly suggest that Stevens is not at all—or not entirely, at least—the conservative/traditional poet Perloff describes, the poet whose work inevitably "subordinates such traditional lyric features as meter and qualitative sound repetition to the articulation of complex and ambiguous meanings" (21). I will not, however, spend much time here delineating these instances; instead, I would like to follow Zukofsky's discovery of Stevens's resistance to convention and rational discourse—to recount, in other words, the narrative Zukofsky sets out in his Stevens talk. The talk begins: "Tho I never met Wallace Stevens

I was interested in him very early. I wanted to read all of him but did not get around to it till I was told I would be giving the Wallace Stevens Memorial Lecture" (*Prepositions* 24). While there is about this introduction an odd bit of resistance and apology—"I *wanted* to read all of him but did not get around to it till I was *told* I would be giving," as if Zukofsky were ordered or forced to "get around to it"—Zukofsky is nonetheless convincing when he describes a newfound attachment to his subject: "I have been at it [reading Stevens] for three months to the neglect of my own work and the occasional reminder of my wife's common sense, *well you know it will last only an hour, how much do you have to do.* But I went on reading him and jotting notations. . . . I felt myself speaking to Stevens for three months. It's really as simple as that" (24). But, of course, it is not just "as simple as that." The sort of relationship with Stevens's poems and letters that Zukofsky describes is tantalizingly complicated. At first, it is: "The contingency of one poet reading another if he gets interested the way I do: I'm not lush about things—I try not to read into things, I try to read, which means that if the page doesn't have it any imagination on my part as to what I might read into it has no significance. I hope everybody would read me the same way . . . just read the words" (24). And then, after some more digressions: "But I won't go into that aspect—simply say, the contingency of one poet reading another that way makes for a kind of friendship which is exempt from all the vicissitudes and changes and tempers that are involved in friendship" (24). This is clearly neither an actual, temporal friendship nor the sort of author-reader "friendship" Wayne Booth imagines but instead a relationship of mutual influence and interchange meditated through texts. The reader reads the author—and the author reads the reader: "When the sense of duration is felt the legend on the page [Stevens in this case] at that time literally reads the reader . . . " (25). The choice of the word "literally" here is odd, since the concept seems so clearly figurative. Mark Scroggins, in fact, claims that "Zukofsky does not want to be taken as implying that he directly influenced Stevens; what is important is that there are moments in which he feels that Stevens's *oeuvre* and his own are 'reading' one another, moments in which the experience of 'duration' is taking place" (75). But while Scroggins's claim seems sensible, Zukofsky does go on in the talk to speculate at length about whether Stevens actually read his (Zukofsky's) poetry and whether he (Zukofsky) might have actually influenced or had an impact on Stevens in some way. It is an odd, comic narrative, full of near misses (Zukofsky applied for a job at Hartford, but Stevens was out of the office), coincidences (Stevens writes about horses; Zukofsky writes about horses), circumstantial evidence (they published in similar places), and gossip: "I understand he was generous to younger poets, and Marianne Moore on her 75th birthday (1962) my wife recalls for this occasion told her that Stevens had been interested in my writing" (26). (Reportedly, Mussolini was "interested" in Pound's writings. Most of us, I suspect, have expressed "interest" in the work of our friends or members of family, whether we found that work congenial or otherwise: an expression of interest is often no more than a gesture of politeness.)

Still, Zukofsky's thesis has a strange sort of logic to it. There are, as he points out, some strong affinities between Stevens's work and his own. Both Stevens and Zukofsky exhibit a playful resistance to conventional wisdom and rational discourse—what Zukofsky describes, in talking about Stevens, as a "gay, lovely skepticism" that "doubts its own skepticism and becomes the only kind of skepticism true to itself" (27). The skepticism that Zukofsky has in mind here is one resistant to conventional and rational abstract truisms, a mind that questions everything but does not finally bog down in philosophy or epistemology.

Two years earlier, in the aforementioned interview with Dembo, Zukofsky describes himself as "doing away with epistemology in *Bottom* [*: On Shakespeare*]" and goes on in the very next sentence to criticize Stevens for "ruin[ing] a great deal of his work by speaking vaguely about the imagination and reality and so on. He can be a wonderful poet, but so much of it is a bore, bad philosophy" (277). After immersing himself in Stevens's poems, however, Zukofsky reverses this judgment entirely, concluding in his Stevens talk that Stevens's poems are not primarily philosophical at all: "Philosophy is not their end, tho they *seem* to be philosophizing" (*Prepositions* 27, emphasis added).

Instead, Zukofsky equates Stevens's work with his own: "Reading him for the last three months I felt my own writing, without being aware of it, was closer to his than to that of any of my contemporaries in the last half century of life we shared together" (27). What I find interesting here is the way this "intensely" felt "kindred" relationship expands in the above-quoted sentence from three months of reading to a "half century of life . . . shared together." The emphasis here is on an intense "closeness" that Zukofsky himself compares to a sort of marriage.

In other places in the talk, Zukofsky describes this relationship as mystical and points out that his previous criticism of Stevens for being too philosophical was wrong: "Coming to his whole work late, I am moved by the fact—as I would wish it in my own work—that his music thruout has *not* been impaired by having philosophized" (30, emphasis added). This uneasiness with "philosophizing" is a problem that both Zukofsky and Stevens work hard in their poetry to "solve." The strategy they both adopt, in this regard, I would argue, is the playful use of humor, the purposeful yoking together of unlike things for comic effect. As Parsons, Peter Quartermain, Guy Davenport, and others have pointed out, "play" lies at the center of Zukofsky's craft.[6] By this, I do not mean—and I don't think Parsons, Quartermain, or Davenport means—that Zukofsky is not also "serious." In fact, the presumed opposition here (between humor and seriousness, play and seriousness, nonsense and sense, etc.) is, in part, what Zukofsky's poetry is all about—it is only by being funny, by playing, by being nonsensical that Zukofsky is able to challenge serious, abstract discourse.

In this regard, it is helpful, I think, to look briefly at some poems. In the Stevens talk, Zukofsky directs us to Stevens's "Primordia," Part 4, where Stevens concludes:

> The trees stand still,
> The trees drink,
> The water runs away from the horses.
> La, la, la, la, la, la, la, la,
> Dee, dum, diddle, dee, dee, diddle, dee, da.
>   [*Opus Posthumous* 26]

Zukofsky compares this to his own "A"-7, where he resorts to similar musical humming:

> Bum pump a–dumb, the pump is neither bum
> Nor dumb, dumb pump uh! hum, bum pump o! shucks!
>   ["A"-7, 41]

There are countless other comic moments where Zukofsky's and Stevens's works intersect. Zukofsky's "Pierrot of Montauk" (section 6 of the sequence "Light"), for example, can be read as a sort of variation on one of Stevens's many clown figures:

> An ornament of sentiment
>
> He's a bit of red and gray—maybe green—rock
> He's Pierrot the clown of Montauk.
>
> He has no eyes, he don't talk—
> He's Pierrot the clown of Montauk.
>
> His cool existence admonishes
> The cool yet bloody of the fishes.
>
> Present him and walk down the beach—
> He has no human tendency to squawk,
> But! He's Pierrot the clown of Montauk.
>
> Declaim his species like the clock:
> Pierrot, Pierrot, Pierrot, PIERROT!—
> He's Pierrot the clown of Montauk.
>   [*Complete Short Poetry* 117–118]

Here, Zukofsky repeatedly stresses the inhuman qualities of the clown: "He has no eyes, he don't talk"; "He has no human tendency to squawk"; "Declaim his species like the clock." Zukofsky pushes this "ornament of sentiment" relentlessly toward pure object and music and, in the process, reminds one of a couple of Henri Bergson's observations about how humor functions. First, Bergson, in his essay on "Laughter," describes the comic effects of repetition, how humor circumvents the rational and creates a sort of mad method all its own. (Here, I am reminded of Zukofsky's advice in "An Objective" that "lunatics are sometimes profitably observed" [*Prepositions* 17].) The "mad method" for Zukofsky is more than just a means to an end; it is, in a sense, the "meaning," "purpose," and "intention" of the poem.

The repeated equations in the Pierrot poem (ornament = sentiment = rock = Pierrot = clown = Montauk = PIERROT! in capital letters) make it difficult to ascertain precisely who or what the "object" of this poem is and leave us suspended somewhere between our conceptions of Pierrot as a human figure underneath a clown's mask and Pierrot as the mask itself. This is where the second Bergsonian observation proves helpful. Bergson claims that "we laugh every time a person gives us the impression of being a thing" and illustrates this claim by describing the performance of two circus clowns who gradually "lost sight of the fact that they were men of flesh and blood like ourselves; one began to think of bundles of all sorts, falling and knocking against each other" (97–98). In the next to last line of Zukofsky's poem, the word "Pierrot" acts in a similarly comic fashion "falling and knocking against" itself.

Stevens's clowns, while generally more corporeal, are nonetheless also embodiments of Bergson's claims. Here I will merely gesture toward such Stevensian comic figures as "The Doctor of Geneva," "Chieftan Iffucan of Azcan" in "Bantams in Pine-Woods," the "metaphysician in the dark, twanging / An instrument" (*Collected Poems* 240) in "Of Modern Poetry," Crispin in "The Comedian as the Letter C," and the Chaplinesque tramp in "Notes toward a Supreme Fiction." [7] Stevens repeatedly uses these clownish characters as mouthpieces for "philosophizing" (lending the "philosophy" a sort of parodic, antiphilosophic bent) and to poke fun at the overly abstract rational pretensions of "the erring brain." For instance, in "Six Significant Landscapes," Stevens writes:

> Rationalists, wearing square hats,
> Think, in square rooms,
> Looking at the floor,
> Looking at the ceiling.
> They confine themselves
> To right-angled triangles.
> If they tried rhomboids,
> Cones, waving ellipses—
> As, for example, the ellipse of the half-moon—
> Rationalists would wear sombreros.
> [*Collected Poems* 75]

These sombreroed rationalists, trapped in their "square" thinking, are as comically devoid of human qualities as Bergson's circus clowns and Zukofsky's "rock" clown ("He's a bit of red and gray—maybe green—rock / He's Pierrot the clown of Montauk").

In the "It Must Be Abstract" section of "Notes toward a Supreme Fiction," Stevens tells a short "nonsense" narrative that concludes with an embrace of precisely the sort of challenging "nonsense" Zukofsky engages in:

> We say: at night an Arabian in my room,
> With his damned hoobla-hoobla-hoobla-how,
> Inscribes a private astronomy
>
> Across the unscrawled fores the future casts
> And throws his stars around the floor. By day
> The wood-dove used to chant his hoobla-hoo
>
> And still the grossest iridescence of ocean
> Howls hoo and rises and howls hoo and falls.
> Life's nonsense pierces us with strange relation.
>   [*Collected Poems* 383]

Stevens here acknowledges the power of "nonsense" to render things "strange" and "new," to shake up our passive acceptance of the transparency of words and rational thought.

Such "strange relation" is, of course, Zukofsky's method *and* subject matter, his comic stock in trade. Zukofsky is forever "playing" with words and their meanings. He writes:

> I'm a fish
> And I dance in your dish.
>
>   Here's ten dollars.
>
> Go and
>   say Hello, Hello.
>   [*Complete Short Poetry* 121]

—and it sounds as if he is about to break into Groucho Marx's "Hello, I Must Be Going" or some similar "nonsense" tune. As Parsons notes, such "nonsense" represents for Zukofsky an opportunity to rethink and remake the poetic process, to reintroduce into poetry the "clear physical eye" and ear.

In addition to his play with "nonsense," Zukofsky's poetry is also often comic in its depiction of characters (see the rather surprisingly pitiful "Tarzan" character in "Light" [*Complete Short Poetry* 115–116], for instance, or the "miserable Catullus" in "Catullus viii" [*Complete*

Short Poetry 88].) There are also several comic moments in Zukofsky's poems where he shares with Stevens a concern about the weather ("Home for Aged Bomb Throwers—U.S.S.R.," for instance) and a fascination with multiple perspectives ("The Old Poet Moves to a New Apartment 14 Times"). All these works, I would argue, use comedy to challenge the overly rational orthodoxy, to display the supremacy of "the clear physical eye" over the perpetually "erring brain."

It's no coincidence, I think, that Zukofsky compares Stevens (and thereby himself) to Shakespeare, perhaps the greatest writer of comedies in the English language. Zukofsky writes of his Stevens-friendship narrative: "If my story has a point regarding Stevens it is as devious as, perhaps I had something in common with Shakespeare: one of my first impressions on reading Stevens would be how much some of his lines recalled Shakespeare. Not imitating Shakespeare, Stevens's work has that kind of passion. It might not be evident to everybody, but it has" (*Prepositions* 28). Elsewhere in *Prepositions,* in "About the Gas Age," Zukofsky summarizes his work on Shakespeare in *Bottom:* "I wrote 500 pages about Shakespeare just to say one thing, the natural human eye is OK, but it's that erring brain that's no good, and he [Shakespeare] says it all the time. Of course, everybody says he says the opposite, but I don't think they read him right" (170). Interestingly, Zukofsky here is redefining Shakespeare as a poet with concerns very similar to his own. Though the "misreading" claim is specifically applied to Shakespeare, when coupled with the essay on Stevens, that claim expands outward to include Stevens, the oft misread twentieth-century poet whose work Zukofsky sees as essentially Shakespearean and finally further outward to include Zukofsky himself, the poet reading and "being read by" both Stevens and Shakespeare.

In their critical comments on Zukofsky's talk, Golding (1985) and Scroggins (1992) suggest some of the intersecting concerns in the poetics of Zukofsky and Stevens. Both critics, though, finally conclude that Zukofsky to some degree exaggerates such intersections in his talk, that the almost Objectivist Stevens whom Zukofsky describes is at considerable remove from the "real" Stevens, whom both critics see as being much more deeply committed to issues of epistemology than Zukofsky allows for.

For Golding, Zukofsky chooses to engage those aspects of Stevens's poetry closest to his own, while simply ignoring the greater body of work at odds with Zukofsky's own thinking about imagination and reality: "[Zukofsky's] selection [of six Stevens poems to read] silently reasserts both his early distaste for Stevens's philosophizing and his preference for the side of Stevens that one would expect an Objectivist poet to appreciate: the Stevens who celebrated the literal, the physical, the external" (131). Golding does an outstanding job collecting instances in Stevens's poetry of the sort "one would expect an Objectivist poet [or critic] to appreciate," and his well-measured argument for a less philosophically handcuffed reading of Stevens is, to my mind, among the more important recent contributions to Stevens criticism. That said, I must add that I see Stevens's presentations of epistemological issues as considerably more problematic than Golding suggests. I read Stevens more as a comic philosopher, an epistemological burlesque artist, who, like Zukofsky, is forever at play and work (the two terms finally form a false antithesis) in the sandboxes and graveyards of our language.

Like Golding, Scroggins describes Zukofsky's talk as a "belated homage to Stevens, which pays only dismissive lip service to the dialectic of 'reality' and the 'imagination' that assumes such prominence in Stevens's criticism (and in Stevens's own prose)" (67). For Scroggins, Zukofsky takes out of context (or, to use Scroggins's term, "recontextualizes") Stevens's poetry in order to support the claim that Stevens's work is consistent with Zukofsky's "clear physical eye" thesis; a similar recontextualization is at work in the lengthy quotations that make up most of *Bottom*: "The passages Zukofsky quotes, taken in their original contexts, by no means argue for such a conclusion [i.e., that Shakespeare favors the 'clear physical eye' over the 'erring mind']; but all of them, in some detail of their language, refer to the problematic with which Zukofsky is dealing, and Zukofsky thereby feels free to recontextualize them into the argument he is mounting" (72). Scroggins sees Zukofsky's descriptions of Stevens as being at odds with Stevens's real thinking; he claims, finally, that, at least in *Bottom,* "practically any passage of Western literature or philosophy that contains one of Zukofsky's key words or concepts—'eye,' 'seeing,' 'blind,' etc.—is fair game" (72) for Zukofsky "regardless of the extent to which that passage endorses—or even pertains to—[his] thesis." While there is a great deal of truth to this claim—certainly in the case of *Bottom*—it is my contention here that Zukofsky has, in fact, identified some important aspects of Stevens's poetics and, in the process, has helped us to understand Zukofsky's own poetics better as well.

It is through the playful, comic use of abstract rational discourse against itself that both Stevens and Zukofsky achieve the sort of "pleasure" that each insists is the essential "test of poetry." According to Zukofsky, quoting his own *A Test of Poetry*, "[t]he test of poetry is the range of pleasure it affords" (*Prepositions* 35). Similarly, according to Stevens, in "Notes Toward a Supreme Fiction," "It Must Give Pleasure." In quoting Stevens's famous dictum in his talk, Zukofsky isolates the source of this "pleasure": "Pleased that the irrational is rational" (35). In this regard, both poets are able to achieve pleasure through the application of the comic trope—the development and surprising resolution of incongruities. Here the pleasing resolution is found in the unlikely equation and interchangeability of two seemingly opposite terms: the rational and the irrational.

In developing what later came to be known as the "incongruity theory" of humor, Arthur Schopenhauer describes why we are "pleased" when the tyranny of reason is overthrown: "In every suddenly appearing conflict between what is perceived and what is thought, what is perceived is always unquestionably right. . . . The victory of knowledge of perception over thought affords us pleasure. For perception is . . . the medium of the present, of enjoyment and gaiety: moreover, it is attended with no exertion. Besides, it is the conception of thoughts that often oppose the gratification of our immediate desires, for, as the medium of the past, the future, and of seriousness, they are the vehicles of our fears, our repentance, and all our cares" (60). Since it is reason that stands between us and pleasure, according to Schopenhauer, we are pleased to the point of laughter when it is unseated by a sensual world that resists reasoning and abstraction: "It must therefore be diverting to us to see this strict, troublesome governess, the reason, for once, convicted of insufficiency" (60). Schopenhauer, in effect, describes the surprising intersection between the poetries and poetics of the apparently Poundian Zukofsky and the apparently "traditional" Stevens—the use of the comic trope as an act of resistance to abstraction.

This comic trope, the sudden, irrational/associational "resolution" of oppositions, is, as I have only briefly sketched here, a favorite of both Stevens and Zukofsky and a trope that appears frequently in both poets' works. The reliance on this trope explains how two such seemingly disparate poets might be seen as being in "close" relationship to one another. Moreover, the recognition of the importance of this trope to adherents of both the Poundian and Stevensian traditions might also serve as a useful bridge between the opposing critical factions described in Perloff's essay.

Notes

1. It is, of course, somewhat ironic that Newcomb criticizes Perloff for her "author-centered specialization" (12) in the introduction to his own book "on" Wallace Stevens, *Wallace Stevens and Literary Canons.*

2. Newcomb, even as he makes an admirable effort to deconstruct this "opposition," obviously is aware enough of, and concerned enough about, these critical disagreements to consider them at great length at the very beginning of his book-length work on Stevens's reception. It is also worth noting here that both of the other critics (Golding and Scroggins) who have written about Zukofsky's talk on Stevens have also addressed the generally perceived differences between Zukofsky's Poundian, "Imagist-Objectivist" poetics and Stevens's "Symbolist"-influenced poetry. Both Scroggins and Golding cite Perloff early on in their respective essays and use her development of a Pound-Stevens split to launch their own explorations of the congruences and dissonances in Stevens's and Zukofsky's poetics. Golding refers to Perloff's article as "invaluable" (123), while Scroggins is somewhat more suspicious. For Scroggins, "Whether [the] rift [Perloff describes] is an actual division within the communities of practicing poets, or primarily a critical formulation . . . , remains an open question" (67). Scroggins, however, goes on to say of Zukofsky and Stevens: "It would be difficult to imagine a bond of kinship among two poets whose poetics are more dissimilar" (67).

3. Similar questions are also addressed in the two previously published critical essays focusing on Zukofsky's talk. Both Golding and Scroggins attempt to account for the surprising fact that Zukofsky, a poet not normally associated in critical circles with Stevens, speaks so highly of Stevens in his talk. Golding asks, "Given their apparently different thematic interests and stylistic affiliations, why should Zukofsky have felt so close to Stevens?" (121). Scroggins, citing Golding, "hope[s], in examining the particular strategies of Zukofsky's reading of Stevens, to show how that reading stands not only as an introduction to Zukofsky's own (arguably idiosyncratic) conception of poetic influence, but as a significant index of the shifts in poets' readerly practice that have accompanied American poetry's postmodern turn towards 'language' " (68). I have found both Golding's and Scroggins's essays invaluable in preparing the present analysis, though (as I will describe later in my argument) I think both tend to discount too easily Zukofsky's claims that there are profound conjunctions between his own work and Stevens's.

4. In the preface to *Bottom,* Zukofsky quotes a similar conceit from Shakespeare's *A Midsummer Night's Dream:* "The eye of man hath not heard, the ear of

man hath not seen, man's hand is not able to taste, his tongue to conceive, nor his heart to report, what my dream was" (*Bottom* 9).

5. Golding provides an excellent accounting of this tendency to read Stevens more for "what" he has to say than "how" he says it. See also Perloff, who keenly traces the willingness of Stevens critics to ignore form, rhythm, and prosody in their readings of their poet.

6. See Parsons's essay on Zukofsky's "A"-24 for a discussion of Zukofsky's "playfulness" with language.

7. For a more thorough discussion of Stevens's Pierrots, I recommend the chapter on Stevens in Robert Storey's *Pierrot: A Critical History of a Mask*.

Works Cited

Bergson, Henri. "Laughter." *Comedy*. Ed. Wylie Sypher. Garden City, NY: Doubleday Anchor, 1956.

Dembo, L. S. Interview with Louis Zukofsky. *Louis Zukofsky: Man and Poet*. Ed. Carroll F. Terrell. Orono, ME: National Poetry Foundation, 1979.

Golding, Alan. "The 'Community of Elements' in Wallace Stevens and Louis Zukofsky." *Wallace Stevens: The Poetics of Modernism*. Ed. Albert Gelpi. Cambridge: Cambridge UP, 1985. 121–40.

Newcomb, John Timberman. *Wallace Stevens and Literary Canons*. Jackson: U of Mississippi P, 1992.

Parsons, Marnie. *Touch Monkeys: Nonsense Strategies for Reading Twentieth-Century Poetry*. Toronto: U of Toronto P, 1994.

Perloff, Marjorie. "Pound/Stevens: Whose Era?" *The Dance of the Intellect: Studies in the Poetry of the Pound Tradition*. New York: Cambridge UP, 1985. 1–32.

Schopenhauer, Arthur. *The World as Will and Idea*. Trans. R. B. Haldane and John Kemp. *The Philosophy of Laughter and Humor*. Ed. John Morreall. Albany: State U of New York P, 1987.

Scroggins, Mark. "A 'Sense of Duration': Wallace Stevens, Louis Zukofsky, and 'Language.' " *Sagetrieb* 11.1–2 (Spring–Fall 1992): 67–83.

Stevens, Wallace. *The Collected Poems of Wallace Stevens*. New York: Knopf, 1954.

———. *The Necessary Angel: Essays on Reality and the Imagination*. New York: Knopf, 1951.

———. *Opus Posthumous*. Ed. Milton J. Bates. New ed. New York: Vintage, 1990.

Storey, Robert F. *Pierrot: A Critical History of a Mask*. Princeton: Princeton UP, 1978.

10

"Words Ranging Forms"
Patterns of Exchange in Zukofsky's Early Lyrics

SUSAN VANDERBORG

> Pound said we live with certain landscapes. And because of the eye's movement, something is imparted to or through the physical movement of your body and you express yourself as a voice.
> —Louis Zukofsky, Interview 267

IT IS DIFFICULT NOT TO read Zukofsky in his own terms as a poet of landscapes, albeit certain fractured and mutable ones. His descriptions of Objectivism are intensely visual, the "objective" itself a term borrowed from optics for a "lens bringing the rays from an object to a focus" (*Prepositions* 12). The early lyrics are filled with light and color out of which a circus horse, an abandoned car, a washstand, momentarily shape themselves. William Carlos Williams would later relegate Objectivism to an "aftermath of Imagism," an attempt to clarify both the object of the poem and the poem as printed object on the page (582). Yet it was not merely the act but the interrogation of imaginative vision that distinguished Zukofsky's poetry of the twenties and thirties from the landscapes of his Imagist predecessors. An awareness that the "eye's movement" can create a hierarchical distance between subject and object led Zukofsky to relocate poetic presence from techniques of sight to those of voice—language in its phonetic and syntactic patterns. This materialistic focus on language, in the attempt to craft a "revolutionary" poetry of community, would define both the formal scope and the limitations of his subsequent work.

"The philosophers have only *interpreted* the world in various ways," Marx had challenged in his *Theses on Feuerbach;* "the point however is to *change* it" (84). Zukofsky counters that each interpretive gaze is inherently an act of changing the world. The ferry crossing described in "29 Poems" is refracted through a range of perspectives, the painterly fascination with lights over the river juxtaposed with the remarks of a tour guide and an economic analysis of tolls, coins, and costs. The observer's error, these multiple narratives suggest, would not be in preferring aesthetics to economics or vice versa but in the very act of choosing, in limiting interpretation to any single version of the event. "An Imponderable," the poet quotes Thorstein Veblen, "is an article of make-believe which has become axiomatic by force of settled habit" (*Complete Short Poetry* 41). Better to snap photographs of one's subject from the vantage point of a moving train, Zukofsky comments in "Immature Pebbles," than to subside into descriptive "irrelevancy" where "one's an accessory to these ways / obliged to accept imponderables" (*Complete Short Poetry* 41).

Nowhere is the danger of reducing observation to classification more sharply challenged than in Zukofsky's images of the poor, who often seem flat symbolic types in Williams and Pound. Zukofsky's vision of heroic peasants from a Diego Rivera mural ("D.R.," *Complete Short Poetry* 39) soon shifts to the workers in "The Immediate Aim" who may become as brutal as the "police dogs" they mistrust if the perspective of their own "eye-pupils" remains too "limited" (*Complete Short Poetry* 54). The patient "beast of the field" in another sequence is playfully rewarded with "geranium" on his "cranium" rather than with being made a fable of maltreated labor (*Complete Short Poetry* 28). These mobile portraits anticipate Zukofsky's fascination with the character Bottom in Shakespeare's *Midsummer Night's Dream,* the laborer-turned-actor-turned-beast whose transformations elude any quick summation by his courtly spectators. "Bottom's Dream has no bottom" or ready meaning to seize upon, Zukofsky reiterates, and thus it forces the audience to respond to each new development (*Bottom* 15).

The difficulty with these imagistic shifts is that they sometimes threaten to halt interpretation altogether. The "almost dreamt" face of a would-be stockmarket player in "29 Songs" narrows down to the nonimage of his final fortunes: "[N]o one is in in No One Inn" (*Complete Short Poetry* 57), where the prepositions, pronouns, and names that should help to guide the reader blur together instead. " '[T]hings' seem to define themselves by their absence rather than by their presence" in Zukofsky's poetry, Burton Hatlen charges ("Poetics of Absence" 93);

as language verges upon the "purely visual," it also "deliberately wills its own destruction" to suggest its limits, its distortion of the world's immediacy ("Poetics of Absence" 82). This extreme questioning of linguistic representation might make it harder to parrot "imponderables." But is a technique of near silence the only method of "unsettling habit" (*Complete Short Poetry* 41) in order to create a more revolutionary poetics?

Revolution is a double-edged term in Zukofsky's early writings, often signifying a return full circle to one's initial premises. To avoid such self-enclosed repetition, Zukofsky turns to the contextual rather than the inexpressible, opening the poem's subjects to "the direction of historic and contemporary particulars" in "a world outside of it" (*Prepositions* 15). "The revolutionary word if it must revolve," he insists, "cannot escape having a reference" (*Prepositions* 16). The attempt to write a poem including history had also impelled Pound to leave the Imagist mode for the narratives and metanarratives of the *Cantos*. Yet Zukofsky's desire "to place everything . . . within a context" (*Prepositions* 15) suggests more than the concatenation of luminous details, or the arrangement of subject rhymes matched across centuries. He invokes history as a matrix of exchanges and connections: "things, human beings as things their instrumentalities of capillaries and veins binding up and bound up with events and contingencies" (*Prepositions* 16). This emphasis on reestablishing connections, underscored in the language of currency and trade, is partly the product of his own historical context during the Depression. He predicted in 1928 that the usual method of "commerce will not complete / Anything" (*Complete Short Poetry* 24), foreshadowing the "weather / Of tears" (*Complete Short Poetry* 37) a year later when an entire system of exchange seemed to have collapsed. That "[n]ight of economic extinctions" would only deepen his desire to write "[o]ne song / Of many voices," the words that could range between disparate forms and speakers ("A"-5, 18). The dilemma for the political artist, "A"-6 implies, was in finding other ways to create a common context with the growing numbers of the poor one portrayed, the new "Bottom" of capitalism's failure.

A poetry that emphasizes a nonhierarchical connection with its subjects was one way for Zukofsky to reaffirm his roots as the son of an immigrant pants-presser as well as his own struggle to find steady work. His "Poem beginning 'The,' " with its immigrant accents and

Marxist ideology, brilliantly satirizes *The Waste Land* by presenting the American fragments left out of its cultural landscape. These images of the dispossessed—the poor, the homeless, and the immigrants—also suggest the poet's anxiety about his vocation, a need to justify word-play as legitimate work that is part of the materialist base rather than the ideological superstructure.[1] "An Objective" envisions "the poem as a job" comparable to the craftsmanship of cabinetmaking: indulging in pure metaphor without attention to the sound and texture of the language is denounced as "[i]dle" (*Prepositions* 15). The street diggers of "A"-7 hail the poet as a fellow worker who offers food for change: "Bother / Brother, we want a meal, different techniques" where there is "no months' rent in arrear" and "no one's cut out" of the exchange ("A"-7, 42). To understand the "different techniques" that poet and subject might share is to move from the visuality of Zukofsky's early poetry to its preoccupation with sound and contextual structures.

From Eye to Ear: The Flight of " 'Mantis' "

The sestina " 'Mantis' " and the "Interpretation" that accompanies it illustrate a critical stage in the transition beyond Imagism. The poem superficially echoes the style of an early Pound or Williams lyric whose central image captures—and sublimates—a vignette of urban squalor. Pound's "In a Station of the Metro" is a concise example:

> The apparition of these faces in a crowd;
> Petals on a wet, black bough.
> > [*Personae* 109]

The slightly frightening swirl of passengers refocuses in the single image of the flower. Pound explained the poem's origin in his glimpse of a beautiful child in a subway (*Gaudier-Brzeska* 88): the underground passage lighted by the flowerlike face recalls the myth of Persephone, the amazed moment when the young girl "gathering flow'rs / Herself a fairer flow'r by gloomy Dis / Was gathered," in Milton's imagery (85). The language of "bottomness" and heights is present not only in the contrast between the meadow and the subway-Hades but also in the very type of figurative language. Metaphor rests on hierarchical levels of meaning—here the factual base and its transformation through the classical allusion to spring imprisoned in winter. "The

'one image poem,' " Pound makes explicit, "is a form of super-posi-
tion, that is to say, it is one idea set on top of another" (*Gaudier-Brzeska*
89). The priority of ideas is clear in "A Station of the Metro," where
the actual faces of the crowd paradoxically become the apparition, and
historical context drops out in the recognition of a literary trope recurring across time.

Zukofsky's " 'Mantis' " also describes an underground subway
scene, juxtaposing a fragile, flowerlike insect with beggars asleep on
stone benches, a newsboy selling papers, and a crowd of self-absorbed
passengers. Here too the narrator feels visually and empathically isolated from the scene, although he regrets that distance more openly:
"I who can't bear to look, cannot touch" (*Complete Short Poetry* 65).
As a result, the mantis's "flights" become increasingly imaginative, the
"Interpretation" tracing the circulation of currency and material that
creates an underclass: " 'Rags make paper / paper makes money,
money makes / banks, banks make loans, loans make / poverty, poverty makes rags' " (*Complete Short Poetry* 71). The analysis might be
better suited to the *Cantos*' sense of history than to an Imagist lyric;
the poem is also more hortatory, with its concluding call to action:
"Fly, mantis, on the poor, arise like leaves," anticipating the "armies
of the poor" (*Complete Short Poetry* 66). Nevertheless, the call still
seems to depend on the insect's symbolic links to the poor and a vocabulary of elevating base material conditions through interpretive
vision. " 'Look, take it up,' "the narrator imagines the mantis begging
him, in order to 'save it!'—as if the author might, through his own
"(thoughts' torsion)!" (*Complete Short Poetry* 65), find a redeeming
meaning in a scene that would otherwise be lost.

A closer analysis confuses the hierarchy of factual base and symbol.
The speaker insists, in the "Interpretation" immediately following the
poem, that these "facts are not a symbol" for the poor: "No human
being wishes to become / An insect for the sake of a symbol" (*Complete Short Poetry* 70). Readers determined to read the mantis as an
emblem, or those who desire only a delicate "grace" in "the visual
sense," do so at the cost of isolating the insect from its past and present
contexts (*Complete Short Poetry* 68). The significance of the mantis
changes as it hops—often arbitrarily within the same line—between
the startled speaker and those he watches, between Old World and
New World poor, between myth and history. In quick succession the
insect is hailed as a *spectre* from European folktales and a *faked flower,*

hardly reassuring images for its role of *guide* or *prophetess*. The note of artificiality in "faked flower" introduces its modern, urban incarnation as *machined wheels* and *android* at the same time it is also an emotional supplicant, *loving beggar*. Neither vision nor symbolism can provide a fully adequate transition for all these transformations. The constantly reimagined mantis, Michael Davidson argues, works to "dereify" the object status of the poor (525).

In spite of the fractured imagery, however, the sestina does not seem formally unstructured or fragmented. On the contrary, the reader is impressed by the dense *presence* of sound patterns in the stanzas as they repeat, and vary the sequence of, the six end words. It was that verbal musicality that attracted Pound to the sestina and canzone forms, the tangibility of a poem that "can be well judged only when heard spoken, or sung to its own measure" (*Spirit of Romance* 26). For Zukofsky, John Taggart asserts, an Objectivist "sincerity," or attention to poetry's measure and sound, becomes the test of the poet's connection with his subject: "If the poet's personal love or compassionate emotion for the poor cannot be finally determined, it nonetheless can be inferred from his love of language, his consciousness of word combinations and their construction to the extent that, in Eric Mottram's phrase, "technique is mythicized" (66). " 'Mantis' " does give the impression of a mythic sestina, multiplying and interweaving the rules of an already difficult form with exaggerated virtuosity as it traces the transformations of both perceiver and perceived. Instead of limiting the repetition to six end words, the poem plays with internal variations of at least seven others, not including homonyms, puns, and near rhymes. In order to have any thematic progression in this intense recycling of material, the words must be continually recontextualized; the poem's ingeniousness lies in its finding so many possible contexts within the space of its lines.

The six end words of the first stanza, for example, are arranged as *leaves / poor / it / you / lost / stone*. Thus placed, they might be minimalist notes for an elegy, with fallen leaves suggesting the plight of the poor, an explanation given of "its" significance for the messenger or poet's "you," and finally a promise to commemorate loss with inscriptions on a monument "stone." But the rearranged endings of the next stanza immediately satirize that reading with the announcement that the memorial *stone / leaves* are themselves *lost*, with *poor / you* left to confront a final, ambiguous *it* that has not been adequately summarized. "Poor you" might suggest the poem's own descriptive poverty, yet it is precisely because these nouns and pronouns are so imagistically reductive that their potential range of referents and narratives is so vast. The recycling of other words adds new combinations to the sequences; the two most frequent additions, "save!" and "new" or "news," pointedly call the speaker to creative action rather than rote repetition.

The individual words and their homonyms create subnarratives as they are transformed from one line context to the next. The subway drafts or artificial *winds* in the first stanza seem to mechanize the mantis into the *windup* toy of the second. But they also anticipate the freeing *wind* that gives *wing* to apes—and, perhaps, to ape-descended men as well—in a conclusion where old constructions are undone. Cold *stone* threatens to crush the mantis and offers little shelter to the beggars; that external environment is assimilated as internal strength when the poor reveal themselves in the closing tercet as "stone on stone." The fallen *leaves* of the first stanza and the fear of being *left* behind without guidance are reassembled as the *leaves* of the narrator's page. *Leave* thus parallels another core word, *lost,* which fulfills its name by dropping out in the tercet as the mantis finds its direction, abandoning fear to rouse the poor from their lethargy.

This process of recontextualizing the word comes close to what Zukofsky imagined in "An Objective" as an alternative to the visual metaphor: "the single word which is in itself a relation, an implied metaphor" (*Prepositions* 14). "Obviously I can't make [a table] eat grass," Zukofsky explained in a later interview, attempting to define his use of "objectification." "I have delimited this thing, in a sense. I call it a table and I want to keep the word for its denotative sense—as solid as possible" (Interview 266). The technique of preserving the word and its concrete referent, and at the same time allowing it to display its own internal possibilities, is the answer to the narrator's ambivalent plea for the poor: 'Save it!'—rescue the oppressed from an endangering situation, but also preserve their force and integrity. Zukofsky projects a revolution *within* the poor; the viewer returns to them as an agent that is always already multiple, requiring only the impetus of fresh associations, rather than an outsider's imagination, in order to display itself. Where Pound's credo was "make it new," Zukofsky watches his subject make itself "Anew," the talismanic word opening one poem about a "people cheated" (*Complete Short Poetry* 79).

Compare the two poets' use of repetition and transformation even on the microlevels of form, their alliterative play with the letters that begin the words "poor" and "beggar." Pound's "In a Station of the Metro" contrasts *p* and *b* sounds to emphasize the softness of the petals and the apparitional faces against the harder, mundane background that threatens to overwhelm them: "*p*etals . . . *b*lack, *b*ough." Zukofsky combines both *p* and *b* sounds to describe a single visual focus, the mantis, in its own multiple aspects, calling our attention to the fact that the two sounds are only voiced and unvoiced variants of the same phoneme. The description of the insect's eyes in line two as "*p*ins, *b*right, *b*lack, and *p*oor" creates an aural chiasmus where the mantis's softer, unthreatening aspects (its slenderness and lack of resources) surround the more boldly distinctive traits ("bright, black"). The mantis is a "spectre," a nearly effaced presence, but it is also the harder sounding, more noticeable "beggar." As the poem progresses, the "softer" sounds themselves betray more menacing qualities. The central homonyms behind the mantis, "praying" and "preying," capture the apparent desperation of an insect whose clasped legs are actually raised to devour others. The interpreter who ignores either the vulnerability or the hidden power of the insect will misunderstand its true potential, just as one might overlook the complex nature of the human poor among whom it travels. The phonetic play allows Zukofsky to make his point explicit: the victimized need only to "voice" the strength they already possess.

The focus on self-transformation within given resources is crucial because it offers a way out of the seemingly closed economic cycles delineated earlier in the poem. The cycles perpetuate themselves by assigning different fixed values to products (paper, rags, money) made from the same material and to agents (banker, pauper) who might be forced to reverse positions, as the depression had already demonstrated. Recognizing the interchangeability of the stages alerts one to the system's artificiality. The final transition to voiced sounds in the tercet of " 'Mantis' " does coincide with a vision of vocalized crowds rising against their oppression:

Fly, mantis, on the poor, arise like leaves
The armies of the poor, strength: stone on stone
And build the new world in your eyes, Save it!
  [*Complete Short Poetry* 66]

The organized "poor" now triumphantly "build," a word whose closing sounds also anticipate a new "world." The tentative injunction "fly" moves to the harder *v* in the command "Save!" while the soft *s* of strength and mantis becomes "arise" and a focus upon the mantis's "eyes," as the power to see and change passes from the watcher to the watched.

Such gestures of exchange seem to offer even the most disempowered a chance to rewrite their situation. The question, however, is whether Zukofsky's particular word games are the most appropriate language in which to invoke a new "collective" of readers (*Complete Short Poetry* 72). If one takes literally the dictum that poetry is "[l]ower limit speech / Upper limit music" ("A"-12, 138), then to work with the phonetics of language should theoretically flatten all communications to equivalent surfaces, a kind of musical ur-language whose accents and rhythms anyone could appreciate. The awkwardness of the insect's "terrified eyes, pins, bright, black, and poor" (*Complete Short Poetry* 65), for instance, might be inferred from the line's harsh, jerky diction. Much of the language in " 'Mantis' " takes the form of simple monosyllables: "Let the poor laugh at my fright, then see it" (*Complete Short Poetry* 66), and its vocabulary is deliberately ordinary: "leaves," "seat," "stomach," "chest."

Yet to depend solely upon sounds or isolated words ignores the question of the poem's semantics. The crowded language, ambiguous syntax, and lack of transitions in " 'Mantis' " make it all but inaccessible at points. "An Interpretation" is less helpful than its title implies, offering not a paraphrase or explanation but a catalogue of abstruse sources in a playful dialogue with the sestina. The most "collective" aspect of the poem still seems to be in the *range* of what it includes— legends from Provençal, West Pacific, and East European immigrant cultures, combined with quotations from Marx, the British Admiralty, and a Wisconsin newspaper—rather than the easy communicability of its language. Indeed, the prospect of "[w]ords ranging forms" ("A"-5, 20) in other lyrics includes contrasting dialects mixed together, instead of one uniform address to the reader. Zukofsky blends street colloquialisms ("Dem Rooshans ain't rational, why!" "A"-6, 34) with fragments of foreign poetry; "Shimaunu-Sān," the melodic creation of a Yiddish poet, rubs elbows with "Ricky, bro'," itself the transformed name of a college boy who committed suicide ("A"-7, 42).

These linguistic strands are intended as more than a modernist collage. Zukofsky believed that sound patterns, if not a semantic code in themselves, could be used as tools to translate between different dialects and different historical contexts. "I think there's a close relationship between families of languages, in this physiological sense," he proposed. "Something must have led the Greeks to say *hudor* and for us to say *water*" (Interview 267). Over a period of eleven years, Zukofsky and his wife translated Catullus through sound cognates and latinate syntax in order "to breathe the 'literal' meaning" of the poetry rather than merely paraphrase (*Complete Short Poetry* 243). As a result, the line "Vale, puella, iam Catullus obdurat," for instance, becomes "Vale! puling girl. I'm Catullus, *obdurate*" (*Complete Short Poetry* 248). If such structural equivalence best preserves the meaning of the poem, then the formal patterns of " 'Mantis' " should be widely communicable to auditors rather than forcing them back upon the exegesis of its "thoughts' torsion" (*Complete Short Poetry* 68).[2]

If the argument seems tortuous, it is because these translations between sound patterns or language families are not always resolvable at the literal level of communication in Zukofsky's poetry. Nor do they offer a clear political praxis for reaching the poor. Zukofsky's lyrics, I have argued, are most political in their insistence that "objective" vision is a fallacy and in their unwillingness to elide referential contexts. Zukofsky's poetry of the twenties and thirties may be among his most *rhetorically* Marxist, adapting a vocabulary of alienation and exchange-value to the use of language as a material commodity. But Zukofsky's verbal exchanges are ultimately inspired by a spiritual perception of language and history rather than the implications of one political ideology. His translations invoke a discourse of originary presence and value, using an almost mystical projection of broken language as a prelude to forming a new community of readers.

Breaking the Word

Zukofsky appended the following note to a selection of love poetry in his aptly named anthology, *A Test of Poetry*, in order to justify the English translations of Ovid: "Good verse is determined by the 'core of the matter,' which is, after all, the poet's awareness of the differences, changes, and possibilities of existence. If poetry does not always translate literally from one language to another, from one time to another, certain lasting emotions find an equivalent or paraphrase in all times"

(60). The "good" translator acknowledges that different linguistic materials are only types of the same principle. Whether the "lasting" emotion is called sincerity, eros, or the Spinozan ethic of love that responds to the alienation of labor in "A"-9, Zukofsky chooses to paraphrase its value in his own poetry by addressing both matter and spirit in an incarnational language of communion.

The early sections of "A" and many other lyrics are structured around the myth of Christ's crucifixion and Easter rising. That act is commemorated in the ritual of communion, where the body broken on the cross is reintegrated into a congregation with the breaking and eating of the sacramental bread. Zukofsky was not committed to a specifically Christian theology per se, but seemed intrigued by the motif of transforming visual absence into another type of presence that could unite a community.[3] The god's absence from the tomb that the mourners open proves his divinity as a Word that will redeem all men universally. "See Him! Whom?" the speaker queries in "A"-7, about "The Son / of Man" ("A" 40). This is not only a quotation from the first chorus of Bach's St. Matthew Passion but also the form of the medieval *quem quaeritis,* the question asked in the procession of Corpus Christi that celebrated the Eucharist: "Whom do you seek? Him who is risen"—and who is manifest even before the search for his image. When Zukofsky's construction-workers in "A"-7 demand "a meal, new techniques" from the poet to enable their own ascension as "Saviours" ("A" 42), they conflate the Eucharist with the materiality of poetic form, as if the writer on his stoop might become a version of the dispensing priest at the altar.

A communional vocabulary helps to explain sequences of " 'Mantis' " that elude a straightforwardly political reading. The narrator's first impression of the insect is the exposure of its vulnerability: "the mantis opened its body" (*Complete Short Poetry* 68). That offering may also be a kind of predation, since the mantis opens itself in lovemaking to devour its partner: "Is it love's food your raised stomach prays?" (*Complete Short Poetry* 66). The violence seems misplaced in a political context unless it is read as the poor's ignorant destruction of their own kind rather than of the masters who threaten them. The sacrifice/predation of a figure linked to the poor becomes more complex through the mantis's association with Christ. This "prophetess," the narrator predicts, will be "[k]illed by thorns (once men)," coming to rest against stone and then rising once more (*Complete Short Poetry* 66). The prayed-for vision of a body consumed in the act of love does lead the poet to find unexpected resurrections around him: "dead, bones, it / Was assembled, apes wing in wind" (*Complete Short Poetry* 66), while the fallen leaves, a conventional trope for human mortality, are suddenly lifted with the insect at the end of the poem. I do not propose " 'Mantis' " as a Christian allegory any more than a Marxist one. What the metaphor of broken love offers the poet is a linguistic strategy, the "Vita Nova" that begins as "le parole" (*Complete Short Poetry* 67). As the narrator tries to reconcile "the simultaneous" and the "diaphanous, historical / In one head"—the apparently self-enclosed present and the larger context that produces it—the leaves of his own text adopt the communional technique of breaking and recombining the word (*Complete Short Poetry* 73).

There are stylistic precedents for the technique in a seventeenth-century religious writer such as George Herbert, whose "Crown" Zukofsky quotes in *A Test of Poetry* as an example of devotional verse. Herbert was also distrustful of imagery, which came from the carnal human imagination and too often glorified the things of this world. Instead of imagistic embellishments, he tried to find remnants of the divine Word by violently breaking apart the sound patterns of human communication through anagrams, puns, alliteration, and call-and-response formats—all familiar techniques in Zukofsky's early lyrics. Breaking the word was partly an act of humility, thwarting the craftsman's pride in his work—and an impartially leveling gesture since all human communication, high and low, was equally fallen. But what he searched for in these reduced pieces of language was the perception that all fragments are united in an originary whole. As Heather Asals observes, Herbert openly adopted the persona of the priest who "breaks the word and letter to expose the many which is one" (12). To indulge in the sensual sounds of language for its own sake would be sinful nonsense, but the melody might be *used,* in the Augustinian sense of use as opposed to enjoyment, to guide readers toward an unearthly beauty (Asals 61). The dialogue between a human questioner and a supernatural "Echo" in Herbert's poem "Heaven" dramatizes that use of broken language:

O who will show me those delights on high?
   Echo.   *I.*
Thou Echo, thou art mortall, all men know.

> Echo.   No.
> . . . .
> Then tell me, what is that supreme delight?
>   Echo.   Light.
> Light to the minde: what shall the will enjoy?
>   Echo.   Joy.
>   [191]

The substance of the holy instruction is repeated from the letters and the sound of the human speaker's own question. "Light" can come from the "delight" of this wordplay, and even the negation of mortality depends upon the expression of mortal knowledge: know/No. Like Zukofsky, Herbert suggests that the problem with our communication is not the corruptness of "what all men know" but the fact that each speaker expresses a partial knowledge, favoring one narrow reading or set of readers. The poet's act of fragmenting and recontextualizing information paradoxically provides more opportunities of glimpsing an immanent structure within it.

Zukofsky uses the same play on delight/light and other equivocations in the word games of "29 Songs," a series of poems that question whether language can restore a community that has lost contact with its labor, its environment, and ultimately the ability to express love. The messenger insect in "Crickets' thickets" anticipates " 'Mantis' ":

> Crickets'
> thickets
>
> light,
> delight:
>
> sleeper's eyes
> keeper's;
>
>   Plies!
> lightning
>
> frightening
> whom . . . ?
>
> doom
> nowhere . . .
>
> where eyes . . .
> air,

are crickets'
air.
        [*Complete Short Poetry* 48]

The words are so elliptically broken that they seem almost swallowed
by the white space of the page. As in Herbert's poem, however, where
multiple leaves are subsumed into something unitary and deathless,
the low "crickets' thickets" combine into one "delight"; the different
"eyes" or perspectives become a single "air," evoking music. What is
found, perhaps, by the "keeper" is a faith in the interconnectedness
of the fragmented language and its users that tempers the lightning
(suggestive both of divine anger and of human weaponry in this pre–
World War II poem), promising "doom/nowhere" for those who are
not too preoccupied to hear the crickets' quieter melody. In a series
of lyrics about possession—that necessarily partial act of appropria-
tion—and the destruction it causes, Zukofsky deliberately makes this
plea for a more open type of exchange with the sparsest possible materials. Celia Zukofsky adds an interesting coda to the crickets' song
that reinforces its message of connection: the poet would send out this
seemingly hermetic poem ten years later as a Christmas greeting to
his friends (Terrell 47).

The lightness of the crickets' song becomes the verbal density of
language in " 'Mantis,' " which breaks down a more worldly narrative
into its lowest common denominator of sounds and syllables: the "use
function of the material" (*Complete Short Poetry* 72). As in the averted
lightning of "Crickets," however, the violence seems directed against
the hubris of creating fixed meanings through language, meanings
that divide because they are partial when taken alone. The readings of
the poor, when they remain "separate" in " 'Mantis,' " are themselves
"too poor," too narrow, to effect change. The newsboy continues to
sell his papers within the system, unable to see the herald insect as
anything but "harmless" (*Complete Short Poetry* 66). "*An Interpretation,*" by contrast, refuses to limit the "thoughts' torsion" that the
mantis provokes by choosing among religious, political, or poetic language for its defining meaning. It is not simply an engagement of
multiplicity for its own sake, Zukofsky insists; what is more important
is how one uses the material, the range of "simultaneous" disciplines,
to reveal their common formulations of presence and loss, the collective and the discrete. The "Head remembering these words" (*Complete*

Short Poetry 73) in all their contexts might trace a relation between the artificer's labored "drafts" of a sestina and the mechanical winds engineered in the subway, or it might reconsider the levels of myth and poetry within Marx's *Manifesto* and the reasons why he chose a "spectre" to represent the onset of communism. These connections do anticipate a possible alliance between the poet and the workers he watches without prioritizing the vision of either.

There are traces of a pattern even in the seeming disorder of "'*Mantis,' An Interpretation*," which echoes the sestina in its repetition of key words. Terms denoting mutability ("movement," "coincidence," "ungainliness") are recycled in counterpoint to ones of "origin" ("original shock," "original title," "original emotion"). It is no coincidence in the schema for " 'Mantis' " that the sestina's last myth is a myth of creation. If the search for revolution does seem to come full circle to a recollection of beginnings, history itself at the end of the "*Interpretation*" becomes "diaphanous," a laden neo-Platonic term from Pound's vocabulary (*Complete Short Poetry* 73). In Canto XXXVI, Pound imagined the "diafan" as a material through which light could be made visible; the process was associated with language, whose fragmentary notes might evoke the memory of a lost coherence (*Cantos* 177). Poetry may not be able to transcribe all "the implications of a too regular form" in Zukofsky's work (*Complete Short Poetry* 70), but neither can it ignore the drive toward "the original which is a permanence" (*Complete Short Poetry* 68) out of the scattered pieces.

For Pound, the forms seen through the diafan translated all material things into light. Zukofsky's focus is slightly different; he emphasizes a collective order within language that is grounded in a material community. In his myth of an incarnational word, there is a nostalgic sense that if we could go back far enough to an originary language, we might also return to a point before bodies were separated into artificial distinctions of class, religion, or nationality—a "Sum" constructed of "voice," where "All thinges is comune" (*Complete Short Poetry* 78). It would be the reversal of Babel, the fall into a false multiplicity where the one language and tribe are supplanted by isolated fragments. The apes of " 'Mantis' " that wing in the wind are taken from a Melanesian legend but also suggest a shared point of evolutionary origin. The narrator in "A"-7 commands the messiah to "[c]hoose Jews' shoes or whose: anyway Choose!" (*Complete Short Poetry* 41), a reminder that the choice of one denomination to express the Word should not matter, just as the first Christian was himself Jewish. Zukofsky's anagrams and number games can in fact be traced further back to their roots in Hebrew kabbalistic traditions, whose vision of God as a broken Name was later incorporated into strands of Christian mysticism.[4]

Ideally, Zukofsky postulates, every reader who learns how to interrogate language could be his or her own redemptor. "[E]ach animal," though compelled to work as "his own gravedigger," the poet notes, "almost / sings," for that elided song is the laborers' knowledge of themselves as the ones who might "walk out / against / the / social / and political / order of / things" (*Complete Short Poetry* 56). The messianic diggers in "A"-7 do learn how to protest their situation because they see what the poet sees: both the ease with which human constructions can be disrupted and a continuity behind them. Although they demand a new system of exchange, the diggers change the confrontational "Bother" to "Brother" ("A"-7, 42) just as the poet replaces the hierarchical command "follow me" with the more collective "fellow me" ("A"-7, 39). The "pump," the working machine, is no longer "bum," that is, faulty, with a double sense of bottom-ness, nor is it acceptingly "dumb" ("A"-7, 41). The awakened diggers are not only able to escape from their symbolically closed-off street ("Seven, Seven Saviours went to heaven—," "A"-7, 42), but to change the order of things, transforming the wooden sawhorses that had blocked human traffic into something fluidly alive:

> . . . And the seven came
> To horses seven (of wood—who will?—kissed
>   their stomachs)
> Bent knees as these rose around them—trot—trot—
>   ["A"-7, 42]

As dead "wood," with its play on the hypothetical "would," gives way to the promised "will," these once static markers seem to epitomize Zukofsky's vision of communion, combining the material and the spiritual within them as a product of *language*. Their physical "manes" pun on the Latin words for ancestral spirits (Hatlen, "Poetics of Absence" 217) as they find their own voice in the poem's conclusion: "Spoke: words, words, we are words, horses, manes / words" ("A"-7, 42). When kabbalistically reduced to nothing but the shape of letters, "two legs stood A, four together M" ("A"-7, 41), they spell the retort of God: I AM what I AM, the preface to all creation (Kenner 190). In human terms, it is also a declaration of pure existence prior to any distinctions in the position of the speaking subject. "No one's cut out" because each face can be "a reflection of the other" ("A"-7, 42) on the slippery material surface of language. As an offer to begin translating between speakers, one could hardly imagine a more equalizing reduction than this: *I am / we are . . . words.*

Face Values

Thematically and formally, "A"-7 is one of Zukofsky's most spectacular displays of patterned language. Its sonnet sequence compresses motifs from almost all of his earlier poetry: sound, light, labor, race, class, revolution, resurrection. It is also a pattern whose rhyme scheme and meter become gradually looser, until it produces sound "reflections" as disjunctive as "techniques" and "stomachs"[5]; the final near rhyme of "came" and "manes" only works if one ignores the concluding phrase, "words," which is displaced below the last line. This formal degeneration with its "words" pointedly left over raises the question of whether Zukofsky can sustain the epiphanic moment of translation, tracing the common forms ranged within different jargons. Certainly he persisted throughout his career in encoding messages through language patterns, from arrangement of *r* and *n* sounds in the opening of "A"-9 by the formula for conic sections (Quartermain 74) to the anagrammic plays on the name of BACH in "A"-12. He would translate the different characters in a play into counterpointed lines in a musical score, a vivid symbol of the one song of many voices. Almost all of these complex patterns, nevertheless, seem incomplete, breaking down at their conclusions or cannibalizing parts of earlier structures as if the holistic form might be glimpsed, but never completely known, through the fragments we arrange.

Zukofsky's lyrics of the twenties and thirties foreshadow the difficulty of maintaining the simultaneous levels of spiritual and material imagery. Kenneth Cox has suggested some of the complications of his linguistic mythology:

> In this view [of language as a descent from a "sacred, universal" speech], language as used resembles money: one *utters* coins. To the diversity of languages there corresponds the diversity of currencies, each tender only within a field where it is accepted by force of faith

SUSAN VANDERBORG

and usage and to some extent supported by law. They are convertible one into another, usually at a discount, and several may be associated in a family, like the romance languages and the sterling area, where some denominations are practically equivalent. Languages and currencies have no intrinsic value, their usefulness depends on acceptance and exchange, but it is possible to imagine an ideal or original value.
[87]

The belief in origins does not seem to circumscribe the artist's creativity *within a* language, where terms have only the significance that faith or use-value imputes to them. The new circulation becomes less fluid in the exchange *between* languages, where one is translated into another "at a discount." Even though Zukofsky's sound games try to level the distinction between different types of speech, for example, the colloquialisms in his poetry often seem like a base structure needing to be embellished themselves. In "Poem beginning 'The' " and the early sections of "*A*", slang passages typically denote the butt of a joke, as in the Poundian spoofs of captains of industry in "*A*"-1: "We ran 'em in chain gangs, down in the Argentine . . . Nothin' like nature for hell-fire!" (5). There are subtle dissonances even within more sympathetic portraits in jargon. Are the lines, "Ricky, bro, Shimaunu-Sān, yours is the / Clavicembalo" in "*A*"-7 (42) a neutral mix bound together by consonance, or is the dialect placed at a faintly comic discount next to the Japanese-cum-Yiddish and Italian allusions, both linked to a high lyric mode? What is the relationship between source and poetic text when the nearly illiterate letters of a "poor pay pfc." are incorporated (in "*A*"-12) within the body of a poem he could not understand? " '*Mantis,' An Interpretation*" seems on one level a parody of the sestina, and yet there is also an odd conferral of authority from the sestina to its commentary when the simple words of the former give way to the Dante quotations and encyclopedic labels of the latter. Zukofsky's praying mantis may be associated with the wholesale breaking of language, but there are clear bottom and top positions within its embrace—a critical distinction for which partner is to survive the mating.

While there is rarely such a death struggle between languages in the early lyrics, poems like " 'Mantis' " do leave the reader with a sense of something inevitably lost in translation, jeopardizing either the message or the medium. Zukofsky writes half-satirically in the "*Interpretation*" that propaganda can be as urgent and real as the evidence of the senses, yet his more bluntly political poems lose the contextual wordplay upon which the transformations of " 'Mantis' " depend. "During the Passaic Strike of 1926" trades complexity for clarity: "For Justice they are shrewdly killing the proletarian / For Justice they are shrewdly shooting him dead" (*Complete Short Poetry* 26). The repetition hammers home the point, but its object is an ominously lifeless and singular noun. Like the marching songs incorporated in "A"-8, the poem works best when read as part of a collection, with surrounding lyrics that question the finality of its vision and language.

Zukofsky's most inclusive statements on poetic language and objectification do acknowledge both the unifying richness and the inadequacy of his translation games. One striking early poem, "To my wash-stand," seems an ideal combination of both Imagist and Symbolist projects; the narrator looks into the mirror of his imagination and sees the face of the object-Other. As in " 'Mantis,' " that visionary identification with the poor is accomplished less by imagery than by a series of word and sound patterns, inspired by an emblematically broken surface:

> so my wash-stand
> in one particular breaking of the
>   tile at which I have
> looked and looked
>
>   has opposed to my head
> the inscription of a head
>   whose coinage is the
> coinage of the poor
>   [*Complete Short Poetry* 53]

"I have / looked and looked": the gazer remains frozen opposite and opposed to its object. The poem focuses instead on the materiality of communication, suggested in the inscribed heads with the prospect of a common currency, as if the poet and the poor were no more than intertranslatable constructions—literally equivalent "face-values."

Why then does the emphasis on language structures seem to block rather than facilitate an exchange? Instead of the two heads confronting one another, when the stanza is broken down carefully there is only the triple mediation of signifiers: the reflected inscription of a head whose coinage is also the coinage of the poor. Acknowledging a common point of origin or speech, the poem speculates, does not in fact balance the two sides of the equation; excess words, and resources, cannot be left out of consideration. The description of the poor as "carefully attentive / to what they have / and to what they do not / have" (*Complete Short Poetry* 53) underscores the far from equal distribution of economic and linguistic currency they have been allowed as their face value. The long, imaginative prologue with its vision of ornamental friezes and circus animals hints that a minimum amount of material leisure may be necessary before one can break down systems to their surface patterns of water, stone, hands, or faces. Oppositions such as top and bottom may ultimately prove to be "invertible counterpoints" (*Complete Short Poetry* 53), simultaneities that can be incorporated within "[o]ne human's intuitive Head" (*Complete Short Poetry* 68). But the position of the translator has not yet become an arbitrary choice. As the poet struggles with the forms he perceives ranged in words, he is aware that others will inscribe "an age in a wash-stand / and in their own heads" (*Complete Short Poetry* 53), with a unique face and a unique paraphrase.

What then " 'is the formula for success?' " the narrator queries in "A"-6 concerning his exchanges. " 'X = work, Y = play, Z = keep your mouth shut' " (23). Pilate had to wash his hands of the decision over the Word, turning his own agency over to the crowd's voice before the communional presence could be manifested. If the ablutions of the poor as they get up each morning are not as dramatic an uprising as the armies of " 'Mantis,' " their "observant watching" is an expectant pause in a poetry otherwise so densely verbal (*Complete Short Poetry* 53). Zukofsky's "Objectivism" begins with the problem of the poet's gaze; its conclusions hinge on the not-yet verbalized response of those who are in the process of finding their own objective. The future dialogue between the two may find "everything lowered to a mutual, common level," or it may be a "mutual slap" ("A"-6, 21). Whatever its form, a response would still validate the contribution of his poetry as an incident which "*can start* / History etc." (*Complete Short Poetry* 70) by "compelling any writing" (67). The new poetry will have "[e]nough worth," he predicts in "*An Interpretation*" if the revisors can remain alert to material differences even while their "emotions" try to "equate" the two sides of the correspondence (*Complete Short Poetry* 70).

Notes

1. Burton Hatlen has an excellent extended discussion of Zukofsky's insistence on poetry as labor in the essay "Art and/as Labor." He sees Zukofsky's public Marxism giving way to a private expression of ethics in the second half of "A"-9, however; I find more continuity between the two sections. Zukofsky invokes a collective presence in language that is immanent in both public and private discourse. See as well Michael Davidson's argument in "Dismantling 'Mantis' " that the latter half of "A"-9 is not a rejection of politics: "It would be more accurate to say that he discovers a more intimate arena in which to study his primary themes of labor and value" (535).

2. Jeffrey Twitchell, in his discussion of abstraction and material language in Zukofsky's poetry, also notes this communicability of sound forms: "For Zukofsky, melopoeia is in part translatable because it is precisely this aspect of poetry in which, as Adorno puts it, 'the subject sounds through language in such a way that Language itself becomes audible' " (62). He analyzes its function as a way of letting random elements enter the compositional process.

3. Zukofsky's comment, in *A Test of Poetry*, on Herbert's devotional lyric suggests that the poem's communicable emotion is a function of style rather than the literal content and therefore accessible to readers outside its belief system: "Recent critics of literature have expressed the opinion that the beliefs implied or held in a poem influence the reader's appreciation. The opposite opinion would be that a poem is an emotional object defined not by the beliefs it deals with, but by its *technique* and the *poetic conviction or mastery* with which these beliefs are expressed" (77–78).

4. I am indebted to Gershom Scholem's discussion of the Shiʿur Komah kabbala, covering the dispersal of the divine name into isolated sounds and the numerical word games that scholars used to "measure" God's dimension. The first chapter of his *The Mystical Shape of the Godhead* traces the adoption of this doctrine in Christian Gnosticism.

5. Peter Quartermain incorporates a detailed discussion of the structural breakdown of "A"-7 in his article on form and crises in the first half of "A"-9. He lists the last rhyme pair more directly as came/words.

Works Cited

Asals, Heather. *Equivocal Predication: George Herbert's Way to God*. Toronto: U of Toronto P, 1981.

Cox, Kenneth. "The Poetry of Louis Zukofsky: '*A*'." *Agenda* 10.1 (1972): 80–89.

Davidson, Michael. "Dismantling 'Mantis': Reification and Objectivist Poetics." *American Literary History* 3.3 (Fall 1991): 521–541.

Hatlen, Burton. "Art and/as Labor: Some Dialectical Patterns in "*A*"-1 through "*A*"-10." *Contemporary Literature* 25.2 (Summer 1984): 205–234.

———. "Zukofsky, Wittgenstein, and the Poetics of Absence." *Sagetrieb* 1.1 (1982): 83–93.

Herbert, George. *The English Poems.* Ed. C. A. Patrides. London: Dent, 1974.

Kenner, Hugh. "Two Pieces on '*A*'." *Louis Zukofsky: Man and Poet.* Ed. Carroll F. Terrell. Orono, ME: National Poetry Foundation, 1979. 187–202.

Marx, Karl. *Theses on Feuerbach.* Appendix to Frederick Engels, *Ludwig Feuerbach and the Outcome of Classical German Philosophy.* New York: International, 1941. 82–84.

Milton, John. *Paradise Lost.* New York: Norton, 1975.

Pound, Ezra. *The Cantos.* New York: New Directions, 1986.

———. *Gaudier-Brzeska: A Memoir.* 1916. New York: New Directions, 1960.

———. *Personæ.* New York: New Directions, 1971.

———. *The Spirit of Romance.* 1910. New York: New Directions, 1953.

Quartermain, Peter. " 'Not At All Surprised by Science': Louis Zukofsky's First Half of 'A'-9." *Disjunctive Poetics: From Gertrude Stein and Louis Zukofsky to Susan Howe.* Cambridge: Cambridge UP, 1992. 70–89.

Scholem, Gershom. *The Mystical Shape of the Godhead.* New York: Schocken, 1991.

Taggart, John. *Songs of Degrees: Essays on Contemporary Poetry and Poetics.* Tuscaloosa: U of Alabama P, 1994.

Terrell, Carroll F. "Louis Zukofsky: An Eccentric Profile." *Louis Zukofsky: Man and Poet.* Ed. Carroll F. Terrell. Orono, ME: National Poetry Foundation, 1979. 31–74.

Twitchell, Jeffrey. "Tuning the Senses: Cavalcanti, Marx, Spinoza, and Zukofsky's 'A'-9." *Sagetrieb* 11.3 (Winter 1992): 57–91.

Williams, William Carlos. "Objectivism." *Princeton Encyclopedia of Poetry and Poetics.* Ed. Alex Preminger et al. Princeton, NJ: Princeton UP, 1974. 582.

Zukofsky, Louis. Interview with L. S. Dembo. *Louis Zukofsky: Man and Poet.* Ed. Carroll F. Terrell. Orono, ME: National Poetry Foundation, 1979. 265–281.

———. *A Test of Poetry.* 1948. New York: C.Z. Publications, 1980.

11

From Modernism to Postmodernism

Zukofsky's "A"-12

BURTON HATLEN

In THIS ESSAY, I WANT to argue that Louis Zukofsky's long poem "A", as it evolved from its beginnings in the late 1920s through its completion in the 1970s, traces a route from modernism to postmodernism. In its ultimate surrender to fragmentation, the modernist long poem (and here I'm thinking especially of *The Cantos* and *The Waste Land*) acknowledges the inability of the individual ego to master history through what Lyotard calls a "grand narrative" (xxiii)—whether a narrative of national origins and identity, as in the traditional epic through Milton, or a narrative of individual development, as in Wordsworth's *Prelude*. The long poems of Pound and Eliot, however, while developing a poetics of disjunction, are still haunted by a nostalgia for a unitary ego which can define itself, in a Wordsworthian manner, against a history that no longer promises a movement toward redemption; and this nostalgia impelled both Pound and Eliot to the mythic politics of fascism or Christian royalism, in search of a plenitude lost. Zukofsky's poetics is closely related to Pound's "Grand Collage," and the first ten sections of "A", all written before World War II, are in many ways still essentially Poundian. But I shall argue here that in his postwar writings Zukofsky moves decisively beyond the modernist mode into a poetics of indeterminacy, interruption, and incompletion that is, I propose, distinctively postmodernist. While I won't here explore this model of Zukofsky's career in as great detail as I might, I believe the moment of this shift is signaled most clearly in "A"-12. This movement begins in a modernist mode that aspires to closure and completion, but in the end it manifests a pervasive structural incompletion, an incompletion that the poet, with a characteristically postmodern "negative capability," is able to accept as inherent to the structure of existence itself.

As a young poet in the late 1920s and the 1930s, the precocious Zukofsky established himself as perhaps the most brilliant of the younger writers influenced by Pound. Pound developed his own collage method in the early 1920s; we see it on full display for the first time in *A Draft of XXX Cantos,* published in 1926. It seems clear that Zukofsky had begun working with a very similar method at about the same time, and by 1930 he had drafted several sections of "*A*", an evolving poem that continued to occupy much of his energies until the end of the 1930s. The poetics of the opening ten sections of "*A*", all of which were complete before 1940, seem to me almost completely Poundian.[1] The method is collage, interweaving fragmentary but intense moments of personal experience—"spots of time"—with contemporary historical events and materials drawn from the poet's reading. But while the method is clearly Poundian, in these sections Zukofsky diverges from Pound in at least four important respects. First, much of the personal material that Zukofsky incorporates in his poem emphasizes his Jewish heritage, an emphasis that pointedly (and intentionally) flies in the face of the implicit (or explicit) anti-Semitism of such modernists as Pound and Eliot. Second, Zukofsky establishes a musical analogy (to Bach's *St. Matthew Passion*) that is more explicit and fully worked through than any such analogy in Pound's poetry, for all the latter's talk of fugue structure. Third, on several occasions Zukofsky interrupts his loosely interwoven collage (I like to think of these sections as "recitative") with very tightly structured "chorale" sections; the alternation of these two different sorts of writing develops a complex system of internal rhythmic and linguistic inter-relations that are quite unlike anything we find in Pound. And fourth, and most significant, Zukofsky grounds his vision of history, not on the farrago of American rural populism, Douglasite economics, and fascist propaganda that we find in Pound, but rather on a careful reading of Henry Adams (on whom Zukofsky wrote a master's thesis for Columbia University) and of Marx. If only because Marxist theory is more rigorous and more fully thought out than anything we can find in Pound, the early sections of "*A*", especially "*A*"-8, display a degree of cogency we rarely find in the historical sections of *The Cantos.*[2]

The Marxian underpinnings of the first ten sections of "*A*" demonstrate that at this stage of his project Zukofsky was still committed to a grand narrative of historical redemption won through the revolutionary struggle of the working class. But the Hitler-Stalin pact shook—if it did not actually dislodge—the faith in Communism of very many American intellectuals and writers; and the Holocaust, if it did not, as Adorno said, make poetry impossible, *did* make impossible a poetry grounded in a myth of secular, political redemption. For various causes that might include these historical exigencies and that certainly involve personal reasons about which I have no information, in 1941 Zukofsky stopped work on *"A"* and did not return to the poem for the better part of a decade. Then, starting in 1948 and finishing in 1950, Zukofsky wrote the second half of "A"-9; in 1950 he wrote the two-page chorale "A"-11; and in the summer of 1951, in what seems to have been only a few months, he wrote by far the longest section of the poem up to that point, "A"-12. In these sections of *"A"* written around 1950, Zukofsky broaches a new theme: if the first ten books of *"A"* were grounded in a mythos of the revolutionary working class, these new sections are grounded in a mythos of the family. It may seem that Zukofsky has simply substituted one myth of redemption for another. In some measure that charge seems to me justified; for the idealized family life presented in the second half of "A"-9, in "A"-11, and in "A"-12 is astonishingly free of conflict, in ways that *no* family in the real world can be, and in this respect Zukofsky's poem is open to the charge of mystification and sentimentality. I want to propose here, however, that despite the limitations that sentimentalism might seem to impose, the domestic idyll of the family Zukofsky, as it is contrapuntally elaborated in "A"-12, allows the poet to accept the contingent, contextual status of the self and thus to initiate a movement beyond a modernist poetics of nostalgia for a lost absolute into a postmodernist poetics of finitude—and thus, of possibility.

The number twelve is rich with significance for any writer of a long poem. For Virgil and for Milton, the twelfth book is the final, summarizing book. Homer's epics are both divided into twenty-four books: two times twelve. More explicitly than either Eliot or Pound, Zukofsky acknowledges the power of this epic precedent; for as he nears the end of "A"-12, he declares,

I've finished 12 "books,"
So to speak,
Of 24—

A kind of childlike
Play this division
Into 24,
Enough perhaps for
12 books in this one
All done in a summer
After a gathering of 12 summers.
          ["A"-12, 258]

The shifting tonalities here are typically Zukofskyan. First, we get a confident proclamation that there *is* a plan, along with an assumption that we will (or should) recognize the epic precedents lying behind this plan and an absolute confidence on the poet's part that he *will* carry this plan through to the end (as he did, for "*A*" belongs with *Paradise Lost* among the handful of long poems in English that are actually *finished*). But then Zukofsky ironically deflates these "epic" claims, acknowledging that this number schema is arbitrary, just a form of childlike play—and indeed it might seem that Zukofsky, in "*A*"-12, has written a text ruled purely by the spirit of *play*, the spirit of the child. (And it's perhaps worth noting that "*A*"-12 is longer than the previous eleven books taken together: had he wanted to make such a gesture, Zukofsky could have divided this long book up into thirteen short ones and then have declared the project complete.) Yet the declaration that these number patterns represent nothing more than "play" in turn gives way to a sense that there are processes at work here that simply must be accepted on faith: a "gathering," a gestation, of twelve years has at last brought forth this new birth. But what "gathers" within time is in truth mysterious. We cannot hope to understand these processes; instead we can only point toward them, as Zukofsky does in the passage just cited.

    The emphasis on epic design in this passage may seem to belie my claim that "*A*"-12 is grounded in a poetics of incompletion and finitude. Indeed, such a label might seem more applicable to *The Cantos,* a project that repeatedly subverted Pound's will to closure, or to *Paterson*: having originally planned it as a four-book poem, Williams carried this project through to completion but then defiantly broke open his own structure by adding a fifth book, at which point the poem instantly became open-ended, so that only the poet's death could "complete" it. Yet while "*A*" is "finished" in a way that *The Cantos* and

Paterson are not, the structure that Zukofsky has here planned and accomplished is *deliberately* broken, incomplete: for the climactic twenty-fourth book of "*A*" was composed, not by the author of the first twenty-three books, but by someone else, his wife, Celia. Furthermore, "A"-24 was completed and named (by Zukofsky himself) before Zukofsky wrote "A"-22 and "A"-23, a fact suggesting that the deliberate self-effacement of the poet in this presumably climactic moment could have been part of the plan from relatively early in the process (though this is a remote possibility). Granted, the words of "A"-24 were written by Zukofsky himself, for Celia Zukofsky has created a "masque" in which four voices speak, contrapuntally or simultaneously, the words of various Zukofsky texts, to the accompaniment of two Handel harpsichord suites. But the implication seems clear: Zukofsky wrote the words and Handel the music, but only Celia Zukofsky has the power to harmonize Louis Zukofsky's various voices, to find the music that plays, tacitly, among all these voices. And so at the end of his poem Zukofsky willingly surrenders control to someone else. "Measure, tacit is," Zukofsky declares in "A"-12 (131). So the person who "sounds" the measure can't hear it—only the listener can do that. Thus to "complete" his life work, Zukofsky must deliberately decide *not* to complete it—to rely on the kindness, not of a stranger indeed, but of his wife. We enter here the territory of a paradox, but this paradox, which first emerges fully in "A"-12, becomes the pivot on which the whole poem turns.

Like the poem as a whole, "A"-12 is grounded on a plan. The plan here, as Barry Ahearn has noted, rests primarily on the number four:

> In "*A*"-12 a quartet is . . . summoned to the poet's aid. Zukofsky's brain trust for this movement: Aristotle, Paracelsus, Spinoza, and . . . Celia. . . . The four appear in shorthand notation at the movement's beginning . . . and end . . . as *B, A, C,* and *H.* "*B*" for Blest (Spinoza), "*A*" for Aristotle (referred to as "Ardent," apparently in recognition of his love of learning), "*C*" for Celia, "*H*" for Hohenheim (Paracelsus's real name was Philippus Aureolus Theophrastus Bombastus von Hohenheim). . . .
>
> . . . what does the world consist of? So far as "*A*"-12 is concerned, it consists simply of the ancient tally of four elements: earth, air, fire, and water.
>
> [125, 126]

And there are also other "fours" in "A"-12 that Ahearn does not mention: the four points of the compass, the four seasons. At this point, we might also find ourselves wondering whether, if *A* represents "ardent" (fr. Latin *ardens, -entis,* present participle of *ardere,* to burn), and if fire is one of the four elements, there might not be some cross-analogies here. Could *C* also be "sea"—thus water, the Great Mother, source of all life? *B* and *H* seem harder, but I'll have some suggestions later. As Ahearn goes on to note, "the family Zukofsky . . . provides a sure footing" (127) for the interplay of elements in "A"-12. But Ahearn neglects to point out that there are also four members of the family Zukofsky, at least as presented in "A"-12[3]: son Paul (regularly associated, as Ahearn recognizes, with fire [213], so he seems to be *A*); Celia, *C,* who may be water; Louis's recently dead father, Pinchos, who seems to be *B* because he was, like Spinoza, "blest" ("Everybody loves Reb Pinchos / Because he loves everybody" [153], and on page 160 the "blest lips that move in the grave" are clearly those of Pinchos), and who is in his grave—thus in the earth; and, of course, Louis himself, who by process of elimination must be *H* for happy, and who busies himself composing airs (poems) (although to see Louis as earth and Pinchos as air would also make sense).

The various fours of "A"-12 interweave, not logically, but musically. "We find Bach and Vivaldi mentioned in the movement," says Ahearn, "but if there is a specific model for '*A*'-12, such as the concerto form, it is well hidden" (212). I believe, however, that there *is* a specific model: the fugue, which usually brings together several voices in an orderly, harmonious exchange; and Zukofsky's model is, I would also propose, a specific composition in this form, Bach's final masterwork, *The Art of the Fugue.* On the second page of "A"-12, immediately after the *Blest, Ardent, Celia, Happy* theme is first sounded, we read: "From the spring of *Art of Fugue*" (127). Zukofsky might refer here to spring as a season and imply that he was studying *The Art of the Fugue* in the spring of 1951; "spring" may also mean source, so Zukofsky may as well be suggesting that he is drawing on the same "springs" as Bach: this common source is, as we will see, desire, or need. The interweaving voices of *The Art of the Fugue* speak together, as Zukofsky suggests in the next line, "like reasonable men / in an orderly discussion." Clearly, Zukofsky hopes his philosophical mentors and the members of his family will talk like that too.

"A"-12 does not, as far as I can determine, model itself on a specific

fugal pattern—double, triple, and so forth—much less on the elaborate overall design of *The Art of the Fugue.* This design works through
virtually every possible fugal form—"simple" fugues, double fugues,
triple fugues, "mirror" fugues, and a quadruple fugue—all based on
or related to a single D minor theme. Language can never, Zukofsky
realizes, achieve the "purity" of music, its reduction of time to a purely
formal pattern. Rather, as the human medium of communication, language is inescapably engaged with history both personal and collective, lived experience: the poem, as Zukofsky puts it in "An Objective," should display "inextricably the direction of historic and
contemporary particulars" (*Prepositions* 12). So things enter "A"-12,
not solely as determined by an *a priori* formal pattern, but rather as
they happen—someone comes into a room and the poem acknowledges this, someone dies and the poem acknowledges this too—and
as they arise within the poet's memory and imagination. But "A"-12
is fugal insofar as it consistently interweaves multiple voices and seeks
to harmonize these voices. Moreover, "A"-12 is, I believe, "musical"
insofar as in it "meaning" is a function, not of the logical or associative
relationships joining together a cluster of "ideas," but rather of the
intervals between and the recurrent patterning of a sequence of
"notes," which may be morphemes or may be words. (In music, pattern becomes significant when we hear it *again.* The same is true, I
suggest, in Zukofsky's poetics.) I will use the word "theme" to denote
such patterned sequences of "notes," but I should emphasize that I am
using this word not in the sense it usually has within literary studies,
as denoting a "central idea," but rather in a specifically musical sense.

The opening lines of "A"-12 offer an example of this musical articulation of materials:

> *Out of deep need*
> Four trombones and the organ in the nave
> A torch surged—
> Timed the theme Bach's name,
> Dark, larch and ridge, night:
> From my body to other bodies
> Angels and bastards interchangeably
> who had better sing and tell stories
> Before all will be abstracted.
> So goes: first, *shape*
> The creation—

A mist from the earth,
The whole face of the ground;
Then *rhythm*—
and breathed breath of life;
Then *style*—
That from the eye its function takes—
"Taste" we say—a living soul.
First, glyph; then syllabary,
Then letters.
                    ["A"-12, 126]

The four words of the opening line, italicized for emphasis, inaugurate that pattern of fours that, as I have already noted, is central to "A"-12. And the first four lines establish a sequence that will recur in various forms throughout the opening lines I have quoted and throughout "A"-12 as a whole: from *need*, to *music* (sound, movement, pattern), to *sight* (the torch), to *word* (Bach's name). This sequence moves from one *body* (and all *need* originates in the lonely body) to *other* bodies, inspiring all these bodies to *sing and tell stories*: the movement from one body to another, it seems, frees all the bodies to sing, in the interlude before the various constituent elements return to their simple, separate (and thus *abstract*) condition. With the words "So goes," Zukofsky proceeds to develop three variations on his initial theme. One sequence, again defined by italics, moves from *shape*, to *rhythm* (here we're in the territory of music and song), to *style* (which Zukofsky associates with the eye, but in this third movement from rhythm to style the process becomes reflexive, as the eye takes the body, the object, as its focus). Interwoven with this sequence, the middle lines of this passage also retrace the process of divine creation: first God shapes man out of the earth, or out of a mist arising from the earth; then He breathes life into His creature; and then the creature looks at the world, names the things of the world, and at this moment becomes a living soul. Zukofsky then retraces the same sequence, in terms of the history of written language as it evolved in Mesopotamia: first the visual sign pictures the thing (*glyph*), then it represents the (auditory) syllable, and finally we arrive at the (purely visual) letter, out of which we can make words.

The next few lines appear to play with or even reverse the basic sequence:

Ratio after
Eyes, tale in sound. First, dance. Then
Voice. First, body—to be seen and to pulse
Happening together.
       ["A"-12, 126]

Here we get bits and pieces of the basic sequence. Reason, discourse, is subsequent to sight; from sight we move to language, the tale in sound. But language, itself musical, also returns us to the middle term (*rhythm* or *syllabary*). In a sense, then, we begin *and end* with dance. We try again to move from dance to voice, but again we collapse back into *body,* where sight and sound happen together: the body is both object of sight and living, pulsing organism. These lines suggest that Zukofsky, like Bach, gives himself the option of breaking his musical themes down into their constituent parts, or even turning them upside down or backward, in counterpoint with the original statement of the theme. But in the final lines of this opening section, the full original sequence returns in yet a fourth form, which we might call philosophical, since it draws on all of Zukofsky's canonical philosophical mentors: Aristotle, Spinoza, and Paracelsus.

Before the void there was neither
Being nor non-being;
Desire, came warmth,
Or which, first?
Until the sages looked in their hearts
For the kinship of what is in what is not
   Or in the heart or in the head?
      Quire after over three millenia.
        ["A"-12, 127]

We begin *before* the void, when there was neither being nor nonbeing. Desire (a condition of the soul) then breeds warmth—or perhaps we move from the physical warmth to desire, for the sequence doesn't seem to matter. In either case, desire–warmth apparently separates being from nonbeing, thus generating the void. And this separation continues until the sages discover within themselves—in their hearts or in their heads—"the kinship of what is in what is not." This philosophical statement of the theme is also grander, more all–inclusive, than the earlier statements and thus constitutes a fitting climax to this passage.

We're seeing here, in all cases, a *pattern of transformations,* which carries us from the immediacy of the given, the physical body and its needs; through a rhythmic articulation of those needs in music, dance, or song—an articulation that necessitates a distribution within time of those elements that make up our life world and thus separates being from nonbeing; to the moment when the eye gives us the world complete again but as *object* now; and finally to language, which has the power to contain *all* the earlier stages of this process but which for that reason is inherently unstable and continually pulls us back toward the earlier moments in the sequence. (Zukofsky's *Bottom* repeatedly— some might say obsessively—describes this same sequence of transformations.) In these opening lines of "A"-12, this basic theme has passed through four variations: poetic, cosmological, linguistic, and philosophical. If we read the passage in this way, we have here a brief theme-and-variations pattern. Or we can read the passage as a prelude to the movement as a whole, designed to introduce the thematic materials that will be developed more fully as we proceed; and indeed, poetic, cosmological, linguistic, and philosophical materials will recur, in a reasonably regular way, throughout "A"-12.

Zukofsky's verse is never transparent, but I feel reasonably safe in asserting that my explication of the opening lines of "A"-12 has tried to account for pretty much everything in these opening lines except: (1) that deeply obscure line, "Dark, larch and ridge, night." I think it's here in large part for its sound values: the heavy, resonant, rolling rhyme on *ar,* the delicate modulation from short *i* to long *i* in "ridge, night," the soft collision of both *i*s with the palatal/plosive consonants. We might note also how the "and" splits the line into two pairs of nouns—although "dark," of course, may be either noun or adjective. "Dark" and "night," at the beginning and end of the line, also balance each other, as synonymous nouns, or as adjective plus noun. And "larch and ridge" establishes something like a visual image, of a tree on a ridge outlined against the darkness. But the placement of the line emphasizes sound over semantics: perhaps, we might even wonder, the four operant words in the line represent the four letters of Bach's name, moving these letters back toward sound, so that they can be set into motion. In this respect the line seems to deflect us back from the movement toward the visual and toward abstraction, to remind us of the inescapable physicality of language. (On the level of "meaning," however, there may also be a hint of the abyss in "dark" and "night.")

(2) And the last line of this prelude also needs some explanation. "Quire" is obviously a pun on "choir": we are hearing multiple voices singing together. But a "quire" is also a set of pages sufficient to make a book, so the pun again blurs the boundary between the textual and the auditory. Why "three millenia"? Because that's the period of time that separates us from the beginnings of literate culture, the invention of the book.

My explication of the opening of "A"-12, however, has elided one other important issue. For while the theme here developed consists of four "notes," the variations I have described above generally seem to break off after *three* notes—at best, the fourth note is muted. Thus we get "shape," "rhythm," and "style," the first three elements of a poetics; but the fourth term, "poetry" itself, is present only by implication. And we move from "glyph" to "syllabary" to "letters"; but again the fourth term, the "word," is present only by implication.[4]

To understand the significance of this tendency to leave the fourth term in these motifs implicit, it will be necessary to look a little more closely at Zukofsky's musical model, Bach's *The Art of the Fugue*. As I have noted, *The Art of the Fugue* builds an impressive musical edifice on the foundation of a single D minor idea. In elaborating this theme, Bach apparently intended (we can't be certain, for he did not live long enough to complete the composition) to work through a broad variety of possible fugal structures, as he had systematically worked through all of the musical keys in *The Well-Tempered Clavier.* In the last fugue (number fourteen in some versions, number nineteen in the one Zukofsky used [according to "A"-12, 130]), scholars have surmised that Bach set out to compose something almost unprecedented, a quadruple fugue: that is, a fugue that would counterpoint and develop four distinct themes. Bach wrote the first three parts of this climactic fugue, basing the third theme on his own name, for the four notes that state the theme are, in order, B, A, C, and H (in German nomenclature B = B flat and H = B natural). Musical logic might at this point call for a return to the original D minor theme—and indeed, several prominent musicologists and composers have composed plausible "completions" of the fugue, by returning to this ur-theme.[5] (The problem, of course, is that there have only been *three* themes presented. Bach is one theme short of a quadruple fugue, and a return to the original theme at this point would make the fugue only a *triple* fugue.)

Bach himself broke off the fugue, however—in performance this moment is deeply disturbing, for we are left suspended in space. What followed is summarized by Zukofsky himself:

> As the countersubject of the fourfold 19th fugue
> Signed on death lightly,
> B, A, C, H,
> Stopped here
> With the last Choral-Prelude
> Told his son-in-law Altnikol.
>   ["A"-12, 130]

Or a little less elliptically: Bach broke off *The Art of the Fugue* to dictate to his son-in-law (a member of the family—and we might remember that Celia Zukofsky typed her husband's poems) a chorale-prelude (or so the story has it—this account, which is widespread, is possibly apocryphal). In translation, this chorale-prelude is titled "I Draw Near Unto Thy Throne"—appropriate enough for a man who was dying. But more interesting for my purposes is the name of the melody on which Bach based this chorale: "When we are in deepest need." For as we have seen, Zukofsky has adapted this phrase and placed it in italics as the first line of "A"-12, "Out of deep need" ("A"-12, 126).

So too, despite all the patterning systems I have already noted, the design of "A"-12, like the design of "A" as a whole, is deliberately *incomplete,* broken. We can see this phenomenon most clearly in the last thirty pages of the movement, a section that might be seen as analogous to the final, unfinished fugue in *The Art of the Fugue.* Starting on page 231, the letters of Bach's name, so important to the whole movement, are introduced in sequence, in large, bold type: *B* on page 231, *A* on page 236, *C* on page 237. But no *H.* Why not? Well, if *H* is Zukofsky himself, perhaps he doesn't need to speak directly, because he is speaking all the time. Perhaps. The *H* does appear, but in ordinary type, as the last word of "A"-12:

> Blest
> Ardent
> Celia
>   unhurt and
> Happy.
>   ["A"-12, 261]

But again the *H* is subtly set apart, linked—as none of the other terms is—with its own negation, for the alliteration on "unhurt" and "happy" is surely calculated. What are we to make of this? With his fascination with fours, Zukofsky was naturally also attracted to the idea of a quadruple fugue: not only four voices but four voices developing four themes, the third of which consists of four notes. That this third theme is built upon the four letters of Bach's own name also obviously fascinated Zukofsky, for he alludes to this famous musical moment in the fourth line of the prelude.

But after introducing the theme built on his own name, Bach, rather than returning to his ur-theme, his originary moment, breaks off; so too, Zukofsky will eventually—and even as early as 1951 he seems to be anticipating this moment—break off after "A"-23, to allow a member of his family to complete his poem, as Bach's son-in-law took down by dictation and tried to piece together Bach's intentions in *The Art of the Fugue.* Most strikingly of all, at this moment of rupture, what erupts, from the gap opened by the interruption, is, simply, *need.* Here is, to return to a motif I have now left suspended for some time, a second sense of "spring," as in "the spring of *Art of Fugue*" ("A"-12, 127): spring as source, starting point. *The Art of the Fugue* springs from "deep need," as does "A"-12 itself. And need by definition points to a gap, an absence. Rather than trying to fill this gap with some form of absolute presence, as Eliot and Pound were still trying to do, Zukofsky, I propose, accepts it as a given, the condition of our existence; and in this respect Zukofsky has, I believe, moved beyond his poetic masters, in a swerve that also carries him beyond modernism itself, into postmodernity.

At this point, having recognized that in the patterns of fours on which "A"-12 is built the fourth term is always partly elided, we begin to understand some of the reasons for such a repeated elision. For example, despite Ahearn's ingenious identification of the four philosophical mentors that preside over "A"-12, it must also be recognized that Celia Zukofsky isn't "really" a philosopher; and while Aristotle, Spinoza, and Paracelsus all speak at length, she says almost nothing. Cosmically, too, the fourth term is partly elided, as we can see in a diagram that Zukofsky offers on page 163. In block capitals we get

MAN $\longrightarrow$ EARTH $\longrightarrow$ WORLDS

with various elaborative phrases grouped beneath each term. And then, down in the corner of the page,

I AM THAT I AM
  and—or
Euhus Euan

As the diagram suggests, we can distinguish three levels or modes of being within the created universe. But the fourth level—the uncreated ground, being itself: Jehovah, whose name is not to be spoken—is simultaneously part of this system and apart from it, unnamable. Within the Zukofsky family, furthermore, there are also various asymmetries, causing the four members of the family to group in various three-versus-one combinations. Louis, Celia, and Paul are alive, while Pinchos is dead. Pinchos, Louis, and Paul are male, while Celia is female. Pinchos, Louis, and Celia are adults, while Paul is a child. Louis, Celia, and Paul are artists, while Pinchos was not. Louis, Celia, and Paul are secularized Jews, while Pinchos was a practicing Jew. And so forth—for there are surely other patterns here that I have not recognized. These various permutations should remind us that family relations are never static. The gap, the void is present within the family system itself.

For the male poet the death of the father—the event that, for Zukofsky, seems to have most immediately triggered this poem—especially opens up this sense of absence. At the beginning of "A"-12, immediately after the prelude, Zukofsky mysteriously writes:

A year, a month, and 19 days before—
  the void in effect—
      ["A"-12, 127]

Later, Zukofsky gives the date of his father's funeral as April 11, 1950 (154). So if he did write "A"-12 in the summer of 1951, "a year, a month, and 19 days" would most probably name the time between Pinchos Zukofsky's death and the moment when his son wrote these lines. Since that death, then, "the void" has been "in effect." The death of the (real or symbolic) father impels many male poets to reinvent the father in the text: see, for instance, Pound's reinvention of Mussolini. But not so Zukofsky. By naming the void, he also accepts it. He accepts as well the transitory, contingent status of his own fatherhood:

And the end is the same:
Bach remembers his own name.
Had he asked me to say Kadish
I believe I would have said it for him.
How fathom his will
Who had taught himself to be simple.
["A"-12, 143]

To remember your name is to let it go. Indeed, we cannot let it go *until* we remember it: so Bach, at last writing a fugue on his own name, has emptied himself of his ego and can now stand naked before the throne of God. The "he" here is both Pinchos and God as well as Bach: "how fathom his will." And in accepting the absolute simplicity that Pinchos has achieved, Zukofsky *has* said kaddish for his father and for that absolute ground of being that the Father claims to instantiate. Accepting the father, Zukofsky can at last say goodbye to him, and thereby he is at last free to become simple himself, simply himself, to become the child he sees in Paul, to play.

To structure "A"-12 around a pattern of four elements is a characteristically modernist gesture, as is Zukofsky's very decision to seek a formal model in a specific baroque musical composition. Such decisions presuppose the closure, the completion that is so integral to the ideology of modernism, from the poetics of the self-contained Imagist observation to the doctrine of poetic "objectification" (and even to the New Critical notion of the "well wrought urn"). In contrast, Zukofsky's transition from modernism to postmodernism, from a teleological poetics of completion to a more open-ended poetics of contingency, discovery, and *play,* is signaled by his disruption of these patterns, his decision to leave his own work, like *The Art of the Fugue,* incomplete, unfinished. The farewell to the father, that "A"-12 enacts is a farewell to Zukofsky's father Pinchos (and to God, and to Bach), but it is as well a farewell to Zukofsky's modernist "fathers" and to the desire for unity that came to characterize the entire modernist project. With "A"-12, Zukofsky launches himself headlong into our own era, and he is with us still.

Notes

1. This is not to say, however, that they are direct *imitations* of *The Cantos.* As Zukofsky makes clear in his correspondence with Pound, he had drafted the first movements of "A" before he had any idea of what Pound was up to in *The*

Cantos: "the dangers," as he puts it, "of being young and too poor to get hold of the books that matter" (Zukofsky, *Pound/Zukofsky* 79). While the collage method clearly owes something to Pound, it also has precedents in Apollinaire, about whom Zukofsky would write a book, and—perhaps as important—in the cinema, a medium in which Zukofsky had considerable interest in the 1930s, as evidenced by his comments to Pound and his essay on Charlie Chaplin, "Modern Times."

2. For a full development of this view of "A"-1 through -10, see Hatlen passim.

3. Of course the Zukofsky family was every bit as extended as the average American family, but none of the brothers, sisters, cousins, and in-laws (some of whom *do* appear pseudonymously in *Little*) are mentioned in "A"-12.

4. *Bottom* can partly help to explain what is happening here: for there it turns out that the final term, the power that must infuse all others if they are to come to life, is *love*—which must, however, remain tacit, born in sight and present in language but never itself an object of discourse. And indeed, the unspoken ultimate term in "A"-12 is also, I believe, *love*.

5. Among them are Donald Francis Tovey, Hugo Riemann, and Feruccio Busoni, whose *Fantasia Contrappuntista,* op. 10, is perhaps the most challenging application of the Bach material. See Geiringer 344–345. I would like to thank Paul Zukofsky for drawing my attention to Busoni's work.

Works Cited

Ahearn, Barry. *Zukofsky's "A": An Introduction.* Berkeley: U of California P, 1983.

Bach, Johann Sebastian. *Die Kunst der Fuge.* Ed. Donald Francis Tovey. London: Oxford UP, n.d.

Geiringer, Karl. *Johann Sebastian Bach: The Culmination of an Era.* New York: Oxford UP, 1966.

Hatlen, Burton. "Art and/as Labor: Some Dialectical Patterns in '*A*'-1 Through '*A*'-10." *Contemporary Literature* 25.2 (Summer 1984): 205–234.

Lyotard, Jean-François. *The Postmodern Condition: A Report on Knowledge.* Trans. Geoff Bennington and Brian Massumi. Minneapolis: U of Minnesota P, 1984.

Zukofsky, Louis. *Pound/Zukofsky: Selected Letters of Ezra Pound and Louis Zukofsky.* Ed. Barry Ahearn. New York: New Directions, 1987.

12

A More Capacious Shoulder
"A"-24, Nonsense, and the Burden of Meaning

MARNIE PARSONS

I

Fig.12.1 ("Z" by bp Nichol is reprinted from *ABC: The Aleph Beth Book* by permission of Oberon Press.)

"A thing to be added."
Oxford English Dictionary

As ADDENDUM. That, suggests William Harmon, in a rather cranky review of Louis Zukofsky's "*A*", is the only way to read "A"-24; it is the long poem's "next most tiresome part" after "A"-21, Zukofsky's homophonic translation of Plautus's *Rudens* (Harmon 15). A dismal failure, "the thing is unreadable," he continues (16). A two-act masque comprising a five-voice synthesis of significant portions of Zukofsky's criticism, drama, fiction, and poetry, all performed simultaneously with selections from Handel's harpsichord pieces, "A"-24 is hardly easy going. My gut reaction, however, is to dismiss Harmon's reading, his failure to see how integral "A"-24 and the index to "*A*", which he also considers ill conceived and flawed, really are to the poem as a whole. I want to name his eye impatient. Surely "A"-22 and "A"-23 (as Don Byrd points out [254]), surely all of "*A*", prepares for, looks to, "A"-24, that final consummation of poem and poet and heart.

Since several movements of the poem are dated later than "A"-24, one could argue that Zukofsky wrote them out of a deep knowledge of where they were going, out of a passion for Celia's own impassioned celebration of his works.

For "A"-24 was not written by Louis Zukofsky: it was written *for* him, composed by his wife, Celia. A de-composition of several of his works but composition nonetheless. Sometimes I wonder if something other than impatience obstructs Harmon's view, and critical views generally, of "A"-24; I wonder if Celia Zukofsky's involvement undercuts the credibility of what her husband seemed to consider this fluid crystallization of his poetics. Perhaps such wondering is unfair; many other readers of Zukofsky write with enthusiasm of the complexity and intricacy of "A"-24. But few write of "A"-24 as itself—as "Celia's L. Z. Masque."[1] The critical tendency is to footnote (or parenthesize) Celia Zukofsky's part in the whole, after or during a discussion of how this final movement complements Louis Zukofsky's poetics. Such discussions are almost always very brief, the footnotes and parentheses briefer still. To me this continued neglect of Celia Zukofsky's tremendous accomplishment in "A"-24 seems outrageous.

Still, what if one gives Harmon some due, listens to him without thinking him either wrongheaded or unwilling to give credit (or critique) where it's owed? Exploring his opinion might be enlightening. So "A"-24 as addendum. Think of the final words of "A"-23: "z-sited path are but us" (563); if one overlooks Zukofsky's clear reference to the structure of "A"-24 just two lines above this ("music, thought, drama, story, poem" [563]—"the" five voices that Celia Zukofsky arranges in the masque), one might read this line as an interesting gesture toward open-endedness. It points both beyond the poem's end (the path leading outward, away from the body of the text) and to the child who will outlive the poet. Michele Leggott notes that Paul Zukofsky, at the time "A"-23 was written, lived on Arbutus Path and that his initials are contained in acrostics in that line (75); Arbutus Path, then, is a z-sited path, a path to z's site, even as "us," the poet's family, is also a path sighted on a letter at once initial and final.[2]

Such possible conflation of alpha and omega in "z" would have been particularly apt as the final gesture of a poem entitled "*A*", whether that "a" be read as the letter itself—a letter that has thus been brought "home"—or as the indefinite article that allows reference to range, indicating not *the* specific thing but *a* diverse set of possibilities, a diversity that "z" clearly contains. It's even more interesting because, as Leggott indicates (52), Zukofsky has built an alphabetic game into the last twenty-six lines of "A"-23 (562–563). He has come, then, to the end of the portion of the poem that he will write, as he has come to the end of the alphabet. What remains to be played out lies beyond the end of his alphabet or at the very least in the interstices of alphabets—the index, which I'm often tempted to read as "A"-25, is a last, witty alphabetic tease on the part of both Zukofskys.[3]

In *On Beyond Zebra!* Dr. Seuss's narrator introduces his young friend Conrad Cornelius o'Donald o'Dell to the letters of *his* post-"z" alphabet:

> "In the places I go there are things that I see
> "That I *never* could spell if I stopped with the **Z**.
> "I'm telling you this 'cause you're one of my friends.
> "*My* alphabet starts where *your* alphabet ends!
> [N.p.]

Seuss's story turns on the limits language sets for imagining or the unlimited imagining of language—the theoretical implications of such imagery extend well beyond the story itself. But what of the alphabet beyond "z"; what if "z" were a beginning, not an end; how does the alphabet construct language, narrative, and world; how might language meander through a different alphabet? Such questions, when added to Harmon's criticism of "A"-24, generate more potential than might initially be apparent. Letters tacked on to the end of the alphabet give Dr. Seuss an opportunity for writing more of his typical Nonsense, for "Umbuses" and "Sneedles" (figure 12.2). That last letter/movement, that "extra" "a,"[4] tacked on to the end of Zukofsky's "alphabet" provides an opportunity for quite another sort of nonsense, for the stretch of language which magnifies its plenitude a hundredfold, for language transposed to another alphabet.[5]

Fig. 12.2 (From *On Beyond Zebra* by Dr. Seuss. TM and copyright (c) 1955 and renewed 1983 by Dr. Seuss Enterprises, L.P. Reprinted by permission of Random House, Inc.)

II

Carroll ultimately refused to commit himself as to whether his
nonsense had any overt meaning. But the nonsense recorded its
own testimony.
> —Louis Zukofsky, "Lewis Carroll" (*Prepositions* 65)

it is an alphabetic wind rises
> —Robin Blaser, "Image-Nation 10 (marriage clothes"

When I suggest that Zukofsky's "extra" "a" generates a nonsensical
language unlike that of Dr. Seuss, I have in mind a rather special-
ized understanding of the term "nonsense," one that Lewis Carroll
would not have anticipated despite his many Nonsense writings.[6] Nor
would Louis Zukofsky have intended it to be used in the context of
his essay on Carroll, though I'd like to think he might have welcomed
its application to others of his works. Generic Nonsense, like that
which Carroll wrote, is protean and slippery, a "verbal sleight of hand"
(Rieke, *The Senses of Nonsense* 157); my own take on nonsense grows
out of a consideration of how language behaves in Nonsense and in
unruly, experimental texts like those Zukofsky wrote.

Such unruly verbal play is not the focus of philosophical nonsense,
nor is philosophical nonsense central to my interest. Certainly nonsense language and philosophical nonsense overlap at times, as the
genre and the philosophical error share areas of accord, but their expectations for and about language's function are enormously different.[7] Nonsense language as I construe it may exploit the weak logic
of philosophical nonsense, but it does so to facilitate the blending,
to expose the symbiosis, of meaning and meaninglessness in all language. Susan Stewart suggests as much in *Nonsense: Aspects of Intertextuality in Folklore and Fiction,* but she speaks of the symbiosis of nonsense and common sense. At once asserting meaning and exposing that
meaning's entertainment of apparent meaninglessness, nonsense engages the possibilities of other meaningful systems. And it urges this
understanding: if (as Wittgenstein suggests in *Philosophical Investigations*) meaning is use, is context, then meaninglessness may rely on use
and context also; if all meaning is meaningless in some other order or
context, then perhaps all apparent meaninglessness is similarly meaningful elsewhere, otherly used.

A model in little is Carroll's nonsensical portmanteau word, described by Humpty Dumpty in *Through the Looking-Glass* as a suitcase sort of word folding two words together to create a third; an example: "mimsy," which Humpty Dumpty glosses as a comingling of "flimsy" and "miserable" (278). In his introduction to the *Sylvie and Bruno* books, Carroll suggests that the most important quality of such portmanteau words is the tangible presence of the original words within the newly formed one; "mimsy" functions successfully as a portmanteau word because both "flimsy" and "miserable" lurk in its wings, oscillate in the shadow of the new.

Gilles Deleuze takes Carroll's notion a tad further in *The Logic of Sense;* he describes the portmanteau word as an intersection of two heterogeneous linguistic series, resulting in a word that means itself without dominating either of its originary words. Using another of Carroll's sample words, "frumious," he argues that "the necessary disjunction is not between fuming and furious, for one may indeed be both at once; rather, it is between fuming-and-furious on one hand and furious-and-fuming on the other. In this sense, the function of the portmanteau word always consists in the ramification of the series into which it is inserted" (46–47). So "frumious" suggests both "fuming" and "furious"; but more important, it also *means* "fuming-and-furious" and "furious-and-fuming," means the tension of both encounter and possibility that this new term represents, and means itself. An extremely various branching off of potential meaning is initiated. That smallish word holds all of those meanings simultaneously; and a reader's smallish mind endeavours to hold as many as it possibly can.

Portmanteau words are characteristic of Carroll's later nonsense (they are absent from *Alice's Adventures in Wonderland*); they could also be seen as characterizing nonsense language. But while Deleuze describes the portmanteau word as the heteroglottic product of the intersection of linguistic *series,* nonsense language results from the intersection of two, three, four, possibly more, separate language *systems,* each rubbing off on the other while still retaining something of their previous selves. This is not simply the intermingling of codes or subcategories—of literary or legal language, French or English or any other subcategory of a verbal system; such mingling enacts a secondary form of nonsense.[8] The more particular, the primary, form of nonsense I have in mind is a tension, a suspension, produced by the attempt to blend alternate *ways* of meaning. Musical and mathematical systems meet with the verbal, in Zukofsky's case, though differing combinations might also include the visual (for instance, concrete poetry or the illustrated limericks of Edward Lear) or the physical (as in the newly emerging deaf poetics).[9] Such systems of meaning are transliterated into or onto one another, suspended in a state of partial alienation: music adopts the terms of a verbal alphabet but doesn't give itself over to the meanings of wholly composed words; words move toward articulating the body without relinquishing their verbal nature, and so on. The upshot? Conventional meaning buckles, entertains such a plenitude of possibilities as to be rendered (almost) meaningless, producing a pluralized, overloaded sense demanding active, imaginative engagement and a new sign in which meaningful systems merge without losing their unique integrity.

Another way to figure this juggling of meanings is as a form of transposition (a term that I hope resonates with equal parts of its musical and its Kristevan senses), a transposition not smoothly accomplished, one that jangles. Julia Kristeva uses the term to replace Bakhtin's "inter-textuality," which is all too often, she says, "understood in the banal sense of 'study of sources' " (60). Transposition is, in Kristeva's theoretical discourse, a *"passage from one sign system to another"* (59). That sign system may be, as she puts it, "of the same signifying material" (59)—entirely composed of verbal language, for instance—but need not be; her *main* concern seems to be not the material of the signing system but the mode of its discourse or articulation. Thus, moving from "a carnival scene to the written text" (59), or in the case of *"A"* from a musical score to a written text, and resituating a line of epic poetry into a lyric context, or a lyric into a historical narrative are equally instances of Kristevan transposition. Each context, Kristeva argues, demands a new articulation and so requires transposition.[10]

My use of "transposition" echoes Kristeva's, but with some significant and peculiar distortions. While for Kristeva the transposition of one language into another, the altering or shifting of the material nature of that language, adds an interesting and demanding wrinkle to the instance of transposition, such a shift is not essential. The material and materiality of the signifying system is, for me, *the* factor. Truly nonsensical transposition involves the relocation of the stuff and structures of one language into another, into an estranging, otherly signifying context. That estrangement elicits singularities, audibly and visibly deforms both the language transposed and the "key" into which it is being transposed. And the result is not just a new articulation: the possibility of a new way of articulating, a new composite sign, glistens in the interstices of this composite language.

One might already sense that this definition of nonsense, this reading of nonsense as a sort of *transpoetics,* could lead to a largish redrawing of what Elizabeth Sewell calls "the field of nonsense." Certainly it suggests that generic Nonsense is not consistently nonsensical and that works not normally classified as Nonsense, take for instance "*A*", are nonetheless nonsense. The latter part of this assertion is of course not new, nor is the equation of Zukofsky with nonsense.

Alison Rieke's *The Senses of Nonsense,* an engaging and immensely useful book, offers a finely honed reading of much of Zukofsky's work in light of her own understanding of nonsense. In the introduction to her book, Rieke claims that "[t]he experimental nonsense of Modernism is privileged, enigmatic speech. . . . It privileges itself by exploiting to the maximum devices of language causing it to mean more rather than less" (19–20). She speaks of a "semantic transformation" that, like the Hatter's Riddle at the Mad Tea-party (seeming first to have no solution, and then in retrospect having several) resists resolution and stability but spawns a proliferation of senses.[11] In the works of Stein, Joyce, and Zukofsky, Rieke locates a "negation and nonsense [that] are repeatedly reidentified as affirmation, as mastery, and as privileged sense," one which is "powerful but duplicitous" (20).

Even this minor juxtaposition of Rieke's "definition" of nonsense with my own should suggest how different our understandings of the term are; a still better indicator of this difference can be found in one of the endnotes supplementing Rieke's discussion of Zukofsky: "I exclude 'A'-24, Celia Zukofsky's 'L. Z. Masque,' a setting of Zukofsky's words to the music of Handel, because it is an entirely different kind of experiment, more musical than linguistic" (260 n. 39). The very movement of Zukofsky's poem that Rieke leaves outside the purview of her nonsensical reading is the one that most visibly embodies nonsense as I construe it. I don't emphasize this difference to diminish Rieke's ideas or her reading of Zukofsky; her take on nonsense is far too useful to be unsettled by my redirection of the term. Rather, I raise Rieke and then set her aside to acknowledge both a debt and a departure: hers was quite literally one of the first works I turned to when I began to think about nonsense's application to twentieth-century literature,[12] yet the more I thought about this application, the more I wanted a sustained, theoretical engagement with the term "nonsense" itself. And if, as Rieke and I agree, nonsense is concerned with the proliferation of senses, then it seems more than apt that "nonsense" itself should illustrate that proliferation, that our senses of "nonsense" should diverge.

III

. . . the efformation, the
dis-creation, the kindness of fragments

the larks of heaven perch and nothing

    —Robin Blaser, " 'the universe is part of ourselves' "

On beyond z(-sited): the embodiment of nonsense? Certainly the embodiment of nonsense in "A" as I define it, although Louis's movements of the poem are not without their nonsensical elements as well. Zukofsky's peculiar attentiveness to the musical and mathematical precisions[13] of verbal language, his near obsession with condensation, and his reveling in pun, etymology, transliteration, and disjunction grow out of the lovingly attentive play with languages that grounds a nonsensical poetics. In fact, one might render the relationship between sense and nonsense throughout Zukofsky's poetry in terms borrowed from his poetic statement in "A"-12 (138) and suggested to me by Charles Bernstein:

$$\int_{\text{sense}}^{\text{nonsense}}$$

An integral
Lower limit sense
Upper limit nonsense.

The switch, from speech to sense, from music to nonsense, is a crucial one, for nonsense is achieved by the "switch" from speech to/ward music. The correspondence isn't clear-cut, though—speech and sense aren't mutually exclusive.

Neither are nonsense and music, of course, and yet when one ponders their presence, their inclusion, in verbal language, one finds the correspondence at once intimate and playful. The very language distortions and estrangements that inscribe musical structures into words elicit witty and teasing word games. For instance, when in "A"-12 Zukofsky builds Bach's name as an acrostic into his poem (261), he transposes Bach's own musical gaming[14] into a verbal context.

The acrostic is a ploy typical of Nonsense, certainly typical of Carroll,[15] but one rarely stretched out and reconceived as variously as it is in this instance; Zukofsky's acrostic is spread, intermittently, over thirty pages and remains essentially incomplete. One realizes in retrospect, if one knows of Zukofsky's BACH antecedent, that the acrostic's letters can also be read as notes. But even for the uninitiated eye, they call attention to themselves. The first indication that a new reading of the letters involved is required is the typeface that first appears on page 231: an extra large, ornate, boldface **B**—**B**lest / Infinite things. "Blest," the English equivalent of Baruch Spinoza's first name, becomes the linguistic instrumentalization of the note/letter. It signals the recurrence of Spinoza, whose works appear frequently throughout the whole poem and who becomes a theme played over several pages; until the next note **A,** for **A**rdent, appears on page 236, followed quickly on page 237 with **C**elia. **A**rdent plays on Nicomachus, father of *A*ristotle, and on the difficult relations between fathers and the sons who resist their *a*uthority. **C**elia's section stretches for twenty-four pages, embraces all manner of elements of poem and home and heart(h). And it ends, on page 261, with the complete, as yet incomplete, acrostic—

> Blest
> Ardent
> Celia
>   unhurt and
> Happy.

This transcription of Bach's name becomes a celebration of Celia's; all the letters, but C, are turned toward her, are adjectives singing her praises. Zukofsky's choice not to include elaborate variations on **H** might be connected to the fact that H, in English notation, is not a musical note—though in Germany it names what we call B natural. Or to an appreciation of the natural cadence achieved through recurrence as (in)completion. One might also read the "exclusion" of **H** as a hint that happy-ness is an outgrowth of Celia, that in this case **C** and **H** are interdependent, inseparable.

However the acrostic is read, it is emblematic of both Zukofsky's transpoetics and his wittily serious play with language. In an article concerning "A"-24, Guy Davenport writes about the importance of play in Zukofsky's writing that "it is crucial to an understanding of his art to single out the wonder of his playfulness, for it sets his work aside (and above) as distinctly as his superb mastery of sound and measure" (18). And Peter Quartermain insists that "[play] lies at the centre of "A"; it is the particular means by which inclusiveness can be achieved, the intent of the poet realised, all the notes sounded at once" (68).[16]

All the notes sounded at once: an eloquent take, particularly appropriate to "A"-24. For Celia's "L. Z. Masque" does, literally, sound all (or a good many) of the notes at once. Zukofsky may have attempted to write counterpoint or fugal structure into his work, but in his compositional notebooks, he concedes (or delights) that "A"-24 answers his question about the possibility of actually doing so: "*Can / The design / Of the fugue / Be transferred / To poetry?*" ("A"-6, 38).[17] Not only has Celia Zukofsky the benefit of using Louis Zukofsky's words, in many of which nonsensical tensions are already at play, but she also orchestrates those words according to musical structures. Her nonsense occurs at a larger, structural level, at (ironically) a more or less generic level, as well as at a linguistic level, and it dominates "A"-24. Her simultaneous use of multiple languages (musical and verbal) and multiple genres, of competing texts, rather than an actual portmanteau-esque blending of languages, *seems* the most disorienting and disruptive aspect of the masque at first glance; in part, this simultaneity of performance or presence does generate "A"-24's nonsense. Celia Zukofsky achieves temporally what her husband achieves spatially, compactly; she accomplishes in the larger field of this movement what Zukofsky himself strives for (and frequently accomplishes) in the moment of the word. And in so doing, she lifts to the surface the tenuous and furtive chaos of his work.

Celia Zukofsky's introductory notes to "L. Z. Masque" make clear that the masque is meant to be performed, that the literal representation of it that comprises "A"-24 is a score for performance. That being the case, the very publication of the masque as "A"-24 exacerbates its nonsensical nature. Musical notation is presented in a forum in which it must be read. Moreover, since the words of the piece, taken from a wide variety of Zukofsky's works, have been arranged and orchestrated along musical structures—not, as so many critics suggest, "set" to Handel's music, but de- and re-composed for their musical/thematic properties[18]—their print status is doubly problematical.

The idea that Celia Zukofsky has engaged in a process of de-composition, of dis-creation, seems to me essential for an understanding of how "A"-24 works. The whole is a tenuous intersection of fragments, of pieces—but one that has been finely tuned. Take the drama for instance; *Arise, arise* is not simply re-printed alongside Handel—rather it is reorganized, recontextualized with Handel as an equal presence. Each character is given one scene of the masque; all of the character's lines are used, in the order in which they appear in the original drama but with none of the sense of conversational interplay that marks the drama. Each character "names" the scene, but so does the musical form with which it is presented. So act 1, scene 1 is "Cousin: Lesson"; their weight is evenly balanced.

The other "Zukofsky" voices are highly selected, given specific positions for resonance and specific and weighty silences. For scene 5 of the masque's first act, for instance, Celia Zukofsky lifts poetry from "A"-8; from what is one of the longer movements of the whole poem, she uses only one line and that not the complete line ("Voice a voice blown, returning as May" [104]), which she repeats fourteen times, although the line in this form appears only once in the original movement. Not only has she chosen this line over the literally hundreds of others in "A"-8, but she has decided how often and when to repeat it, has in fact established it as a musicalized motif running throughout the scene. The "poem" voice in this scene has large gaps of silence that complement and draw attention to the repetition of the words "Voice a voice blown, returning as May" and the continual alteration of their presentation in terms of pitch and duration; these silences could also be read/heard as establishing the *absence* of most of the body of "A"-8. Considering how important silences are in music, one might make an interesting study based on the absences in "A"-24—both the actual moments of silence in the piece itself (which are surprisingly many) and the absent/silent texts that they might be said to represent.[19]

Writing of the difficulties besetting composers who set texts to music, David Burrows says "the challenge . . . is to construct something comparable by demolishing the poem as poem and absorbing what remains—certain words in a certain order—in a new affectively centering structure" (87). Clearly Celia Zukofsky has done this, has "demolish[ed] the poem as poem" or the story as story, the drama as drama, the thought as thought and "absorb[ed] what remains." But the words enter a new order as well as "a new affectively centering structure"; it is the order of collage, of intersection and interweaving; it is an order quilted from the fabrics, the materials, of Zukofsky's creative life. But as in any good crazy quilt a new design unifies the whole.

Moreover, Celia Zukofsky has also attempted something that Burrows says sets music off from verbal texts. She has organized the verbal texts not just as words recomposed to the tune of music, but rather as *words recomposed as music*. Burrows writes: "The modern European notation of music reflects a concern with the exact management of relative duration according to an array of fixed units related to each other by simple rations. Their flow is controlled by a background of steady pulses and groups of pulses (measures). . . . Verbal notation, on the other hand, shows no more concern for relative duration than it does for pitch (making an exception for the arrangement into lines and stanzas of verse)" (69). Celia Zukofsky's directions for the performance of the masque, however, include very specific instructions about pitch and duration for its voices: "The metronome markings for the music determine the duration of each page for all the voices on each page. The speed at which each voice speaks is correlated to the time-space factor of the music. The words are NEVER SUNG to the music. Dynamics are indicated by type point size—(14pt = loud; 12pt = moderate; 10pt = soft)" ("A"-24, 564). She has tried, then, to organize the verbal notation as if it were musical notation, to rewrite the stuff of verbal language in/to the structures of musical language. That this "transposition" has then been printed as part of a verbal construct, "A", to be read as part of that construct means that the verbal language that was rendered music has been rerendered as verbal language.[20]

When performed, "A"-24 seems inchoate, just next door to indecipherable and not necessarily guaranteed to please or ease the casual listener. Guy Davenport offers the wonderful, welcoming analogy of "a family reunion of [Zukofsky's] work, inside and outside the poem, a grand Jewish family affair, with everybody talking at once" (22). Not all listeners are so kindly disposed toward the masque, however. Hearing part of the masque performed, my stepson's immediate reaction was annoyance—he recognized, he admitted, that the sounds of the words were meant to flow together like music, but the intersection made him feel uncomfortable, tense. As if, he continued, the music were in a minor key. The observations seem rather astute from one who knew nothing about the piece except that it was supposedly part of a poem. He immediately recognized that these words were being presented *as* music, being rendered in an entirely other language system, but he also associated the music with a key culturally encoded with dis-ease.

Despite sounding (or looking) inchoate, "A"-24 has sense, many senses intersecting and interfering with and spawning the process of making sense. These senses are instigated by the words themselves, by the implications of Celia Zukofsky's choices, the fragments she splices, the precision with which she times one voice to start, one to stop, one, two, three, four to overlay. The way she measures so that certain sounds collide, collude, so ribbons of sound braid together, or a single voice rises to the stillness of a solitary phrase. These senses are augmented as well by a more Kristevan sense of transposition implied in the composer's use of the masque form, the genres she incorporates in it, and the various musical forms that are integrated into and name each scene: lesson, prelude and allegro, suite, fantasia, chaconne, sonata, capriccio, passacaille, and fugues. Each voice brings contextual meanings, generic meanings, historical meanings. And the simultaneity of these meanings, their concurrent presentation and thematic inter-resonances, supplement the "nonsense" of the garrulous overlapping of tongues.

Each word spoken by each voice becomes a node, a momentary crystallization of all those vectors of possible meaning and association born of word and voice and genre; it becomes a point of conflict and conflation, a grace note. And yet each is orchestrated as much for the pull of its tidal sound (or noise) as for its thematic resonances. Countered and counted by the classical order of Handel, these words move as a wash of sound, a musical fluidity at once reinforcing and relativizing crystallized linguistic nodes. Listening to "A"-24, I am struck by how the Handel occupies my ear, how the words become almost a background to the music as often (and sometimes inappropriately) music may become a background for words or pictures. It's an inversion that seems crucial: when "A"-24 is performed musically, music dominates because it is the known quantity, an ear is accustomed to negotiating its complexities; when "A"-24 is presented visually, the words dominate because the reading eye (certainly the eye of the musically untrained) knows how to negotiate them (see figure 12.3).

In an article about the complexities of performing "A"-24, Bob Perelman suggests that the analogy of "language approaching music" is actually misleading (292). Music and verbal language occupy time differently; unlike music, whose "units are instantly 'transparent,' so to speak," a word's "phonemes, the units of 'verbal music,' aren't transparent, can't be superimposed without ambiguity"; "a phoneme doesn't sound like a word" (292–293). Rendering the meanings of musical and verbal language ultimately irreconcilable, the difference Perelman identifies underscores my take on "A"-24's nonsense. For music and verbal language *do* mean differently. The two cannot form a chord, though they may reach a delicate balance, a point of accord: the ear awakens to the fact of words's daily inhibitions about their own musicality, of music's inhabitation of Zukofsky's words. Musical and verbal languages interpenetrate, collide. Words move to accommodate music, music to accommodate words, though such movement is always circumscribed by an inevitable and intensely interesting inability to complete itself. Nonsense is born in that tension, in that slippage not away from meaning but toward absorbing another form of meaning, almost.

In a manner reminiscent of the way *"A"* as a whole entertains its various plenitudes, "A"-24 bears the burden of such slippage and of all those extracontextual, generic, historical meanings; Quartermain writes that "[from] the very first line *"A"* presents complexities of interrelationship, and [Zukofsky's] aim is to achieve a simultaneity of multiples, political, aesthetic, historical, economic, linguistic" (61). Celia Zukofsky's use of concurrent voices opens out her husband's very condensed form to air such interrelationships. In a sense, she reverses the process of his writing to provide another *type* of simultaneity, to dramatize at an immediate visual and aural level what is masked by the seemingly simple line of Zukofsky's text.

IV

"If there's no meaning in it," said the King, "that saves a world of trouble, you know, as we needn't try to find any. And yet I don't know," he went on, spreading out the verses on his knee, and looking at them with one eye; "I seem to see some meaning in

Fig. 12.3 (From Louis Zukofsky, "*A*". Copyright 1993, pages 722–723. Reprinted by permission of the Johns Hopkins University Press.)

The nonsense recorded its own testimony —

You can't deny I have talked to my niece for

bird sang in the late afternoon,   and as he searched for it,

O   head,   think,   how

the   insistence   of   the   Queen   of   Hearts

fifty   minutes   and that she has not peeped a word to

he wished he knew its name.

climbing,   you   would   be;   /

that   the   sentence   be   given   before   the   verdict,

answer   your   aunt.   You've   an   impious,   stubborn   hussy   of   a

He heard his name pronounced with

O   heart,   /

them, after all. ' — *said I could not swim* ;' you ca'n't swim, can you?" he added, turning to the Knave.
—Lewis Carroll, *Alice's Adventures in Wonderland*

"Aunt: Passacaille" is the eighth section (third scene of act 2) in the masque. I'm drawn to look a bit more closely at it because here Celia Zukofsky uses her husband's 1935 essay on "Lewis Carroll," here "the nonsense record[s] its own testimony." In the Carroll essay, Zukofsky juxtaposes, with rather typically elliptical pastiche, quotations from "A Broken Spell"[21] and "Journal of a Tour in Russia in 1867," two of Carroll's more sensical works; he jostles some sense out of Carroll's Nonsense by setting it in a broader context.[22] That sense? Society and the law, even reasoning and culture, are guilty of a laughable self-importance, frequently of tyranny. Carroll flinched at publicly pronouncing his Nonsense's senses, but Zukofsky prods the *Alice* books and *The Hunting of the Snark,* represents them as fostering sharp criticisms of the deeply mired social, political, and legal institutions of Carroll's day—and perhaps, by extension, his own. Yet meaning, sense, because it is inherently political, inevitably shaped by the beliefs of its fabricator, has its own self-importance, its own tyrannies. These are the tyrannies that nonsense can exploit and explore by recontextualizing sense(s)'s materiality.

The presence of that Carroll essay in "Aunt: Passacaille," then, its introduction of "nonsense" into this field of nonsense, offers a node of thematic coherence, a foothold for reading this scene. Overlaying snippets of the Carroll essay with the aunt's dialogue from *Arise, arise,* bits of "Ferdinand," "Thanks to the Dictionary," and "A"-6, and Handel's Passacaille from Suite 7 in G minor, Celia Zukofsky plays variously over self-inflating tyrannies of government, of family, of meaning, and over the hope for release from them. As a musical form, the passacaille is rather well suited to this particular poetic incarnation; its relentless ostinato bass and the three-quarter time signature that underscores its harmonic variations offer an alternative governance, one of both control and release.

Historically, the form hearkens back to Spanish street dances, its name built on "pasar" (to pass) and "calle" (street): a lovely joke on Celia Zukofsky's part, I suspect, since two of the three quotations from Carroll's "Russian Journal" that Louis used in his essay involve movement in the street—movement not of dance but of policemen escorting a child to jail, of a lone cop's shoes squeaking on his beat. This musical pun already suggests something about the results of transposition: the literary context of (in)justice, of rigid policing of the streets, is repositioned against a musical context of the street dance—itself a controlled movement but with implications vastly different from those that Zukofsky explores in his essay. The juxtaposition of different material senses and contexts, then, allows for the partial defusing of one form of control when it is placed within the context of another. What such transposition suggests about *authorial* control—Zukofsky's or his wife's or Carroll's, for that matter—will have to be considered in another essay.

Reading the scene, one can locate points of thematic crossover and conflation. The aunt = the Queen of Hearts? the nephew = the Knave? Such one-to-one correspondences, such single-mindednesses, are too easy to be definitive of the whole, though certain aspects of the characters connect in a limited way. But what about the interplay between "Nephew, you're a witness" (722) and the trial scenario of quotations from the Carroll essay (723–724); some aspects of the drama seem more than relative to cross-examination, and a verdict about the niece (she's "an impious, stubborn hussy" [723]) is given, not before the sentence, but at the same time as the idea of passing judgment. In fact, *passing* judgment could be said to focus many of the goings-on in this scene, and so to render the passacaille that much more appropriate.

But all these vectors of meaning are based on a sustained reading, and they all seek a form of discursive sense for which music is not responsible (Burrows 70). Don Byrd suggests that "A"-24 can be read "vertically"[23] as well as "horizontally," that simultaneity as well as discursiveness operates in understanding this intricate piece (239). Reading it vertically emphasizes its polyphonic nature, its simultaneity, and saves a lot of frantic flipping back and forth. While resonance of word and theme might continue (it's hard for a meaning-seeking mind not to strike up some connection, ironic or not, when the phrases "picking a pocket" and "profit-sharing" are overlaid [730]), vertical reading allows the words to exist as phonic representations, moves them toward expressions of a moment and away from constructions over time.

What I'm suggesting is that, while the masque exists most fully in performance, as Byrd rightly argues (241), reading it "vertically" suspends the masque between performance and print. And even as the masque is somehow suspended between forms, so the sense(s) that a reader/listener seeks are also suspended between those expected of literature and verbal language and those expected of performative arts and music. It is no less significant, then, that "sell" and "selfishly" (724) or "as she" and "measures" (724) or "You'll do that" and "tell you that" (725) are interconnected by the force of instant and proximity, than that the character of the aunt recalls the Queen of Hearts. Musically, these cross-currents are *more* significant.

The testimony that this nonsense records is not only about injustice and the tyranny of Sense; it is also a testimony of and *to* the possibility of meaningful systems. Although I suspect that when Zukofsky used the word "recorded" he had only its documentary/textual meaning in mind, Celia Zukofsky's repositioning of the word in this movement of "*A*" seems more than appropriate. The verb is itself replete with meanings that animate the paradox of "A"-24. "To record": "to get by heart,"; "to take to heart"; "to practise (a song, a tune)"[24]; "to sing of or about"; "to call to mind"; "to meditate, ponder (something) *with oneself*"; "to tell or relate orally"; "to declare as one's verdict"; "to relate in writing"; "to bear witness to." All of these senses *record* the nonsense of "A"-24, its testimony, and Celia Zukofsky's composition, her "taking to heart" of Louis Zukofsky's works.

V

> the gift—
> she hears
> the work
> in its recurrence
> —Louis Zukofsky, "A"-24

As Zukofsky's works become more experimental, more opaque, passive models of reading become increasingly ineffectual. One great strength of *Reading Zukofsky's* 80 Flowers, Michele Leggott's impressive study of Louis's later work, is her insistence that Zukofsky's writing demands new strategies of reading, new *ways* to read; another is the creation of one such strategy for approaching *80 Flowers*. But what to do with the visually (and aurally) multiple "A"-24, that epitome of poetic simultaneity, of (as Zukofsky suggests) poetry as fugal counterpoint? Perhaps the trick of reading "A"-24 lies in the artfulness with which Celia Zukofsky created it.

At the end of this last movement, Zukofsky rededicates to his wife what she has, with dedication, composed for him:

> "A"-24
> Celia's
> L. Z. Masque
> the gift—
> she hears
> the work
> in its recurrence
>   [806][25]

"In its recurrence": a predictably eccentric dedication? Perhaps, but recurrence is what I think best characterizes the reading and the understanding of this text—what best characterizes its nonsense.

Reading "A"-24, one's eye strays, dances in out up down backward forward; it seeks out echoes and equivalencies, verbal cousins, mothers, fathers, sons (the relations of *Arise, arise* and *"A"* embodied in words, as words). A sustained, linear reading is impossible; one must turn, and turn again, to the pages, the voices, the words that have already been read. This is not simple repetition. "[T]here can be no repetition because the essence of that expression is insistence," Gertrude Stein writes in "Portraits and Repetitions" (167). And if nothing else, "A"-24 is insistent, requires a tenacious insistence of its reader.

But insistence is hardly a reading strategy, and "recurrence" and its linguistic sister "recurrent" mean severally, conflate a variety of disciplines in one word. *The Century Dictionary*, long one of Zukofsky's favorite resource books, lists not only the familiar definition of "returning from time to time; reappearing" but also some more intriguing and, to my mind, more useful definitions: "In *anat.*, turned back in its course, and running in a direction the opposite of its former one In *entom.*, turning back toward its base: as, a *recurrent* process." When applied to Celia Zukofsky's "L. Z. Masque," these definitions suggest not only how one reads the text—always flipping back to previous pages—but suggest as well that, in hearing the work in its recurrence, Celia Zukofsky has effectively reversed the process of her husband's writing, expanding his intellectualized condensation. In so doing she makes visible, palpable, to a reader the substrata of senses in Zukofsky's words, makes visceral the possibilities for resonance inherent in his dense, distillate work.

Even more pointed are two other usages of the words "recurrent" and "recurrence." One is the *Century's* definition of "recurrent" from the study of crystals: "noting a crystal which exhibits an oscillatory combination of two sets of planes." Such a recurrent movement might be analogous to a nonsense that oscillates to combine languages, forms of sense, that moves between linguistic planes, between musical and verbal meanings.

The final form of recurrence has to do with that musical meaning, is one of the structures, in fact, *of* musical meaning. In *Emotion and Meaning in Music,* Leonard Meyer claims that meaning in music is "a product of expectation" (35), an expectation sometimes met and sometimes frustrated. Such expectation is partly historical, cultural, and generic, of course, but it is also complemented by the patterns of repetition, reiteration, and recurrence within any given piece. "Recurrence," Meyer explains, "is repetition which must be distinguished from "reiteration." Recurrence is repetition which takes place after there has been a departure from whatever has been established as given in the particular piece. There can be a return to a pattern only after there has been something different which was understood as a departure from the pattern. Because there is departure and return, recurrence always involves a delay of expectation and subsequent fulfillment" (151–152). Recurrence, then, is crucial to thematic and motivic repetition and variation, closely linked, by Meyer, with the relaxation of tension (caused by frustrated expectations) and often, though not always, with closure (152, 153).

Locating such recurrence in "A"-24, or perhaps more appropriately considering "A"-24 *as* such recurrence, is to regard this movement as an orchestration of thematic, phrasal and motifal units (all terms, of course, that have literary as well as musical senses), as an orchestration of sound patterns, whose recurrence here occurs both *within* the movement (as, for instance, "Voice a voice" is repeated in act I, scene 5) and *without* it (the reuse of Louis's work and of Handel's).

The recurrence that animates a reading of "A"-24, then, is one of insistent turning and returning to fundamentals, of oscillation between planes of meaning, and of meaning-creating repetition. When "A"-24 is read as a continual recrystallization of constantly shifting senses, as an oscillation between planes of meaning, ways of establishing (and undercutting) expectations for meaning, the act of reading ceases to be a search for sense *per se.* Reading itself becomes recurrence, is fractured, split into vectors of possible association at a myriad of levels; language becomes a series of movements: of pages, of phrases. And this oscillation, this patterning of expectation and frustration in which meaning is established by its own frustration, hints that linguistic meaning is constantly on the move, is contingent upon other meanings, other languages that mean differently, that underscore and undermine sense, that enable and debilitate it.

The burden of meaning in "A"-24 is not cast off as much as shifted to a broader, a more capacious shoulder—one that carries the several possibilities of sense and nonsense. Reading it not with an eye to finding a single, a tyrannical, sense but rather as a playing over and under and around and with various meanings, various ways of *making* meaning—this at once liberates the reader and sings true with the work itself.

At the end of Seuss's *On Beyond Zebra!* Conrad Cornelius o'Donald o'Dell is converted, so to speak—

> Because, finally, he said:
> "This is really great stuff!
> "And I guess the old alphabet
> "*ISN'T* enough!' "
> [N.p.]

If "A-24 is the nonsense that follows on beyond "z-sited," then Celia Zukofsky's nonsense suggests that *one* alphabet isn't enough. And I am converted.

Notes

A Postdoctoral Fellowship and an Initiatory Research Grant from the Social Sciences and Research Council of Canada and Wilfrid Laurier University, respectively, facilitated the research and writing of this essay. My thanks to both institutions. An earlier version of this paper was delivered at the University of Maine, Orono, in June of 1993 and was published with minor changes in *West Coast Line,* Fall 1993; both were titled "The nonsense recorded its own testimony." An "Ur" version containing some of these ideas titled "The Harmonics of Addenda" was delivered at the University of Western Ontario in March of 1993. Thanks to various audiences and readers for useful prodding and suggestions and to the members of Damjana Bratuz's "Interdisciplinary Research in Music" course at the Centre for the Study of Theory and Criticism, University of Western Ontario.

1. Originally "A"-24 was named "L. Z. Masque"; Celia Zukofsky com-

posed it as a surprise gift for Louis Zukofsky, completing it in 1968. While she did the arranging and structuring herself, Paul Zukofsky offered suggestions about the typography and Handel. I do not mean to make light of critical commentary on the masque; what exists is, for the most part, exceedingly useful. My concerns, which I cannot explore as fully here as I would like, are both the problem of authorship that the masque's inclusion in "*A*" raises and a critical tendency to shy away from such an inquiry.

2. Leggott engages in similar wordplay with "z-sited" in her discussion of this line, though the resonances she evokes are slightly different. This difference is proof, surely, of the richness of the line itself. See *Reading Zukofsky's* 80 Flowers, p. 75.

3. Peter Quartermain indicates in *Disjunctive Poetics* that initially Zukofsky listed only the words "a," "an," and "the" in the index; Celia Zukofsky extended it, and her husband revised the work (208).

4. I'm aware that designating "A"-24 as "extra" flies in the face of Zukofsky's plan from the outset to write a poem in twenty-four movements; I use the notion in response to Harmon's comments, not in an attempt to rewrite Zukofsky's project.

5. It is well worth noting that the first volume of *Bottom: On Shakespeare,* that written by Zukofsky himself, ends with his lengthy "Alphabet of Subjects"; Celia Zukofsky's musical setting of Shakespeare's *Pericles* follows as volume 2. Here again one finds Celia's music as the fullness beyond Louis's alphabet. The centrality of her works to Zukofsky's own, to the possible stretch of language, was once again diminished when only the first volume of *Bottom* was republished by the University of California Press in 1987.

6. In the discussion that follows, I will be attempting to make distinctions between generic Nonsense, such as Dr. Seuss writes, and a nonsensical quality in language often identifiable, though not exclusively located, in poetic language. To help facilitate these distinctions, I will use an upper case *N* when referring to generic Nonsense, and a lower case *n* when discussing other forms of nonsense.

7. For a more sustained discussion of this difference see my book *Touch Monkeys: Nonsense Strategies for Reading Twentieth-Century Poetry.* The most frequent question (or challenge) I face regarding these ideas about nonsense has to do with its political orientation. Since sense is inherently political, one can hardly consider nonsense as anything less. Often I backpedal, saying that nonsense is a(ll)political, combining a pervasive politicality with blatant apoliticality even as it combines meaning and meaninglessness. The more I consider the problem, however, the less satisfactory I find this playful reasoning, for both "meaning" and "meaninglessness" are proscribed by the politics of using those terms. For now, I leave my answer open-ended, admitting that nonsense, because of its participation in the sense that it at once exposes and reestablishes, is itself a political construct.

8. This secondary nonsense pervades Zukofsky's work: witness his translit-

erative poetics—the infamous translations of Catullus, done with Celia Zukofsky, and his rendering of Latin, Hebrew, and Ojibwa (Quartermain 63) into their English phonic equivalents in various sections of "*A*".

9. Brenda Jo Brueggeman's paper on deaf poetics, delivered at the University of Louisville's Twentieth-Century Literature Conference in February 1993, considered this poetics in terms of postmodernism; her discussion made connections with nonsense seem viable as well.

10. Kristeva's ideas about transposition are more complex than I can (or need to) articulate in the context of this essay. Her entire theory of poetic language proves useful when engaging nonsense; while I do extend and revise certain aspects of her theory when reading it alongside of nonsense, I am indebted to it. For a more extended discussion of the relationship between Kristeva and nonsense than I give on these pages, see the second chapter of *Touch Monkeys*.

11. The Hatter's riddle "Why is a raven like a writing-desk?" seems to have no solution; indeed none is offered in *Alice's Adventures in Wonderland*. When pressed, Carroll suggested in the preface to the 1896 edition of *Alice* that, while the Riddle originally "had no answer at all," "a fairly appropriate" one might be " '[b]ecause it can produce a few notes, though they are *very* flat; and it is never put with the wrong end in front!' " (quoted in Huxley 21). Huxley provides other, and much wittier, answers—"Because Poe wrote on both"; "Because the notes for which they are noted are not noted to be musical notes"; "Because it slops with a flap"; "Because 'Each' begins with an E" (22). The riddle meant to have no solution, now has no resolution because it has too many answers.

12. At that time I was studying *Finnegans Wake* and was able to locate a copy of Rieke's doctoral dissertation, "Sense, Nonsense, and the Invention of Languages." The dissertation was revised and extended to become *The Senses of Nonsense*.

13. Michele Leggott's *Reading Zukofsky's 80 Flowers* provides an exceedingly useful and interesting discussion of Zukofsky's use of mathematical structures in his later works.

14. J. S. Bach on occasion "wrote" his own name into his musical compositions, using the German musical letter system: B (b flat), A (a), C (c), H (b natural).

15. See, for instance, the poems that frame *Through the Looking-Glass*.

16. The relationship between nonsense and play is one that has been considered in some detail by a variety of critics; for a thorough discussion of this connection, see any of the following books: Sewell, Stewart, Tigges, or Parsons.

17. For the exact quotation from Zukofsky's notebooks, see Leggott 57.

18. This distinction between composition and setting becomes clearer when one considers Celia Zukofsky's settings for some of her husband's poetry in *Autobiography* or her setting of Shakespeare's *Pericles* as the second volume of *Bottom: On Shakespeare*. The nature of these works is hugely different from that of the masque.

19. An exceedingly interesting place to start such an inquiry would be the stage directions for *Arise, arise*: visible but silent speech—both on the page and on the stage (if the performer reading the dramatic line acts out the gestures).

20. Louis Zukofsky's decision to use "L. Z. Masque" as "A"-24 is theoretically another transposition accomplished by Zukofsky himself. Whether that transposition is an act of writing or of citation is a good question.

21. Zukofsky lists this story by its subtitle; it is more commonly known as "Novelty and Romancement." The story, originally published in 1856, is a satirical poke at the romantic effusions of a poetaster who has misread an advertisement for Roman Cement. The quotation Zukofsky uses is the narrator/poet's discussion of his "philosopher" uncle, who (like the poet whose talent his uncle alone recognizes) remains unappreciated by the world at large. A convenient quotation, it conflates the satire of both insipid poetry and weak reasoning. This story and Carroll's "Russian Journal" can be found in *The Russian Journal and Other Selections from the Works of Louis Carroll*.

22. Deleuze finds Carroll's often obvious drive toward sense (a word Deleuze rather elaborately redefines in *The Logic of Sense*) detrimental to Nonsense and, in *Anti-Oedipus,* names him "the coward of belles-lettres" (Deleuze and Guattari 135). To outline all of Deleuze's concerns with Carroll's Nonsense would require more time and space than can be allotted in this context. Briefly, however: Deleuze suggests that Carroll's Nonsense plays with sense superficially, merely to affirm its rigors and so confirm the status quo. He contrasts it with Antonin Artaud's work, designating the latter as an example of accepted sense structures being irrevocably shattered by the confrontation between language unhinged and what he refers to as the "schizoid" body. Jean-Jacques Lecercle's *Philosophy Through the Looking Glass* gives a useful overview of Deleuze on this matter. I hesitate over Deleuze's ideas because all nonsense, no matter how radical, stands in reflective relation to sense, informs and is informed by it. Carroll is far less conservative than is traditionally assumed; see, for instance, Lisa S. Ede's doctoral dissertation for an excellent rereading of the works. But even if Carroll does stand at the conservative end of a nonsensical spectrum, his engagement of sense can be read as far more creative, far less straitlaced, than Deleuze suggests.

23. The BACH acrostic method mentioned earlier in terms of Louis's work is, of course, read vertically.

24. This use is specifically with reference to birds.

25. In the 1972 separate publication of "A"-24, Zukofsky's dedication appears at the beginning, not the end, of the movement. One can speculate on the reason for its repositioning at the end of the movement when all of "A" was published in a single volume; perhaps this new position was to allow for greater weight to be placed upon the dedication, to offer it not only as recognition of Celia Zukofsky's accomplishment but also as cadence for the volume as a whole.

Works Cited

Bernstein, Charles. Letter to the author. March 1992.

Blaser, Robin. "Image-Nation 10 (marriage clothes." *The Holy Forest.* Toronto: Coach House P, 1993. 129–135.

———. " 'the universe is part of ourselves.' " *The Holy Forest.* Toronto: Coach House P, 1993. 234.

Brueggeman, Brenda Jo. "Deaf Poetics: The Significance of Silence, Poetics of Presence, and Voice of Vision." A paper presented at the Twenty-first Twentieth-Century Literature Conference, University of Louisville, Louisville, Kentucky, 25–27 February, 1993.

Burrows, David. *Sound, Speech, and Music.* Amherst: U of Massachusetts P, 1990.

Byrd, Don. *The Poetics of the Common Knowledge.* Albany: State U of New York P, 1994.

Carroll, Lewis. *Alice's Adventures in Wonderland* and *Through the Looking-Glass.* 1865, 1872. Harmondsworth, England: Puffin-Penguin, 1962.

———. "Introduction to *Sylvie and Bruno.*" *The Complete Works of Lewis Carroll.* 1936. New York: Vintage-Random House, 1976.

———. *The Russian Journal and Other Selections from the Works of Lewis Carroll.* Ed. John Francis McDermott. New York: Dutton, 1935.

The Century Dictionary: An Encyclopedic Lexicon of the English Language. Ed. W. D. Whitney et al. New York: Century, 1900.

Davenport, Guy. "Zukofsky's 'A'-24." *Parnassus* 2 (Spring-Summer 1974): 15–24.

Deleuze, Gilles. *The Logic of Sense.* Trans. Mark Lester and Charles Stivale. Ed. Constantin V. Boundas. New York: Columbia UP, 1990.

Deleuze, Gilles, and Felix Guattari. *Anti-Oedipus: Capitalism and Schizophrenia.* Trans. Robert Hurley, Mark Seem, and Helen R. Lane. New York: Viking, 1977.

Ede, Lisa S. "The Nonsense of Edward Lear and Lewis Carroll." Diss. Ohio State U, 1975.

Harmon, William. "Eiron Eyes." *Parnassus* 7:2 (1979): 5–23.

Kristeva, Julia. *Revolution in Poetic Language.* Trans. Margaret Waller. New York: Columbia UP, 1984.

Lecercle, Jean-Jacques. *Philosophy Through the Looking Glass: Language, Nonsense, Desire.* La Salle, IL: Open Court, 1985.

Leggott, Michele. *Reading Zukofsky's 80 Flowers.* Baltimore: Johns Hopkins UP, 1989.

Meyer, Leonard. *Emotion and Meaning in Music.* Chicago: U of Chicago P, 1956.

Nichol, bp. *ABC: The Aleph Beth Book.* Ottawa, Canada: Oberon P, 1971.

———. "Phrasing." *Truth: A Book of Fictions.* Stratford, Ontario: Mercury P, 1993.

The Oxford English Dictionary. Oxford: Oxford UP, 1971.

Parsons, Marnie. *Touch Monkeys: Nonsense Strategies for Reading Twentieth-Century Poetry.* Toronto: U of Toronto P, 1993.

Perelman, Bob. " 'A'-24." In *The L=A=N=G=U=A=G=E Book.* Ed. Bruce Andrews and Charles Bernstein. Carbondale: Southern Illinois UP, 1984. 292–293.

Quartermain, Peter. *Disjunctive Poetics: From Gertrude Stein and Louis Zukofsky to Susan Howe.* Cambridge: Cambridge UP, 1992.

Rieke, Alison. "Sense, Nonsense, and the Invention of Languages: James Joyce, Louis Zukofsky, Gertrude Stein." Diss. U of Kentucky, 1984.

———. *The Senses of Nonsense.* Iowa City: U of Iowa P, 1992.

Seuss, Dr. (Theodor Seuss Geisel.) *On Beyond Zebra!* New York: Random House, 1955.

Sewell, Elizabeth. *The Field of Nonsense.* London: Chatto & Windus, 1952.

Stein, Gertrude. "Portraits and Repetition." *Lectures in America.* 1935. Boston: Beacon, 1957. 165–206.

Stewart, Susan. *Nonsense: Aspects of Intertextuality in Folklore and Fiction.* Baltimore: Johns Hopkins UP, 1978.

Tigges, Wim. *An Anatomy of Literary Nonsense.* Amsterdam: Rodopi Editions, 1988.

Wittgenstein, Ludwig. *Philosophical Investigations.* Trans. G. E. M. Anscombe. 1953. London: Blackwell, 1958.

13

A Fractal Music
Some Notes on Zukofsky's Flowers

KENT JOHNSON

for Michael Heller and Armand Schwerner

For out of olde feldes, as men seyth,
Cometh al this newe corn fro yer to yere,
And out of olde bokes, in good feyth,
Cometh al this newe science that men lere.
—Chaucer, *Parliament of Fowls*

1　What follows are selections from a collection of notes begun five or six years ago on Zukofsky's last work. While it has been periodically expanded and rearranged, the engagement has stubbornly retained its notational quality. It is a kind of intuitive and associational musing, an ongoing "thinking with" Zukofsky's *80 Flowers*,[1] one of the most linguistically idiosyncratic and semantically dense texts in American poetry. The density of these poems resides not just in the way that their words suggest a multitude of relationships between them but also, and most deeply, in the way that Zukofsky offers each word as one part (one petal) of a hidden semantic and auditory whole. We might read the "Epigraph" to *80 Flowers* as intimating that the word opens, "gaping," into *time,* each offered as an unlocking into a labyrinth of etymology and music that is "unwithering" in its transmutations of signification and sound. No previous poet writing in English had so insistently directed attention *into* words, and there is no other extended work in the language previous to it that moves so insistently beneath our conventions of syntax and sense:

Heart us invisibly thyme time
round rose bud fire downland

bird tread quagmire dry gill-over-the-ground
stem-square leaves-cordate earth race horsethyme
breath neighbors a mace nays
sorrow of harness pulses pent
thus fruit pod split four
one-fourth ripens *unwithering* gaping
                    ["Epigraph," *Complete Short Poetry* 325]

2   While so much of "*A*" unfolds from the intricacies of Bach's
music, Zukofsky's late work—in its radical distillations of syntax and
its rigorous eight-line/five-word count—can be seen as moving in
the direction of composers like Schoenberg, or Webern, where fugal
technique moves away from a recurrence of harmonic or thematic
phrasing and toward more widely distributed and nonlinear patterns
of repetition and combination. The dominant tonal centers and thematic keys that guide the progression of "*A*" are replaced in the *Flowers*
by a singular attention to the serial repatternings of sound between
words and their components and between words and their *histories* as
sound. What Susan Buck-Morss has argued as Schoenberg's aesthetic
and ethical ground is equally relevant to *80 Flowers:* the impulse of
serial, ideogrammic forms of composition arises from a faith that
knowledge and value, meaning and spirit, are not qualities to be nar-
rated from the depths of the individual subject, but discovered—as potential—in the *material* itself (Buck-Morss 56). In this regard, Michael
Heller's felicitous comparison of the prosody of "*A*" with baroque
musicality is even more apt in relation to the affinity Zukofsky's final
work shares with the compositional modalities of high modernism:
"The sense of totality or completeness of such music is in its absence
of a residue, in its simultaneity of means and ends" (Heller 27).

> "Privet" (*Complete Short Poetry* 328)   †

3   But the premodern is still very much present in these poems.
Zukofsky's hand throughout the *Flowers* project is guided by an obsessively philological eye, and citation and transliteration from Homer,

† In the spirit of the printed version of Zukofsky's lecture "For Wallace Stevens" (*Prepositions*
24–38), the reader is invited to refer elsewhere to the poems whose titles appear between sections
of this essay. As in Zukofsky's sequential arrangement in that lecture of his own writings in
relation to some of Stevens's, these works bear a kind of antiphonal relationship to what precedes
and follows them.

Theophrastus, Diogenes Laertius, Apollodorus, Hesiod, Virgil, Horace, the Hebrew Bible, Su-Shih, Chaucer, the Provençal lyric, and his beloved Shakespeare—but a partial list—suffuse the fabric of the book.[2] It is in their redemption of the gestural and percussive that the architectonics of these sound-fields seem to reach back from the Renaissance transition and into earlier prosodies. As in the Anglo-Saxon, or Skelton's "tumbling verse," melos and lexis exalt their oneness:

> "Windflower" (*Complete Short Poetry* 343)

4　Or as in the Chinese. That the dominant formal configuration of the *lu-shih* ("regulated poems"), the preferred form of eighth- and ninth-century poets, was also eight line and five character seems more than coincidence, and Zukofsky's last project might be read as a pilgrimage to the origins of the American ideogrammic line—those literal transcriptions of T'ang poetry in Fenollosa's notebooks that so influenced Pound. And further clues suggest that the Chinese Connection, if not explicitly acknowledged, is intentional on Zukofsky's part: on a looseleaf sheet, now in the poet's archive at the University of Texas, the opening schema for the *Flowers:*

> *Plan.* Beginning at 70 to finish for my 80th
> 　birthday a book of songs called *80 Flowers.*
>
> *Substance.* Only those flowers I have actually
> 　seen and whatever botany I can learn
> 　in 10 years. ("drive"—horses cf *Anew* poem
> 　　33 & "A"-7)
>
> *Form.* 8-line songs of 5-word lines: 40 words
> 　to each poem, growing out of and con-
> 　densing my previous books, "A", *All,*
> 　*Arise, arise, Bottom: On Shakespeare,*
> 　*Catullus, Little* etc.[3]

Zukofsky's term, "songs," is precisely the classical meaning of "shih." That definition, along with much else on the qualities of T'ang verse, is present in Herbert A. Giles's *A History of Chinese Literature,* a book essential to Pound and one of Zukofsky's major sources in the preparation of "A"-22 and -23, where his regulated five-word line becomes an insistent formal device.[4] And exactly in the middle of the first line of *Starglow,* the first of the *Flowers,* is the word "china." But direct example may best suggest the link. With a few more botanical references, the following literal translation of a shih by Wang Wei would clearly be at home among the *Flowers:*

Late years only love peace
Myriad things not woven mind
Self reflect no long-term plan
Simply grasp return gnarled woods
Pine wind blow loosen girdle
Mountain moon beam play zither
Your question failure success principle
Diver's song enter estuary deep

As Giles notes, in a page Zukofsky surely read:

A Chinese poem is at best a hard nut to crack, expressed as it usually is in lines of five or seven monosyllabic root-ideas, without inflection, agglutination, or grammatical indication of any kind, the connection between which has to be inferred by the reader from the logic, from the context, and least perhaps of all from the syntactical arrangement of the words. . . . For purposes of poetry the characters in the Chinese language are all ranged under two tones, as flats and sharps, and these occupy fixed positions just as dactyls, spondees, trochees, and anapests in the construction of Latin verse. As a consequence, the natural order of words is often entirely sacrificed to the exigencies of tone, thus making it more difficult than ever for the reader to grasp the sense.
[144]

In the Chinese, tone or relative pitch operates as a phonemic element, and in the *lu-shih,* euphonic interlacings are created following involved procedures for the vertical and horizontal linking of characters. But these aural interlockings are in no way overlaid as mere formal device; they serve, rather, as procedural and generative foundation of a complex grid of semantic couplings and intertextual allusions, through which the reader is invited to move as much by attention to the multiplicity of nonlinear textures as by normative, syntagmatic sequence. Such a prosody has much to teach us about the *Flowers.*[5]

5   If there are few American texts more carefully conducted and painstakingly philological than *80 Flowers,* there are, at the same time,

few examples that more insistently speak to language's autonomous nature and to its potential for reproducing beyond the conscious intentions of author or reader. Paradoxically, Zukofsky's late writing may be seen as intersecting most closely with John Cage's chance-driven mesostics or aspects of Jackson Mac Low's work, where "meanings" are proposed as tonal components, fully inborn to their aural matrix. And this is increasingly the sense in Zukofsky's later writing—that the signified fully cohabits the sign of music: "How much what is sounded by words has to do with what is seen by them—and how much what is both sounded and seen by them crosscuts an interplay among themselves—will naturally sustain the scientific definition of poetry we are looking for" (*Prepositions* 8).

6 This and other statements from "Poetry," published in 1946, along with others in "A Statement for Poetry" (1950), complicate some of the earlier phenomenological projections of "An Objective," from 1931, itself a document full of wonderful complications.[6] And in fact, Objectivist poetics may be regarded as a Janus face of sorts: one gaze turned in "faith" toward the referential vectors of the sign, the other toward the larger energies of textuality and an exaltation of cognition's deep implication in its field. While there is no sharply defined turn in Zukofsky's later criticism (as some critics find in that of the Wittgenstein he so admired), the concerns of the late poetry clearly highlight that "other" gaze. The insistent deferral of imagistic rest from "A"-22 on foregrounds each sign's embeddedness in an open *field* of relations (as any occasion of nature is so embedded); each particular—each chord—both infused by and charging context, creating, to quote Mutlu Konuk Blasing (herself quoting Hugh Kenner), "a universe of 'patterned integrities' [that] work above or below the horizontal grid on which mere analogies are plotted" (147).

> "Hyacinth" (*Complete Short Poetry* 343)

7 "Hyacinth ends with the italicized words "gladden gladwyn gladwin glad." And one might posit "glyphs," as a further consonance, perhaps, in that the alphabetic is pushed toward an almost surreal object-status. Eliot Weinberger's observations on pre-Columbian "writing" resonate remarkably with *80 Flowers*:

[The Maya glyphs] were laid out on a grid that could be followed in a variety of directions. . . . There were . . . nearly endless ways to write any given word, and Mayan scribes were valued for their punning and ability to coin new variations while strictly adhering to the rules. . . . This meant not only that each word was an *assembled object,* but that each object was in a state of perpetual metamorphosis, its meaning only comprehensible for the moment it is seen in the context of the other object-glyphs. . . . In the poetry of the Aztecs, the poet becomes the poem itself, which becomes a plant growing within the poem; the plant becomes the fiber of the book in which the poem is painted; the fibers of the book become the woven fiber of the mat. . . . Octavio Paz's 'Hymn among the ruins' ends with this famous line: 'words that are flowers that are fruits that are acts'.
[19–22]

> "Spirea" (*Complete Short Poetry* 344)

8   And Zukofsky, suggestively: "[M]ost Western poets of consequence seem constantly to communicate the letters of their alphabets as graphic representations of thoughts—no doubt the thought of the word influences the letters but the letters are there and seem to exude thought" (*Prepositions* 17). And in *Bottom: On Shakespeare,* quoting the medieval John Scotus Erigena: "Grammar begins with the letter, from which all writing is derived and into which it is all resolved" (119).

9   Zukofsky seems to have come to the idea of the word as both particle and wave, at once essential to any constitution of meaning, yet without fixed essence or any certainty of measure. And in their semantically indeterminate nature, the *Flowers* instantiate a basic tenet of poststructuralist thought: that our 'sense' of things arises, as Robert Scholes puts it, "only by establishing our own connections within the network of textuality that enables our thinking and perceiving in the first place. . . . human interaction with the world is . . . always mediated by signs that can be interpreted only by connecting them to other signs, without ever leading to some final resting place . . . that might be called Reality or Truth" (153). The problematics of epistemology, so central to Zukofsky's prior corpus, are, in a sense, settled in the *Flowers through* an acknowledgment of the unbounded problematics of language—the world and the mind's movement find their literal oneness in the endless unfolding and blossoming of the word. The intuition is prefigured in "Poetry": "[P]oets measure by means of *words,* whose effect as offshoot of nature may (or should) be that their strength of suggestion can never be accounted for completely" (*Prepositions* 7).

10   But Zukofsky resists being reduced to some instinctive precursor to the idea of language as a groundless *mise-en-abîme.* In the quote above, he is speaking to the complex *histories* of words and asserting that language at its primary levels is deeply marked with meaning from within, independently and in advance of how those elements are positioned in any syntactic chain. If such meanings "can never be accounted for completely," that is, they are not so easily dispersed or deferred into absolute "absence." In Zukofsky's late work the single word or phoneme is itself decidedly *text,* is a site where meaning is always percolating up through underlying layers of language and time (or as Zukofsky has it in the Epigraph above, *thyme*). Freed from hypotactic bounds, the sign is offered as a kind of temporal fissure that tunnels back into voices and thoughts from a purportedly dissolved past. In the *Flowers,* then, meaning is far from the neat package we normally take it to be, but meaning is—if paradoxically—*there,* the more meaningful for its unsuspected inwreathings and upwellings inside the most elemental components of writing. The *Flowers* stand, in all their apparent distance from "common speech," as rooted in a faith that words *do* lead back, if not toward an identifiable "Reality" or "Truth," then toward some communal ground that is anterior to, and greater than, the mediated "senses" of the present. "The story, as Zukofsky says, "must exist in each word, or it can't go on" ("*A*" dust jacket).

> "Bearded Iris" (*Complete Short Poetry* 345)

11   Zukofsky's archaeological *and* musical push, in growing relief in the last movements of "*A*" and insistently afterward: to write downward, against the strata of representational conventions, toward forgotten shards of sense and sound in and among the words—toward the richnesses history deposits in them. And how, actually, such a project seems necessarily plotted toward a recognition that the semantic and aural energies of language from the beginning overwhelm, are *in excess of,* gestures to configure the sign in a willed "sincerity."

12   "Late" Zukofsky begins with "A"-22, where the five-word line becomes the generative structure of all his succeeding work. The poem begins:

> Others letters a sum owed
> ages account years each year
> out of old fields, permute
> blow blue up against yellow
> —scapes welcome young birds—initial
>
> transmutes itself, swim near and
> read a weed's reward—grain
> an omen a good omen
> the chill mists greet woods
> ice, flowers—their soul's return
>   ["A"-22, 508]

Michelle Leggott, in her mind-boggling investigation of Zukofsky's late poetic, reveals that "A"-22 unfolds as a permutation of the poet's brief valentine poem to his wife Celia and son Paul:

AN   ERA

ANY   TIME

OF   YEAR

In his notebook, as he is preparing "A"-22, Zukofsky enters a diagram:

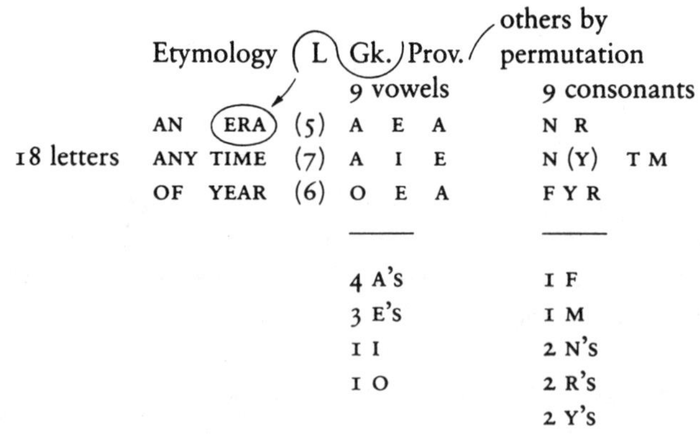

	Etymology (L Gk.) Prov.		others by permutation		
			9 vowels	9 consonants	
	AN (ERA) (5)	A E A	N R	
18 letters	ANY TIME (7)	A I E	N (Y) T M	
	OF YEAR (6)	O E A	F Y R	
		4 A's	1 F	
		3 E's	1 M	
		1 I	2 N's	
		1 O	2 R's	
			2 Y's	

Fig. 13.1 (Quoted in Leggot 41.)

And by this division begins, obsessively, to explore the paragrammatic and anagrammatic associations hidden in the poem.[7] For example:

AN   ERA

A N Y   TIME

OF   YEAR

ANNO (Latin for "to pass through a year" or "to swim toward or alongside") may transmute, through paragrammatic combination (Zukofsky traces these possibilities in the "A"-22 notes), to ANNONA, ANNUO (the Latin *u* stands in phonetically for the English *y*), ANNUE, ANA, NEYO, ANANEYO, ANANEOMAI, NA. The terms mean, respectively, in a literal or transliterated sense, from Latin, Greek, or Provençal, "yearly produce"; "to nod to" or "point out by a sign" (*annue* is the verb's imperative form); "a" (a prefix whose force is always contextualized); "to nod or beckon, as a sign, to nod or bow in token of assent"; "to come to the surface" or "to throw back the head in token of denial"; "to mount up"; and "lady," all of them inwreathed into "A"-22 and beyond, opening, in turn, into other meanings and thematic resonances.[8] The valentine poem is, in Leggott's words, an "audio-semantic goldmine," a model for all he would do later, in coming into communion with a past whose subliminal breaths ceaselessly give life and form to the present. Zukofsky's words, as he leads into "A"-22 bear repeating:

> Others letters a sum owed
> ages account years each year
> out of old fields, permute

13 The movement of Zukofsky from some of the philosophical certainties of "An Objective" to the late work bears suggestive comparison with the experience of someone to whom, in retrospect, he seems closely intellectually akin: Ferdinand de Saussure's move from *The Course in General Linguistics,* upon which the corpus of structuralism rests, to the unfinished study, begun in his last years, of anagrams and paragrams in classical Latin, Greek, and Vedic verse.[9] From the epochal investigations of *The Course,* where Saussure's attention is devoted to the systematized differences that give structure to language, there is a move into a preoccupation with buried semantic conflations that *defy* any systematization. Such a shift would seem, on one level, to reinforce Saussure's central emphasis on the arbitrary nature of the sign and thus, by implication, of the separation of language from the world of "real things." But in fact, the opening to indeterminacy may be seen as a manner of U-turn in his late concerns: language, in the end, breaks out of its synchronic frame and enters the deep-flowing realm of time and chance, becoming—as opposed to objective, regulating system—fully immanent in the unfolding of a reality that transcends the delimitations of any structure. "Chance—," as Saussure puts it in one of the anagram notebooks, "for anyone who has given any measure of attention to the material fact—becomes the inevitable foundation of everything" (quoted in Starobinski 101).

The single word, in the context of such an ontology, becomes much more than an empty assemblage of marks excreting a differentially produced signified: it is uncovered as a vessel latent with resonances of history, collective memory, and emotion, none of which are so easily reduced to the mere effects of a structure. What is suggestive about the comparison, then, is this: the rational framings and spatial closures that enact the epistemologies of the best-known work of Zukofsky and Saussure are subsumed, in the final projects of both, by an apprehension of language as an infinite, nonlinear network of meanings scaling in time. The turn, that is, is away from the concern with the ways in which language as definable system, may focus and objectify the world, and toward a fascination with the ways in which words are always profoundly unsettled, always numinous and unbounded in an ocean of signs whose dimensions reach beyond the delimitations of any functional mapping. Writing of the implications of Saussure's 139-notebook project, Steve McCaffery comments, "[E]merging from the multiple ruptures that alphabetic components bring to virtuality, meaning becomes partly the production of a general economy, a persistent excess, non-intentionality and expenditure without reserve through writing's component letters. Through a very specific project, Saussure seemingly hit upon the vertiginous nature of textuality, seeing in this paragrammatic persistence an inevitable indeterminacy within all writing" (208). And it is this "vertiginousness," quantum-like in its nature, that Zukofsky, too, seems to hit upon in the end.

14 Zukofsky, in section 3 of "The Old Poet Moves to a New Apartment 14 Times": "All the questions are answered with their own words" (*Complete Short Poetry* 223). His and Celia's phonic translation

of *Catullus,* in particular, may be read as such an answering—as a pro-
posal that every "question" or poem is expectant, in its innermost being, with the code of an antiphonal response. And as the body of syntax
falls away in the final work, such latencies begin to show through as
the very *spirit* of his writing.

15   A statement by Roman Jakobson has been quoted in recent
years until it has become almost a cliché: "The poetic function projects the principle of equivalence from the axis of selection to the axis
of combination" ("Closing Statement" 358). But it is unavoidable in
discussing Zukofsky's late work, which is an enactment, as is Schoenberg's music, of Jacobson's maxim with a vengeance. Indeed, the grids
of the *Flowers* are woven with a hyperattention to the multiple axes
of combination that traverse the text: rhythm and percussiveness, pro-
toanagrammatic formations, etymological connotations within words,
and the ways in which words may unlock into others to reveal unseen
or hidden meanings. It is in this sense, to return to the beginning, that
the *Flowers* stand as one of the most radically disjunctive poems in the
language. Combinatory association, along a multiplicity of vectors, is
all. And it is the paradox of such obsessive attention to the factual,
material valences of *la langue* that we are taken simultaneously inward,
toward a music that has no absolute origin, circumference, or end.

16   Which returns us to the matter of fugal structure. Roland
Barthes, writing of it, states: "[R]hetorical continuity resists returning
to what it has set forth, while (formal) continuity of its nature returns,
recalls: the new is ceaselessly accompanied by the old: it is, one might
say, a fugal continuity, in the course of which identifiable fragments
ceaselessly reappear" (*Critical Essays* 181, quoted in Conte 196). This
is an apt definition not only of fugal structures but of mathematically
fractal systems as well. Indeed, the former may be seen as an example
of fractal form in their instantiation of structures self-similar in symmetry across scale and their paradoxically endless transfiguration
within a formally circumscribed area. But the idea of fractalization,
as it relates to the *Flowers,* is made more complex by the fact that we
are dealing with the medium of language. Fractal pattern, in this case,
may be conceived in terms not only of pure sound or the scaled re-
cursions of physical form but of patterns of phonemic signifying units,
or in Saussure's phrase, "sound-images," that are phenomenally appre-

hended by speakers as carriers of meaning.[10] The "identifiable fragments" that "ceaselessly reappear" are laden with the "old," with the
sounds and meanings of the past: a few dozen phonemes recrystallizing
up through time into an infinity of possible texts.

It is possible in this sense, then, to understand Saussure's and Zukofsky's interest in the anagrammatic and paragrammatic crossings inherent in poems as an intuitive opening to language's fractional dimension, and that both apprehended that this dimension, in that it
enfolds endless meaning beyond the phenomenal or intentional scale
of the subject, transcends the bounds that any "objective" or structural
frame would impose.

> "Aloe" (*Complete Short Poetry* 349)

17   A quotation from James Gleick's often quoted *Chaos* may help
set a context: in discussing the work of Benoit Mandelbrot and Christopher Scholz, pioneers in the science of nonlinear dynamics, Gleick
states:

> Geophysicists looked at surfaces the way anyone would, as shapes. A
> surface might be flat. Or it might have a particular shape. You could
> look at the outline of a Volkswagen Beetle, for example and draw
> that surface as a curve. The curve would be measurable in familiar
> Euclidian ways. You could fit an equation to it. But in Scholz's de-
> scription, you would only be looking at that surface through a nar-
> row spectral band. It would be like looking at the universe through
> a red filter—you see what is happening at that particular wavelength
> of light, but you miss everything happening at the wavelengths of
> other colors, not to mention that vast range of activity at parts of
> the spectrum corresponding to infrared radiation or radio waves.
> The spectrum, in this analogy, corresponds to scale. To think of a
> Volkswagen in terms of its Euclidean shape is to see it only on the
> scale of an observer ten meters or one hundred meters away. What
> about an observer one kilometer away, or one hundred kilometers?
> What about an observer one millimeter away, or one micron?
>   [105]

As in our perception of the "real," we have been conditioned to
regard language in a "Euclidean manner," where signifiers have a
seemingly neutral and more or less inevitable relation to their referents.

But Zukofsky's late work proposes that each sign, to quote Joseph Conte commenting on serial form, is "one cork of many bobbing in the open sea of simultaneity," and that "to attempt to isolate an element of causality or a linear sequence is to violate the nature of that reality" (26). In his last work, Zukofsky's radical excision of the horizontal pull of syntax foregrounds the graphemic nature not only of each complete lexical unit but of each word's phonemic and morphemic essence. By so doing, Zukofsky brings us, if we are willing, to a relationship with language beneath its referential, linear vectors and into its *inner space*. In the *Flowers,* the asyndetic form opens up the semantic axis of the text and releases each word and the linguistic "bits" within them to be shuttled, multidirectionally, throughout the fabric of the overall poem. That is, the semantic openness of the *Flowers* swells the carrying capacity of the phonemic understructure; the repetitions and equivalences of pure sound that insist their presence throughout the poems weave phonic branchings and permutations, resonating a combinational interplay that reaches back into and *beyond* those texts that form the spiritual and citational universe of Zukofsky's final work.

It's in this sense that the concept of fractal scale as continuum puts Zukofsky's transfiguration of premodernist sources in a new light. While in modernist poetics citation and quotation tend to be entered as hidden clue or learned allusion to a more enobling past, Zukofsky permutes words and phrases of his multiple sources as strands in a fluid, nonlinear, and nonhierarchical field. Words of the present and the past are enfolded anew into the "open sea of simultaneity."

18   *Not,* that is, that we could ever fully account empirically for such self-embedding complexity and pattern.[11] But that, one might propose, is the allegorical horizon of the *Flowers*: language seems to be in our control only at a certain *spectral band*; "perfect rest" or the "resolving of words and their ideation into structure"—ideals argued for in "An Objective"—are revealed, when we look inward, as limited frames superimposed upon a vast, inwreathed music that we can barely begin to comprehend. The determined prosody of this late poetry, then—its symmetrical word and line count—is not an expression of "rested totality" but rather something akin to the figure of a net, pulled up through the endlessly thick latency of linguistic combinations that underlie all writing and thought. We are asked to regard something alive and pulsing, brought up from the boundless subrosa realm where all meanings are constituted. The *Flowers* stand as the Koch Curve or the Cantor Dust of poetry, showing that an infinite quality may be contained within a mathematically or prosodically limited area. In that they do, they sustain, with a good deal of prescience, "the scientific definition of poetry" for which Zukofsky was looking.

19   New research carried out by the Linguistics of Altered States of Consciousness (LISS) group at Moscow University suggests that ancient linguistic structures are cross-culturally embedded in the deepest layer of mind of all contemporary speakers. The particularly original proposal of LISS—and one that it supports with extensive experimental data[12]—is that texts that foreground material below the conventions of narrative or syllogistic discourse often represent sudden focusings of this archetypal reservoir. In an article on the work of LISS, Mikhail Dziubenko offers an extensive quotation from Roland Barthes (and the quotation does have fugal resonances with his preceding one) by way of introduction to some of the group's theoretical concerns:

> The writer, in this case alone, special, and in opposition to all those who speak or who write the language in order to communicate, is the person who does not allow the obligation of his language to speak for him, who knows and feels the deficiencies of the particular language he is using and has a utopian vision of a total language in which *nothing is compulsory.* The writer thus makes a number of borrowings, through his discourse, and without knowing it. He takes from Greek the middle voice, as when he assumes responsibility for his writing instead of leaving it vicariously to some sacred image of himself. . . . He takes from Nootka the amazement of a word in which the subject does nothing more than predicate, *in extremis,* under the form of a secondary suffix, the most trivial information, which is, for its part, pompously enshrined in the root. He takes from Hebrew the (diagrammatic) figure whereby the person is placed before the verb, according to whether it is directed to the past or to the future. He takes from Chinook a discontinous temporal which is unknown to us (the past tense is indefinite, recent or mythical), etc. All the linguistic practices, at the same time as they form as it

were the vast imagination of language, bear witness to the fact that it is possible to construct the relationship between the speaker and the statement by centering or decentering it in a way that is unheard of for us and for our mother tongue. This total language, brought together beyond all normal linguistic practice by the writer, is not the *lingua adamica,* the perfect, original, paradisiac language. It is, on the contrary, made up from the hollowness of all languages, whose imprint is carried over from grammar to discourse.

[quoted in Dziubenko 26–27]

Barthes would probably have found the *Flowers* brimming with the kinds of syntactic and morphological breakthroughs into other languages he mentions above. But Zukofsky goes perhaps a step further, proposing the possibility that the smallest particles of all, the "sound-images," also provide a fold, or wormhole, through which we might touch the universe of other languages and times. In "Poetry," Zukofsky proposes that composition, at its most difficult and rewarding levels, sets itself the task of releasing realms locked up in the "parts" of language: "[A] case can be made for the poet giving some of his life to the use of the words *the* and *a*: both of which are weighted with as much epos and historical destiny as one man can perhaps resolve. Those who do not believe this are too sure that the little words mean nothing among so many other words." And elsewhere in the same essay: "Felt deeply, poems like all things have the possibilities of elements whose isotopes are yet to be found. Light has travelled and so looked forward" (*Prepositions* 4). One can imagine him being interested in the proposals of the new Russian linguists. Indeed, Dmitri Spivak, founder of LISS, is extremely interested in Zukofsky. After spending time with samples of *80 Flowers,* Spivak remarked: "These are most beautiful. The poems, you see, are written in the poet's true native tongue, but I don't mean English in the restricted sense of it. I mean, you see, that the language has been made pure to reveal the endless glossolalia at its heart."[13]

> "Snowdrop" (*Complete Short Poetry* 342)

20   And the LISS group has been most attentive to the work of John Cage. Andrew Schelling, quoting Eliot by way of Shakespeare, pays tribute to him here, though he could as easily be writing of Zukofsky:

> [Cage] demonstrates so incontrovertibly that the "authors" of verse dwell many places beneath, beyond or beside the poet's personal volition. Those are pearls that were his eyes. Call them what you will—daemons, flavors, angelic powers, *rasas*—the poetic intelligences pervade an immense mutable web that weaves its way through everyone: Language. When they appear they display a playfulness, a mutable wisdom attributable to no one man or woman. Tens of thousands of years of linguistic experiment emerge in their gestures.
>
> The writer's task, one suspects, is but to entice them to an open field.
>
> [228]

And the paths of the two poets cross with the surprise of a mesostic in *80 Flowers*: it is a book of Cage's, published by Steinhour, that prompts Zukofsky to send his last manuscript to that press.[14]

21   Jean Starobinski, at the end of his major study on Saussure's investigations into the anagram, observes:

> Thus, one comes to the conclusion . . . that the words of a work are rooted in other, antecedent words, and that they are not directly chosen by the formative consciousness.
>
> To the question What lies directly beneath the line? the answer is not the creative *subject* but the inductive word. Not that Ferdinand de Saussure goes so far as to erase the role of artistic subjectivity, but it does seem to him that this subjectivity can produce its text only by passage through a *pretext*. . . .
>
> It is . . . the discovery of the simple truth that language is an infinite resource, and that behind each phrase lies the multiple clamor from which it has detached itself to appear before us in its isolated individuality. . . .
>
> This leads one to ask whether all discourse which has provisionally the status of an ensemble cannot be regarded as the subsemsemble of a "totality" which has not yet been recognized. Each text encloses and is enclosed. Every text is a productive product.
>
> [121–122]

> "Snow-Wreath" (*Complete Short Poetry* 342)

22   Phoneme::Phenomena. It is a chance occurrence, surely, but a strange one. Was Zukofsky aware of it? The only alphabetical difference marking such a seemingly vast divide is a single "A."

23   Hugh Kenner: "By some miracle of fourth-dimensional topology, Zukofsky routinely folded universes into matchboxes" (quoted in Leggott 47).

24   And it is because of the "foldedness" of these poems that intention or "craft," though brought to a pitch, does not set itself *over* language but seems a means of *yielding* to its field—of allowing deeper and multivalent prosodies to surface that might call forth that which is beyond the self. Such a stance has little to do with the "formalist" tag so often hung on Zukofsky's work. It has everything to do with mystery and with devotion for a world that reveals itself in the barest and most fragile ways.

> "Zinnia" (*Complete Short Poetry* 351)

Notes

1. Published by the Steinhour Press in 1978, in a limited edition of eighty copies.

2. Michele J. Leggott's stunning investigation, *Reading Zukofsky's* 80 Flowers, offers a minutely detailed tracing of the intertextual dynamic of Zukofsky's late poetic.

3. My references to unpublished Zukofsky materials in the Harry Ransom Humanities Center, University of Texas at Austin, are drawn from Michele J. Leggott's *Reading Zukofsky's* 80 Flowers (27). Unpublished Zukofsky materials are copyright Paul Zukofsky and may not be quoted by third parties without express permission of the copyright holder.

4. Leggott notes Zukofsky's use of Giles (404 n.9). My thanks to Eliot Weinberger for pointing out, in correspondence with me, Pound's close familiarity with the Giles book.

5. See, for example, Stephen Owen's *Traditional Chinese Poetry and Poetics: Omen of the World,* or James J. Y. Liu, *Language-Paradox-Poetics* for excellent discussions of classical Chinese prosody.

6. With *Bottom: On Shakespeare,* these are Zukofsky's central statements on poetics.

7. Some of Zukofsky's notes from the "A"-22 notebook are cited in Leggott

41. See Leggott (particularly 34–72) for a fascinating discussion of Zukofsky's intricate sowing of etymological permutations in his late poetry.

8. Much of my discussion here is paraphrased from Leggott 43–45.

9. While the lectures that constitute *The Course* were given between 1907 and 1911, a time roughly concurrent with the anagram research, it is logical to conceive of the developed and formulated material of *The Course* (as product of long research) as antedating the tentative and unfinished investigations of the anagram notebooks. The major study of this phase of Saussure's career is Jean Starobinski, *Words Upon Words: The Anagrams of Ferdinand de Saussure.*

10. I gloss here from Schleifer, "Ferdinand de Saussure."

11. Such empirical limits, actually, inhere in most fractal systems. Benoit Mandelbrot, in discussing the fractal mapping of coastlines, for example, states that any effort to achieve a model at all scales is "doomed to failure, because each coastline is molded through the ages by multiple influences that are not recorded and cannot be reconstituted in any detail. The goal of achieving a full description is hopeless, and should not even be entertained." The point is that chance and alterity are fundamental constituents of fractal dimensions. See Mandelbrot, *The Fractal Geometry of Nature* 210. Mandelbrot does, however, demonstrate that at certain levels scaling dimensions in language *can* be empirically discovered and mapped: relative word frequency, for example, within sufficiently large discourse samples, will generally constitute statistically fractal dimensions (see 344–347).

12. See, for example, Mikhail Dziubenko, " 'New Poetry' and Perspectives for Philology."

13. As stated to me by Spivak in Leningrad, August 1989.

14. My thanks to Paul Zukofsky, who showed his father the volume in question, for this information.

Works Cited

Barthes, Roland. *Critical Essays.* Trans. Richard Howard. Evanston, IL: Northwestern UP, 1972.

Blasing, Mutlu Konuk. *American Poetry: The Rhetoric of Its Forms.* New Haven: Yale UP, 1989.

Buck-Morss, Susan. *The Origin of Negative Dialectics.* London: Macmillan, 1977.

Conte, Joseph M. *Unending Design: The Forms of Postmodern Poetry.* Ithaca: Cornell UP, 1991.

Dziubenko, Mikhail. " 'New Poetry' and Perspectives for Philology." *Poetics Journal* 8 (June 1989): 24–31.

Giles, Herbert A. *A History of Chinese Literature.* New York: Appleton, 1928.

Gleick, James. *Chaos.* New York: Penguin, 1987.

Heller, Michael. *Conviction's Net of Branches: Essays on the Objectivist Poets and Poetry.* Carbondale: Southern Illinois UP, 1985.

Jakobson, Roman. "Closing Statement." *Linguistics and Poetics*. Ed. Thomas A. Sebeok. Cambridge: MIT P, 1960. 350–377.

Leggott, Michele J. *Reading Zukofsky's 80 Flowers*. Baltimore: Johns Hopkins UP, 1989.

Liu, James J. Y. *Language—Paradox—Poetics*. Princeton: Princeton UP, 1988.

McCaffery, Steve. *North of Intention: Critical Writings, 1973–1986*. New York: Roof, 1986.

Mandelbrot, Benoit. *The Fractal Geometry of Nature*. New York: W. H. Freeman, 1983.

Owen, Stephen. *Traditional Chinese Poetry and Poetics: Omen of the World*. Madison: U of Wisconsin P, 1985.

Schelling, Andrew. "Hobson-Jobson: An Account of Sanskrit Poetics in Homage to John Cage." *Sulfur* 33 (Fall 1993): 224–229.

Schleifer, Roland. "Ferdinand de Saussure." *The Johns Hopkins Encyclopedia of Literary Criticism*. Ed. Michael Groden and Martin Kreiswirth. Baltimore: Johns Hopkins UP, 1994. 651–655.

Scholes, Robert. "Canonicity and Textuality." *Introduction to Scholarship in Modern Languages and Literatures*. Ed. Joseph Gibaldi. New York: Modern Language Association, 1992. 138–158.

Starobinski, Jean. *Words upon Words: The Anagrams of Ferdinand de Saussure*. Trans. Olivia Emmett. New Haven: Yale UP, 1979.

Weinberger, Eliot. "Lost Wax / Found Objects: Brian Nissen's Bronze Relics." *Sulfur* 21: 17–26.

Contributors

Barry Ahearn is associate professor of English at Tulane University. He is author of *Zukofsky's "A": An Introduction* and *William Carlos Williams and Alterity* and editor of *Pound/Zukofsky: Selected Letters of Ezra Pound and Louis Zukofsky* and *Pound/Cummings: The Correspondence of Ezra Pound and E. E. Cummings.*

P. Michael Campbell is assistant professor of English at Georgetown College, Georgetown, Kentucky. He is author of a book of poetry, *The Weight of the Male Walrus,* and is editor of *Palmer/Davidson: Poets and Critics Respond to the Poetry of Michael Palmer and Michael Davidson.*

Norman Finkelstein is professor of English at Xavier University, Cincinnati, Ohio. He is author of *The Ritual of New Creation: Jewish Tradition and Contemporary Literature* and *The Utopian Moment in Contemporary American Poetry* as well as two volumes of poems, *Restless Messengers* and *The Objects in Your Life.* He has also written many essays and reviews on modern and contemporary American poetry and twentieth-century Jewish writing.

Burton Hatlen is professor of English at the University of Maine. He edits the journal *Sagetrieb* and is director of the National Poetry Foundation. He is editor of *George Oppen: Man and Poet* and has written a book of poems, *I Wanted to Say.* He has also published many essays on modern and contemporary American poetry.

Kent Johnson teaches English and Spanish at Highland Community College in Freeport, Illinois. He is a practicing poet, has published widely on modern and contemporary American poetry, and has edited the anthologies *Third Wave: The New Russian Poetry* and *Beneath a Single Moon: Buddhism and Contemporary American Poetry.*

Ming-Qian Ma is assistant professor of English at the University of Nevada, Las Vegas. He has published various articles on modern and contemporary American writers, including George Oppen, Gustaf Sobin, Susan Howe, and Saul Bellow.

Alec Marsh is assistant professor of English at Muhlenberg College, Allentown, Pennsylvania. He has published poems and critical work on Wallace Stevens, William Carlos Williams, and Ezra Pound.

Ira B. Nadel is professor of English at the University of British Columbia, Vancouver. He is author of *Biography: Fiction, Fact, and Form, Joyce and the Jews: Culture and Texts,* and *Various Positions: A Life of Leonard Cohen.* The volumes he has edited include *Gertrude Stein and the Making of Literature* (with Shirley Neuman), *The Letters of Ezra Pound to Alice Corbin Henderson,* and the forthcoming *Cambridge Companion to Ezra Pound.*

Marnie Parsons is assistant professor of English at the University of Western Ontario, London, Ontario. She is author of *Touch Monkeys: Nonsense Strategies for Reading Twentieth-Century Poetry* and of various articles and reviews concerning contemporary Canadian and American poetry and children's literature. She is also an editor at Brick Books, a press specializing in contemporary poetry.

Peter Quartermain is professor of English at the University of British Columbia, Vancouver. He is author of *Disjunctive Poetics: From Gertrude Stein and Louis Zukofsky to Susan Howe* and *Basil Bunting: Poet of the North.* He has edited several volumes of the *Dictionary of Literary Biography* and is currently editing Basil Bunting's *Selected Prose* and, with Rachel Blau DuPlessis, *The Objectivist Nexus,* a collection of essays on the Objectivists. He has published numerous essays and reviews on American, British, and Canadian poetry.

Mark Scroggins is assistant professor of English at Florida Atlantic University. He is a practicing poet and has published essays and reviews on various modern and contemporary poets, including Wallace Stevens, Louis Zukofsky, and Ian Hamilton Finlay. His *Louis Zukofsky and the Poetry of Knowledge* is forthcoming.

Steve Shoemaker is a doctoral candidate at the University of Virginia. He has published articles dealing with Saul Bellow, Carl Rakosi, and the Objectivist movement as a whole.

Susan Vanderborg is assistant professor of English at the University of South Carolina, Columbia. She has published two essays on Susan Howe and has written on contemporary American poetry, science fiction, and the gothic.

Index

Byrd, Don, 138, 230, 247
Byron, George Gordon, Lord, 86

Cage, John, 17, 148, 261, 271–72
Cahill, Holger, 113
Carman, Bliss, 9
Carroll, Lewis (Charles Ludwig Dodgson), 233, 238, 247, 254 (n. 22); *Alice's Adventures in Wonderland,* 234, 243–46, 253 (n. 11); "A Broken Spell," 246, 254 (n. 21); *The Hunting of the Snark,* 246; "Journal of a Tour in Russia in 1867," 246, 254 (n. 21); *Sylvie and Bruno,* 234; *Through the Looking-Glass,* 234, 246, 253 (n. 15)
Casillo, Robert, 32, 74–75
Catullus, 157
Cavalcanti, Guido; "Donna mi prega," 46, 96, 100, 106–8
Century Dictionary, 249–50
Chambers, Whittaker, 45, 52; "You Have Seen the Heads," 52
Chaplin, Charlie, 9, 229 (n. 1); *Modern Times,* 62 (n. 9)
Chaucer, Geoffrey, *Parliament of Fowls,* 257, 259
Civil Works Administration (CWA), 80
Clark, Herbert H., 133
Clarvoe, Jennifer, 132, 136
Clay, Henry, 119–21
Coleridge, Samuel Taylor, 35
Columbia University, 33–35, 45, 48, 116, 120, 215
Columbus, Christopher, 122–23
Communist Party (CPUSA), 45, 49, 53, 55, 56, 58, 84–86
Confucius, 109, 132–33; *The Great Digest,* 132
Contact (periodical), 24, 42 (n. 1), 55
Conte, Joseph M., 154, 269
Coolidge, Clark, 8, 169; *The Maintains,* 161
Corman, Cid, 159
Cowley, Malcolm, 58
Cox, Kenneth, 2, 6, 208–9
Creeley, Robert, 2, 18 (n. 1)
Crozier, Andrew, 2
Cuddihy, John Murray, *The Ordeal of Civility,* 69
Cummings, E. E., 2, 9, 51–52, 81

Dahlberg, Edward, 48, 50, 91 (n. 2)
Daily Worker (periodical), 56, 86
Dante, 135–36, 209
Dasenbrook, Reed Way, 149 (n. 11)
Davenport, Guy, 1, 2, 45–46, 183, 239, 241
David, King, 159–68, 170, 172 (nn. 16, 20)
Davidson, Michael, 47, 53, 95, 110 (n. 3), 197, 212 (n. 1)
Davis, Stuart, 58
Deerfield, Historic, 88
Degli Atti, Isotta, 143–44
Deleuze, Gilles, 234, 254 (n. 22)
Della Francesca, Piero, 155
Dembo, L. S., 125 (n. 3), 138, 179, 180, 182
Derrida, Jacques, 129, 140, 142, 145, 147–48, 149 (n. 9)
Diepeveen, Leonard, 130–31, 134, 142, 146, 148 (n. 2), 149 (nn. 4, 8, 12), 150 (n. 17)
Diogenes Laertius, 259
Direction (periodical), 159
Donne, John, 35; "Elegie on the Lady Marckam," 35
Douglas, C. H., 109. *See also* Social Credit
Dryden, John, 155
Duncan, Robert, 2, 138, 148
Durant, Alan, 141, 144, 145
Dynamo (periodical), 50, 55
Dziubenko, Mikhail, 270, 274 (n. 12)

Eagleton, Terry, 65–66
Ede, Lisa S., 254 (n. 22)
Eisenstein, Sergei, 54
Eliot, T. S., 8, 34, 36, 47, 48, 53, 74, 129, 132, 138, 155, 157, 215, 216, 226, 271; "The Metaphysical Poets," 131; "Philip Massinger," 131–32; *Prufrock and Other Observations,* 131; "Tradition and the Individual Talent," 131, 155; *The Waste Land,* 8, 99, 195, 214
Ellison, Ralph, 91 (n. 2)
Emerson, Ralph Waldo, 13, 109, 149 (n. 6)
Engels, Frederick, 82, 84, 86
Erskine, John, 34
Evans, Robert, 90
Exile, The (periodical), 23–24

Fearing, Kenneth, 91 (n. 2)
Federal Art Project, 81, 92 (n. 2), 112–13
Federal Writers' Project, 81, 91 (n. 2)

Paracelsus, 218, 222, 226
Parker, Dorothy, 58
Parsons, Marnie, 179–80, 183, 191 (n. 6), 252 (n. 7), 253 (nn. 10, 16)
Partisan Review (periodical), 50
Pater, Walter, 5, 7
Paulson, William, 137, 139, 142, 150 (n. 15)
Paz, Octavio, 262
Pearce, W. Barnett, 145
Penberthy, Jenny, 61 (n. 1), 62 (n. 8)
Perelman, Bob, 243
Perloff, Marjorie, 2, 19 (n. 2), 140, 175–77, 190, 190 (nn. 1, 2), 191 (n. 5)
Peters, Hugh, 119
Philo Judaeus, 34
Phyfe, Duncan, 89–91, 119
Physiocrats, 103–5, 110 (n. 5)
Plato; *Cratylus,* 169
Plautus; *Rudens,* 230
Poe, Edgar A., 122
Poetry (periodical), 55, 59, 66–68
Polk, James K., 119
Polleta, Gregory, 145
Popular Front, 56, 58
Possibilities (periodical), 159
Pound, Ezra, 5–7, 8, 10, 14–15, 17, 23, 31–33, 34, 36–41, 42 (n. 3), 47, 49, 50–52, 53, 54, 55, 61 (n. 1), 71–72, 74–77, 80–81, 83–85, 89, 91, 92 (nn. 3–5), 95–109, 114, 120, 129–36, 138, 139, 141, 145, 148 (n. 3), 149 (nn. 7, 11), 155, 175–78, 182, 193, 198, 206, 215, 216, 226, 227, 259; *ABC of Economics,* 37–38; *ABC of Reading,* 130–31, 140, 141; "The Approach to Paris, v," 148 (n. 1); "The Bowmen of Shu," 52; *The Cantos,* 2, 38, 47, 73, 95–97, 100, 109, 133, 160, 194, 214–15, 217, 228–29 (n. 1); Canto 6, 134; Canto 7, 135–36; Canto 13, 132–33; Canto 35, 106; Canto 36, 100, 106, 206; Canto 38, 97–98, 106; Canto 42, 143; Canto 43, 143; Canto 74, 142–44; Canto 75, 143; *A Draft of XXX Cantos,* 215; *Gaudier-Brzeska,* 195–96; *Guide to Kulchur,* 41, 114, 121; "Henry James," 31, 135; *Hugh Selwyn Mauberley,* 54; *I Gather the Limbs of Osiris,* 44; "In a Station of the Metro," 195–96, 199; *Jefferson and/or Mussolini,* 37–40; *Oro e lavoro (Gold and Work),* 102–3, 108; "The Ren-

aissance," 110 (n. 5); "A Retrospect," 98; "The Serious Artist," 94, 123; *The Spirit of Romance,* 197
Pound, Thaddeus Coleman, 102
Prynne, J. H., 154, 158, 167, 168, 172 (n. 21)

Quartermain, Peter, 2, 19 (n. 2), 47, 183, 208, 212 (n. 5), 239, 243, 252 (n. 3)
Quesnay, François de, 103, 110 (n. 4)
Quinn, Kerker, 159, 161, 170 (nn. 9, 12), 172 (nn. 15, 16)

Rainey, Lawrence J., 133, 138, 141
Rakosi, Carl, 26
Rasula, Jed, 18 (n. 2)
Red Eric, 122
Redman, Tim, 110 (n. 6)
Reed, John, 47
Reeves, Ruth, 81, 112
Reisman, Jerry, 92 (n. 7), 159, 170 (n. 4)
Rexroth, Kenneth, 2, 48, 81
Reznikoff, Charles, 26, 71–72; "Depression," 90
Ricardo, David, 108
Richards, I. A., 167, 172 (n. 22)
Rieke, Alison J., 144, 233, 236–37, 253 (n. 12)
Riemann, Hugo, 229 (n. 5)
Rivera, Diego, 193
Rockefeller, John D., 88
Rodker, John, 155
Roosevelt, Franklin Delano, 55, 80
Roskolenkier, Harry, 52, 81
Rourke, Constance, 112–13

Sacco and Vanzetti, 53
Salem Witch Trials, 123
Sartiliot, Claudette, 142
Saussure, Ferdinand de, 144, 265–66, 268, 272, 274 (n. 9)
Schappes, Morris U., 59, 61 (n. 6)
Scharfstein, Ben-Ami, 146, 147
Schechner, Mark, 77
Schelb, Edward, 47, 148
Schelling, Andrew, 271–72
Schimmel, Harold, 26, 42 (n. 5), 71
Schleifer, Roland, 274 (n. 10)
Schoenberg, Arnold, 155, 258, 267
Scholem, Gershom, 212 (n. 4)
Scholes, Robert, 262

Scholz, Christopher, 268
Schopenhauer, Arthur, 189
Scotus Eriginas, John, 105, 262
Scroggins, Mark, 181, 187–88, 190 (nn. 2, 3)
Seidman, Hugh, 2
Seneca, 141
Serres, Michel, 146, 149 (n. 13)
Seuss, Dr. (Theodore S. Geisel), 232–33, 251, 252 (n. 6)
Sewell, Elizabeth, 236, 253 (n. 16)
Shakespeare, William, 35, 53, 187, 259, 271; *A Midsummer Night's Dream,* 190–91 (n. 4), 193; *Pericles, Prince of Tyre,* 252 (n. 5), 253 (n. 18); *Troilus and Cressida,* 125 (n. 4)
Shannon, Claude E., 137
Sharp, Tom, 62 (n. 13)
Shelburne Museum, 88
Sieburth, Richard, 149 (n. 7)
Silliman, Ron, 2, 13, 17
Simon, Linda, 48
Sitwell, Edith, 155
Skelton, John, 259
Sklar, Martin J., 109 (n. 1)
Smith, Adam, 108; *The Wealth of Nations,* 110 (n. 4)
Smith, Paul, 14
Social Credit, 77, 97–99, 101, 143, 215
Sollers, Phillippe, *Numbers,* 149 (n. 9)
Sordello, 135
Spanish Civil War, 56
Spector, Herman, 52, 54
Spenser, Edmund, 10–11, 155; *The Faerie Queene,* 154
Spinoza, Baruch, 31, 76, 95, 100, 109, 202, 218–19, 222, 226, 238; *Ethics,* 47
Spivak, Dmitri, 271, 274 (n. 13)
Stalin, Joseph, 53, 103
Stanley, Sandra Kumamoto, 19 (n. 2), 62 (n. 12)
Starobinski, Jean, 272, 274 (n. 9)
Stein, Gertrude, 116, 155, 236; "Portraits and Repetition," 249
Steiner, George, 8
Steinhour Press, 272, 273 (n. 1)
Sternberg, Meir, 132, 133–34, 136
Stevens, Wallace, 8–9, 17, 44, 48, 175–90, 190 (nn. 2, 3), 191 (nn. 5, 7); "Bantams in Pine-Woods," 185; "The Comedian as the Letter C," 185; "The Doctor of

Geneva," 185; *Harmonium,* 178; *Ideas of Order,* 48; "The Noble Rider and the Sound of Words," 180; "Notes Toward a Supreme Fiction," 185–86, 189; "Of Modern Poetry," 185; "Primordia," 183; "Six Significant Landscapes," 185
Stewart, Susan, 233, 253 (n. 16)
Storey, Robert, 191 (n. 7)
Surrette, Leon, 106
Su-Shih, 259

Taggart, John, 2, 17, 18 (n. 1), 148, 150 (n. 19), 197
Tennyson, Alfred Lord; "Tiresias," 8
Terrell, Carroll F., 136, 143; *Louis Zukofsky: Man and Poet,* 13–14
Theophrastus, 259
Tigges, Wim, 153 (n. 16)
TO, Publishers, 37
Tomas, John, 42 (n. 5), 74, 150 (n. 18)
Tomlinson, Charles, 2
Tovey, Donald Francis, 229 (n. 5)
Trotsky, Leon, 58
Twitchell, Jeffrey, 212 (n. 2)

Veblen, Thorstein, 193
Virgil, 135–36, 216, 259
Vivaldi, Antonio, 219
Vogel, Joseph, 91 (n. 2)
Von Hallberg, Robert, 18 (n. 2)

Wald, Alan, 46, 61 (n. 4), 62 (n. 11), 72
Wallace Stevens Memorial Lecture, 177, 181
Wang Wei, 260
Washington, George, 122
Watten, Barrett, 159, 172 (n. 21), 172–73 (n. 24)
Webb, Electra Havemeyer, 88
Webern, Anton, 258
Weinberger, Eliot, 261–62
Wheelwright, John, 52, 55, 62 (n. 11)
Whitman, Walt, 25, 112, 155; "By Blue Ontario's Shores," 112, 125 (n. 1)
Wiener, Norbert, 136
Willard, Emma Hart, 119
Williams, William Appleman, 109 (n. 1)
Williams, William Carlos, 8, 16, 18, 23, 51–52, 72, 114, 116, 120, 129, 178, 192, 193; *George Washington [The First President],*

116, 171 (n. 4); *In the American Grain,* 114, 119, 121, 122–25; "A Morning Imagination of America," 52; *Paterson,* 8, 217–18; "The Pure Products of America," 52; *A Voyage to Pagany,* 23; *The Wanderer,* 8

Williamsburg, Colonial, 88

Wisconsin, University of, 116

Wittgenstein, Ludwig, 261; *Philosophical Investigations,* 233; *Tractatus Logico-Philosophicus,* 140

WNYC Radio, 119

Wordsworth, William; *The Prelude,* 214

Works Progress Administration (WPA), 16, 81, 99, 112–13, 116

Yeats, William Butler, 47

Yehoash (Solomon Bloomgarten), 41, 73

Yiddish language, 26, 65–70, 71, 73

Zacchi, Romana, 130, 147

Zipf, George Kingsley, 155–56, 158, 171 (n. 7)

Zukofsky, Celia, 17, 24, 45, 118, 205, 218, 219, 225, 226, 227, 231, 236, 238–43, 246–51, 251–52 (n. 1), 252 (nn. 3, 5), 253 (n. 18), 254 (n. 25), 264, 266. *See* Zukofsky, Louis, "A"-24 ["L. Z. Masque"]; *see also* Zukofsky, Louis, *Catullus,* and Shakespeare, William, *Pericles, Prince of Tyre*

Zukofsky, Louis

POETRY: *29 Poems,* 193, 194; *29 Songs,* 97, 114, 204; *55 Poems,* 102; *80 Flowers,* 8, 11, 13, 18, 114, 248, 257–73; individual poems of *80 Flowers:* "Aloe," 268; "Bearded Iris," 263; "Epigraph," 257–58, 263; "Hyacinth," 261; "Privet," 258; "Snowdrop," 271; "Snow-Wreath," 272; "Spirea," 262; "Starglow," 259; "Wind-flower," 259; "Zinnia," 273; *"A",* 1, 3, 6, 13, 16, 25, 29, 33, 48, 51, 56, 62 (n. 12), 89, 90–91, 104, 114–16, 155, 170, 202, 209, 214, 216, 217–18, 228 (n. 1), 229 (n. 2), 230–31, 235, 237, 239, 249, 252–53 (n. 1), 258, 259, 263; individual movements of *"A": "A"*-1–7, 52, 59, 89, 165, 209; *"A" 1–12,* 159; *"A"*-1, 52, 114; *"A"*-4, 73–74, 165; *"A"*-5, 170 (n. 4), 200; *"A"*-6, 60, 100, 170 (n. 4), 194, 200, 211, 239; *"A"*-7, 2, 114, 158, 165, 170 (n. 4), 183, 195, 200, 202, 206–8, 209, 212 (n. 5); *"A"*-8, 56–61, 62 (n. 14), 78, 81–83, 85, 87–91, 96, 99–100, 104, 114, 125 (n. 1), 158, 165, 210–11, 240; *"A"*-9, 46–47, 53, 77–78, 83, 95–96, 100, 106–9, 115, 124, 158, 171 (n. 5), 208, 212 (nn. 1, 5), 216; *"A"*-11, 216; *"A"*-12, 3, 17, 29–30, 33, 76, 82–83, 114–15, 116, 117, 120, 124, 147, 150 (n. 19), 156, 169, 170, 200, 208, 209, 214–28, 229 (nn. 3, 4), 237–38; *"A"*-13, 2, 116, 154; *"A"*-14, 117, 129; *"A"*-15, 158, 170 (n. 2); *"A"*-17, 114; *"A"*-21, 230; *"A"*-22, 11, 18, 125, 129, 150 (n. 19), 161, 230, 259, 261, 264–65, 273 (n. 7); *"A"*-23, 8, 11, 150 (n. 19), 226, 230, 231, 232, 259; *"A"*-24 ("L. Z. Masque"), 17–18, 191 (n. 6), 230–51, 251–52 (n. 4), 254 (nn. 19, 25); "Index" to *"A",* 114, 117–18, 252 (n. 3); "ABC," 11–12; *All,* 259; *Anew,* 198, 206; *Catullus* (with Celia Zukofsky), 201, 253 (n. 1), 267; "Catullus viii," 185–86; "Crickets' thickets," 204–5; "D. R.," 193; "During the Passaic Strike of 1926," 210; "Ferry," 114, 193; *First Half of "A"-9,* 107, 115, 171 (n. 8); "Home for Aged Bomb Throwers—U.S.S.R.," 187; "Immature Pebbles," 193–94; "The Immediate Aim," 193, 207; "I's (pronounced *eyes*)," 11, 179–80; "Light," 183–86; " 'Mantis,' " 2, 17, 53, 86, 195–206, 209–10; " 'Mantis,' An Interpretation," 86–87, 101–2, 124, 196, 200–201, 202–3, 205–6, 209–12; "March Comrades," 57–61, 62 (n. 14); "No One Inn," 193; "The Old Poet Moves to a New Apartment 14 Times," 187, 266; "Poem beginning 'The,' " 16, 17, 23, 33–37, 41–42, 48, 51, 71, 74–75, 117, 129, 136–40, 144–48, 149 (n. 9), 150 (nn. 18, 19), 194–95, 209; "Song 27" ("Song—3/4 time [*pleasantly drunk*]"), 97, 101, 104; "This Fall, 1933," 101; "Tibor Serly," 194; "To my wash-stand," 210; "Wire," 4–5

OTHER WORKS: "About the Gas Age," 187; *About Some Americans,* 83, 116; "American Ironwork, 1584–1856," 118; "American Kitchenware," 88, 118; "American Poetry, 1920–1930," 129, 178; "American Tinware," 118–19; *Arise,*